Storytelling

Storytelling

RUTH TOOZE

Director, Children's Book Caravan

Englewood Cliffs, N.J.

PRENTICE-HALL, INC.

Current printing (last digit):
15   14   13   12   11   10   9   8

PRINTED IN THE UNITED STATES OF AMERICA

85085-C

Preface

S torytelling is a simple, down-to-earth presentation of storytelling for all who would like to tell stories well—at home, in a classroom, in a library, or by a campfire.

Storytelling was one of the earliest means of communication. Throughout man's early development, it was a great medium for sharing experience, for teaching, and for handing down from one generation to another ideas, ideals, values, and standards of behavior; it was also a superb form of entertainment. Consequently, it developed into a real art. It is still an art that may well be practiced by all who are concerned with children.

But storytelling is not limited to use with children. Does not every good speaker frequently use a story to establish rapport with his audience, no matter how serious the import of his speech? Or to illustrate a vital point? Or to capture and hold the attention of his audience? Or to climax or finish an important message? Storytelling is still valuable in today's patterns of communication.

However, this book is concerned primarily with telling stories to children and young people as a means of sharing, teaching, and entertaining. The four chapters in Section I discuss storytelling as a resource in your own way of living with children. Chapter 1 is concerned with the significance of our rich heritage. Chapter 2 indicates ways in which anyone can build a valuable background in the fields of literature, psychology, and child development. Chapter 3 discusses how to tell stories well —the importance of the voice, its placement, pitch, and quality, correct breathing, timing, and other relevant factors. Chapter 4 gives careful consideration to the kinds of stories that are good to tell, what makes them good to tell, and offers some guidance in their selection.

Section II includes some twenty stories, a story poem, and three ballads which are good for telling—not once but many times—to children of all ages.

Section III is an extensive bibliography of books that will help the storyteller build background and understanding, of stories new and old, from earliest myths and legends to modern tales, and of some ballads and poetry. The traditional material is grouped by countries. The modern stories are classified by age level, with brief annotations that may prove helpful. Poetry, religious stories, and special holiday material are also included.

My indebtedness is great: to storytellers of the past, to storytellers of the present, such as Ruth Sawyer, Gudrun Thorne-Thomsen, Richard Chase, and Marie Shedlock; to some of the modern authors of short stories, such as Katherine Mansfield, Katherine Porter, and Isak Dinesen—all great tellers of tales; and to the many children who have shared wonderful hours with me and helped me grow both in skill and love of storytelling.

RUTH TOOZE

Acknowledgments

Bishop, Claire, and Kurt Wiese, for a selection from *The Five Chinese Brothers*, copyright 1938 by Claire Huchet Bishop and Kurt Wiese. Reprinted by permission of Coward-McCann, Inc.

Bryson, Lyman, for a quotation from *The Next America*, by permission of Harper & Brothers.

Carrick, Valery, for "The Bun" and "The Little House" from *Picture Tales from the Russian* (translated by Nevill Forbes). Reprinted by permission of J. B. Lippincott Company.

Chase, Richard, for a quotation from *Grandfather Tales*, by permission of Houghton Mifflin Company; and for "Wicked John and the Devil," copyright 1951. Reprinted by permission of and arrangement with Houghton Mifflin Company, the authorized publishers.

Coblentz, Catherine Cate, for a quotation from "The River Song," in *The Blue Cat of Castle Town,* copyright 1949, by permission of Longmans Green and Company, Inc.

Colum, Padraic, for a selection from *The Golden Fleece,* copyright by The Macmillan Company. Reprinted by permission of the Macmillan Company.

Dinesen, Isak, for four quotations from *Last Tales,* copyright 1957, by permission of Random House, Inc.

Eichenberg, Fritz, for a quotation from *Art and Faith,* by permission of Pendle Hill Pamphlets, Wallingford, Pennsylvania.

Gibran, Kahlil, for a quotation from *The Prophet,* copyright 1923 by Kahlil Gibran; renewal copyright 1951 by Administrators C. T. A. of Kahlil Gibran Estate, and Mary G. Gibran. Reprinted by permission of Alfred A. Knopf, Inc.

Hazard, Paul, for a quotation from *Books, Children and Men,* by permission of The Horn Book, Inc.

Jones, Elizabeth Orton, for a selection from *Ragman of Paris,* copyright 1937, by permission of Henry Z. Walck, Inc.

Kipling, Rudyard, for "The Sing-Song of Old Man Kangaroo," from *Just So Stories.* Reprinted by permission of Mrs. George Bambridge and Doubleday & Company.

Klem, Grace, for a selection from *Serena and the Cookie Lady,* copyright 1948 by Pierce and Smith. Reprinted by permission of Abingdon Press, Publishers.

LeGrand, Henderson, for a selection from *Why Cowboys Sing in Texas,* copyright 1950. Reprinted by permission of Abingdon Press, Publishers.

Le Sueur, Meridel, for a selection from *Chanticleer,* copyright 1951 by Meridel Le Sueur. Reprinted by permission of Alfred A. Knopf, Inc.; and for a selection from *Little Brother of the Wilderness,* copyright 1947 by Meridel Le Sueur. Reprinted by permission of Alfred A. Knopf, Inc.

Lucas, Mrs. Edgar, for the translation of Hans Christian Andersen's "The Emperor's New Clothes," from *Hans Andersen's Fairy Tales* (Children's Illustrated Classics). Reprinted by permission of E. P. Dutton & Co. and J. M. Dent & Sons Ltd. (London).

Mitchell, Lucy Sprague, for "How the Engine Learned the Knowing Song," from *Here and Now Story Book,* copyright 1921 by E. P. Dutton & Co., Inc.; copyright renewal 1948 by Lucy Sprague Mitchell. Reprinted by permission of E. P. Dutton & Co., Inc.

Nathan, Robert, for the poem "Dunkirk," from *The Green Leaf: The Collected Poems of Robert Nathan,* copyright 1941, 1950 by Robert Nathan. Reprinted by permission of Alfred A. Knopf, Inc.

Newell, Hope, for a selection from *The Little Old Woman Who Used Her Head,* by permission of Thomas Nelson & Sons.

Peck, Leigh, for "How Pecos Bill Began," from *Pecos Bill and Lightning,* copyright, 1940. Reprinted by permission of and arrangement with Houghton Mifflin Company, the authorized publishers.

Rickert, Edith, for a condensation of *The Bojabi Tree*, copyright 1923 by Doubleday, Page & Company, copyright 1922 by D. C. Heath & Company. Reprinted by permission of Doubleday & Company, Inc.

Riesman, David, for a quotation from *The Lonely Crowd*, by permission of Yale University Press.

Shapiro, Irwin, for an adaptation of *How Old Stormalong Captured the Mocha Dick*, originally copyrighted 1942 by Irwin Shapiro. Reprinted by permission of Julian Messner, Inc.

Steele, William C., for a quotation from "The Long Hunter and the Tall Tale," by permission of The Horn Book, Inc.

Storyland, for "The Drum That Saved Lambkin," by permission of The University Publishing Company.

Ward, Nanda and Lynd, for *The Black Sombrero*, copyright 1952 by Nanda and Lynd Ward. Reprinted by permission of Farrar, Straus and Cudahy, Inc.

Watts, Mabel, for a selection from *A Cow in the House*, by permission of Follett Publishing Company.

Weil, Lisl, for a selection from *Jacoble Tells the Truth*, copyright 1946. Reprinted by permission of and arrangement with Houghton Mifflin Company, the authorized publishers.

Welch, Jean Louise, and Ruth Carroll, for a selection from *The Animals Came First*, copyright 1948, by permission of Henry Z. Walck, Inc.

Contents

SECTION I. STORYTELLING AND YOU

SECTION II. SOME GOOD STORIES TO TELL

SECTION III. BIBLIOGRAPHY

Introduction

Storytellers are indispensable agents of socialization. They picture the world for the child and thus give both form and limits to his memory and imagination.
                        —David Riesman, *The Lonely Crowd*

S TORIES are of the stuff of life. Stories are one of man's chief means of communication. Stories are to teach, to learn, to entertain, to enjoy, to inspire. Stories are to tell. Telling stories is sharing life experience, real and imaginary. So stories are to tell by everyone with experience to share with those who have ears to hear. The teller and the listener together create the story, for, like a song that lives only when it is sung and heard, a story lives only when it is told and heard.

Great storytelling, like great singing, is an art—an art which can be cultivated. But not only great artists sing. Anyone with a song in his heart sings at work, at play, at going-to-sleep time, bringing comfort in sorrow and joy in living to any who may listen. Great storytellers, such as Homer or an Irish bard or English minstrel of olden time, or Marie Shedlock or Ruth Sawyer or Gudrun Thorne-Thomsen in our time, share their gifts with listeners who have ears to hear and hearts and minds to appreciate. But all those with a story in their minds and hearts and on their lips also tell their stories to children or the friends with whom they work and play. They tell their stories in terms of their heritage, their experience, their ability, their willingness to satisfy the needs of others. It is for this group of storytellers—teachers, mothers, librarians, social workers, playground workers, camp leaders—all who work and live with children (of all ages)—that this book may prove of value. The world needs great storytellers, but it also needs those who tell stories well in their everyday living.

Storytelling is probably as old as man's power of speech and as new as the words that come from a teacher's lips today. It should have a significant place in today's complex pattern of living and learning. Storytelling is a creative act in which the story garnered from the stuff of life passes through the teller, as light passes through a prism of glass to reveal all the colors it holds, to return to the stream of life itself. It becomes part of the life stuff of all the listeners as it completes the circle. It is no accident that the circle is a symbol of life's fullness. As one small boy once said in discussing the letters, "I like 'O' best because it is all there." The circle is the completed cycle. Good storytelling completes a cycle.

The diffusion of light reveals all the colors in the prism. It takes all the facets of the prism to reveal all the colors—violet, indigo, blue green, yellow, orange, red. So good storytelling will take all the facets of varied experience, all the facets of a rich background, all the facets of sensitive awareness, all the facets of understanding and insight, all the facets of the skills in using voice and body, all the facets of putting the words together, all the facets of the stories themselves.

Any and every storyteller has a long, rich heritage behind him, a resource on which to rest, from which to draw.

Any and every storyteller can become a *good* storyteller.

Any and every storyteller may learn to use all the means of telling a story well.

Any and every storyteller must know a rich variety of stories to tell.

Storytelling and You

1

The Heritage

Sans stories the human race would have perished as it would have perished sans water.
—Isak Dinesen, *Last Tales*

IN man's first days upon the earth, he hunted and fished and brought back food to his family. Undoubtedly a man returning with his prey or his catch eagerly told of his adventures to all who would listen. His story would be told in the first person:

"I, the clever one—"

"I, the strong one—"

"I, the skillful one—"

"I killed this beast."

"I caught these fish."

It is easy to imagine campfires blazing, spirals of smoke ascending, eager faces reflecting the firelight as the listeners relived his experiences with the victorious hunter. Such vicarious sharing was perhaps the only excitement in their lives. The story meant almost as much, sometimes more perhaps, as the food in their satisfied stomachs. This must have been true as men settled all over the earth: in Mesopotamia and Persia, in Egypt and Arabia, in Greece and Italy, in China and India, in Brazil and Peru, in Canada and in the United States—on the plains, on the mountains, by the lakes, by the rivers, on the islands. Men and men and men sharing their life experiences with men and women and children—all growing in skills and knowledge and wisdom.

> The divine art is the story. In the beginning was the story. . . .
> But you will remember that the human characters do come forth on
> the sixth day only—by that time they were bound to come, for where
> the story is, the characters will gather!
>
> —Isak Dinesen, *Last Tales*

The storyteller now as then widens experience for his listeners. Here and there—near a rock in Wales, at a crossroads in Ireland, on a street in Japan, at an Indian dance in North America —one may hear a storyteller who belongs in this great tradition. I sat the better part of a night beside such a one, an old musicmaker of the Ute tribe of Indians in Utah. It was early spring— the season for the annual bear dance. The corral of willow twigs was built and the long tin drum, about six feet by two by two, was sunk in the ground, with a hole at least two feet deep below the tin box drum itself. What resonance this gave! All about wandered men and women waiting for the moment when again a woman would choose her mate for the year ahead. The musicmaker sat beside his drum, resting his long notched stick lightly on it. He fingered the assorted dry bones which he soon would rub up and down that stick in rhythmic patterns so beautiful, so various one wondered how his art could ever be called primitive. Slowly, slowly he began his drumming; slowly, slowly he began his singing, actually the telling of a long, long story. It took many hours and everyone became part of the adventure.

Beside me sat an old friend who translated the story now and then—but somehow I needed little translation. Knowing not a word of the Ute Indian language, I understood so much from the rise and fall of his voice, the change in tempo, the change in expression as he took us all on and on through a tale of love as old as time, as young as the maid and youth who found each other first that night and walked back and forth, back and forth in their rhythmic dance. Such ceremonies and festivals enable us to go back in time and deepen our understanding of this creative art of storytelling that has played so important a part in man's development.

As time went on, these first-person narratives of personal adventure changed even as man changed in his living and grew in his thinking. Occasionally, the story would be told in the third person. Gradually this came to be the accepted form, the stories remaining essentially action tales. Often they were rhythmic in form—the beginnings of poetry. Sometimes the teller accompanied himself on a drum or on a crude stringed instrument of his own making. Sometimes, as he moved about in his talking, the rhythmic pattern became a kind of dance. Certain forms and patterns were more effective, gradually became more acceptable, and eventually were accepted. Poetry, music, and dancing were closely associated with storytelling, all contributing to the development of the art. But always there was a great variation in the telling, for each teller told his story in his own way, using his special skills to the greatest advantage.

It was natural that this teller of stories should gradually become important in his group, his village, his tribe. Often he was relieved of other tribal duties and was chosen to tell the experiences of many others. Sometimes he added comments of his own. Consequently, he developed into an interpreter of experience, not just a narrator. He became the wise one or the leader, eventually the medicine man or priest. Not only did he tell stories, but he invented chants for those who went forth to do battle, chants to propitiate the gods who controlled man's ways.

Such a leader tends to become more and more important to his fellow man—and this is just what happened to the story-teller. As tribes went in search of better hunting grounds and grazing lands, they came into contact with other groups, which often resulted in conflict and struggle. The storyteller was likely to be the one chosen to communicate with others. He would be sent forth to tell the story of his group, to present their side of a controversy. So a storyteller became a leader, a leader be-came a representative, a representative became a mediator, and a mediator became a man of importance to those in his group. In his goings and comings, and all that he told of life outside his group's experience, he widened their horizons, lengthened their point of view, and even deepened their understanding. And if he had great skill, something of the story entered into their very souls, their essential beings and became a part of them. If a story becomes part of the experience of many people, this quality of universality makes it live.

As men then developed into thinking people who steadily widened their contacts with others, stories developed far be-yond the earliest narrative accounts of actual experience. Some of man's wondering as well as some of his wandering entered into the stories. Because of man's wondering about himself and his universe, many of the earliest stories which were told over and over again from one generation to the next and the next and the next were stories of man's origins and his gods. He fash-ioned these gods in his own image, the chief difference in power between the divine and the human being one of degree, not of kind. The cloth was the same, but the patterns were different. Almost every people had its story of creation, many of which have come down to our generation. One of the greatest of these is the beautiful story in the book of Genesis in the Bible, the story handed down by the Hebrews who lived in the middle eastern part of the world. From India, far to the east, come the Ramayana, stories of Siva, Brahma, and Vishnu. From southern Europe, the myths of Greek gods—Zeus, Poseidon, Apollo, Athena, and many others—have survived in all their beauty. From northern Europe, the myths of the Norse gods—Odin, Freya, Baldur, Thor, Siegfried, Brunhilde, and others—are still told in story and sung in opera. On the American continents north and south, the Indians told and still tell myths of the creation of man. In the north, in the south, in the east, in the west, where men lived and worked and thought and wondered, the stories of how they came to be, developed. The Angle, the Saxon, the Norseman, the Dane; the Egyptian, the Hebrew, the Roman, the Greek; the Persian, the Babylonian, the Hindu and Philippine; the Indian, the Mayan, the Incan, the American; all of them told stories to their children and children's children, of their gods, of their beginnings, of their greatness and power and strength.

They also told tales of the achievements of their heroes. Sometimes a hero tale developed into a long epic of adventure, such as that of the famous Ulysses. Legends grew up about such heroes, some of them true in their beginnings, adding much that was imaginary, in their growing. A legend is more likely to be a story that grows and grows about a great human being rather than about a god. Myths and legends, hero tales and epics evolved in the days of man's greatest wondering about himself and his origin. Religion and magic and explanation of life were often intermingled. Out of all these came great stories, many of which still live in books of religion, in grand operas based on the old myths and legends, in epic stories and collections of myths and legends.

Animals always played an important part in man's life. Men killed wild ones for food, they tamed others as servants and pets. They observed animal ways and animal traits, often comparing these to like traits of the human. It was natural and inevitable that they should tell stories about animals. Some shaped their tales of a fox or a hare or a tortoise to point a moral. Two nations—Greece and India—seem to have been most successful in creating these tales of animals to point a moral, which came to be called fables. The fables of Aesop probably originated in Greece about the seventh century B.C. and by tortuous paths have come down to us via Rome, Spain, France, Germany, and England. In the eighteenth century, following the great revival of classic learning, Gay in England, Ivarte in Spain, Lessing in Germany, and La Fontaine in France all told fables. They raised the fable from folklore to literature. Probably the best known are the ancient fables of Aesop and those of the French fablist, La Fontaine.

In India, too, the fable became not just folklore but true literature. The ancient animal tales, the Jatakas, seem to have begun in about the fourth century B.C. and the Pancha-tantra, further tales, began about a century later. All these still exist and have influenced the Persian, the Syrian, the Hebrew, the Greek. Gradually the oriental influence extended to the Danish, the Dutch, the Spanish, the Italian, the French, the German, the English. In these fables certain characteristics came to be attributed to the same animals. The fox was always sly, the tortoise slow but persistent. Sayings such as "sly as a fox," "slow as a tortoise" came to be applied to human beings since fables were often used to point a moral or show the results of a certain kind of behavior. Fables, jataka tales, and those of the Pancha-tantra still survive and will hold a listener's interest.

As ethical values slowly evolved and standards of behavior of a cultural group developed, the story became a good means of communicating such values and standards, especially to the young. The story became a full extension of life experience, a means for answering questions, a means for stimulating growth in desired directions. If the true story of a hero was inadequate, a lively imagination could easily enhance the tale with all the skill and artistry at the teller's command. But always the tale was characteristic of the cultural group, the people, the folk, one of whom was telling the story of a hero or an animal, of an exciting adventure, a mysterious experience, or a journey into the "wild blue yonder" (which today would simply be called space). Thus such tales came to be called folk tales, which grew as man's need to express himself and his capacity for enjoyment of expression grew. As a folk tale was handed down from one generation to another by word of mouth, it became highly disciplined, all extraneous words being chiseled away even as the stone is cut to reflect the colors within.

Fairly fixed patterns began to be established for these tales. The pattern of most folk tales is similar to that of many a folk song or other form of folk art. There is a brief introduction:

"Once upon a time there lived . . ." or "In the deep forest where no paths ever were made by man or beast. . . ." Then the chief characters and their problems are set forth. In music this is the development of the theme. The plot is developed by contrast and repetition in both story and music until a climax is reached in which the problem is resolved. Then follows an ending (in music a coda), which often returns to the introduction, sometimes repeating much of it exactly. One of the best illustrations of this old form of story is that of the peddler whose caps were stolen by monkeys (see page 81). It is worth careful study. Here is the introduction.

"Once upon a time there was a peddler who sold caps."

Then comes his problem—distress at being unable to sell any caps one day and the dire results of his taking a rest near a tree in which there were monkeys. The theme is wonderfully developed by contrast and repetition.

At the end he replaces his tower of caps exactly as they were in the introduction and returns to the village calling, "Caps for sale!" Even the colors and their order in the tower of caps is noteworthy: yellow, blue, green (blue and yellow), red—the primary colors. Always *red* on top. It is still the favorite color of most children.

Here is an ageless story. It is good to tell to children of all ages. It is good to use in creative writing classes in the elementary school or in college to study form and to discover how to build a story effectively. Perhaps one of the significant results of hearing a good story well told is an increasing awareness and appreciation of form, beauty of design and pattern, sequence and relatedness, which are of the essence of every good art.

I have found that not only folk tales but also stories by authors such as Rumer Godden, Isak Dinesen, Katherine Mansfield, and Katherine Porter have refined my sense of form. These and many others may also help you in developing a feel for form and increase your appreciation of all that form means to a story.

The folk song and the folk dance evolved in like fashion, revealing people's need for expression in songs for joy or sorrow, for the high road or the low, for going to sleep or waking, and for expression in movement of both grace and strength. So they are inevitably one of the keys to understanding the people from whom they came. They reflect their own people's lives, telling what they did and how.

"*Savez-vous planter les choux?*" ("Do you know how we plant cabbage?")

"*Il était une bergère*" ("Once there was a shepherdess")

"*Bergère, bergère*" ("shepherdess, oh shepherdess")

"*Sur le pont d'Avignon, on y danse*" ("On the bridge of Avignon, they dance this way and that")

These few first lines of well-known French folk songs are good illustrations of patterns of life in France. All such folk songs and folk tales reveal the interests, values, aspirations, sense of humor, and love of beauty of their creators. Therefore, we may know any people better as we become acquainted with the expression of their needs, desires, and ideals in the many forms of their folk art.

In a young country like the United States, where everything seems bigger and better, the folk tales that flourish best are tall tales of tall heroes, rare mixtures of true achievement and imaginary adventure—of a cowboy, lumber jack, railroad worker, sailor. Often the story becomes the extreme expression of a powerful compelling desire which seems quite beyond our own powers.

Now in some countries, people invent special little people who are gifted with powers rare and magical to fulfill wishes which they themselves have not the power to fulfill. So there were fairies, elves, pixies, trolls, dwarfs, gnomes, brownies, goblins, and leprechauns. Most of those whom we know best dwell in northern Europe and many are the tales about them—the elves who did the work of the needy German shoemaker while he slept at night or the pixie folk in their ring in Wales or the kindly leprechaun in Ireland.

Hans Christian Andersen created some of our best loved tales of imagination, which we usually call fairy tales: "The Ugly Duckling," "The Steadfast Tin Soldier," "The Emperor's New Clothes." The German brothers Grimm told stories called *Household Tales*, probably adapted from old folk tales rather than being original creations like those of Hans Andersen. We seem to know best the French version of "Cinderella" by Perrault, but many lands have the story of a young stepsister's abuse by older stepsisters and how she finds a prince charming. Because the names folk and fairy tales are sometimes used interchangeably, it is difficult to differentiate between them. On the whole, folk tales are likely to be tales of a way of life, and fairy tales, those told by one author about magic ways of making wishes come true. Even so-called authorities, such as folklorists and literary scholars, do not all agree on these questions of semantics: some differentiate the myth, the legend, the hero tale, the folk tale, the fairy tale; others talk of myths and legends and folk and fairy tales in the same context. But our discussion here has shown the minor differentiation in origin and development of each group, which may help both in understanding other people's terminology and in being thoughtful about one's own usage.

Often stories were told in metrical form, especially the adventures of a bold hero or lover, known as ballads. They often recreate actual episodes in history, tell of a deed of chivalry or a tale of romantic love. So beloved is Robin Hood, the chivalrous hero of the Song of Robin Hood, not only in Merrie England but by the young of heart everywhere that no one is quite sure whether or not that gallant outlaw actually once lived in Sherwood Forest. Switzerland has its William Tell, France its Roland, America its Paul Bunyan. Storytellers and singers keep such heroes alive. People, transplanted from one country to another take their stories with them, a good way of keeping vital the heritage from the land of their birth. Today it is interesting to find more Jack Tales alive in our southern Appalachian mountain country than in England itself. Many old English ballads such as "Barbara Allen" and the swapping songs are better preserved in these mountains than in England. Cecil Sharp came to these regions from England to collect old ballads, folk songs, folk dances, folk tales. Families like the Ritchies keep them alive with their "singin' times" and through such books as *The Swapping Song Book*. Richard Chase has collected many Jack Tales and other folk tales, folk dances, folk songs from these same mountain people who came long ago from England. In the bayou country of Louisiana, on the streets of New Orleans, in the wilds of French Canada, one still may hear old French ballads, songs, and stories.

Over and over one sees the arts of music, poetry, dance, and storytelling interwoven, perhaps nowhere more than in the ballad. The ballad probably reached the height of its development in Europe of the Middle Ages when wandering newsbearers and entertainers became numerous and wielded great influence. In Scandinavia they were called skalds; in Ireland and England, minstrels; in Germany, minnesingers; and in France, troubadours and *trouvères*. A troubadour often had a *jongleur* or juggler who did much of his work and entertained with clever agility at feasts and festivals. The trouvère usually wrote his own stories and ballads. There are many interesting stories of trouvères such as William the Duke of Guieme, Adam de la Hale, Richard the Lion Hearted, and his close friend and companion, Blondel de Nesle. Once when Richard was imprisoned, Blondel recognized his singing from a high tower and was able to rescue his friend, the King. Roland, the nephew of Charlemagne, was another famous trouvère in France. There is a modern version told from the old ballad, "The Song of Roland."

Neithart von Reuenthal was a well-known minnesinger in Germany in the thirteenth century. Today we probably know more about these minnesingers because of Wagner's opera *Die Meistersinger* (*The Master Singers*), the story of a contest in which the goldsmith's beautiful daughter, Eva, was to be given in marriage to the winning singer. Young Walter von Stolzing was not a member of the guild but Hans Sachs, an older meistersinger, helped him to sing his song and win the contest. Walter's song is still one of the most beautiful of all love songs.

Troubadours, trouvére, minstrels, and minnesingers had very high standards for their profession, and organizations of guilds in which apprentices learned through long, disciplined training. Some became very wealthy and wielded great power, but many remained poor wanderers, dependent for their living upon their skill in "singing for their supper." "Adam of the Road" by Elizabeth Janet Gray is a delightful story of a minstrel in medieval England.

From time to time, there is a great revival of interest in these medieval storytellers, news-bearers, and singers, especially in the ballad forms they used—not just on the part of collectors and scholars but among popular singers and writers. This has a significance far beyond the music or story itself. Burl Ives, Richard Dyer Bennett, Jean Ritchie, Susan Reed, Woody Guthrie, Harry Belafonte are not just entertainers. They are carriers of the folk tradition in America at its best.

Shepherds, pilgrims, crusaders, adventurers, gypsies, troubadours, minnesingers, trouvères, settlers of new lands, mothers, teachers, artists—all have taken their songs and stories with them wherever they went.

They told old tales, often modifying them to fit new circumstances. The great Lord Randal in England became plain Johnny in America.

They told new tales. Some stemmed from the old way of life. Some sprang from the new ways of life.

Everywhere, everywhere people need stories to answer the questioning of every human heart "Who am I?" "Where did I come from?" "Why am I here?" "Whither am I going?" Always, always people need stories—to tell them, to hear them. Storytelling for both teller and listener is an affair of the heart as well as of the mind, and beyond both, of the spirit.

Human experiences of need, longing, sorrow, joy are universal. So the story that arises here and there and everywhere from basic human experiences is universal. Anyone, anywhere, may enjoy a Spanish, Irish, Chinese, or Turkish story. The story itself could have happened anywhere, but the details are characteristic of the locale. The don is Spanish, the actor is Chinese, the leprechaun is Irish, and the hodja exists only in Turkey. The essential universal story lives on and on and may become known and loved in a country far from its origin. Sometimes it is easy to determine the origin of a story. Greek myths could come only from Greece, the Nibelungen from Germany, Viking tales from Norway and Denmark. But take our story of the peddler and the monkeys. It appears in a number of places in American books. In one it is called "a Russian folk tale," in another "an old tale from Brazil." But a few years ago, the Metropolitan Museum of New York acquired a beautiful old Persian vase, dated by scholars several hundred years before Christ. Around its sides is a vivid portrayal of the peddler, the monkey stealing his caps, his strenuous efforts to regain them, and the final recovery of the caps! Peddlers are very old in the history of man, probably having come into existence when first any exchange of goods began between two groups. So we might find peddler stories of like nature almost anywhere in the world.

Almost every people has some form of the flood story. Noah has many counterparts, probably because all human beings at sometime wish they could wipe the slate clean and begin all over again. So here is a wish fulfillment story that assures the sinner, the needy one, the unhappy one that his Creator believes in him and will give him a chance to begin again. All the life experience from birth to death, in this world and out of it, is the warp and woof from which great storytellers weave their story tapestry.

All the world's great teachers have known this and have used the story or parable (a story shaped to teach some special lesson) to teach and to inspire their students. So, too, have leaders of the world's great religions—Moses, Confucius, Buddha, Mahomet, Jesus—used stories and parables to explain to their followers their concepts of God and man and man's relationship to both his God and his fellow man. Every follower and disciple tells these stories and parables again and again unto all generations.

When men began to keep records of that which they cherished and wished to hand on to future generations, some beloved stories were inscribed. No one is really certain when that time was. Probably the earliest actual records we have are the Egyptian papyri with the Tales of the Magicians, which scholars believe go back as far as 4000 B.C. In these, supposedly, the sons of Cheops, the great pyramid builder, entertained their father with stories, each picking up where the other left off. Thousands of years later, this device of a group of stories suspended on a central framework was used in the *1001 Tales of the Arabian Nights,* and still later in Chaucer's *Canterbury Tales.*

Stories will always be one of the great means of communication between man and his fellow man—myths, legends, hero tales, epics, sagas, fables, parables, folk tales, fairy tales, ballads, stories of real life then and now, stories rare and magical—for stories are of the stuff of life.

This is our heritage. It goes back to the beginning of time and is as rich as the total of human experience—a wide, wide river flowing onward and onward. It is the heritage of everyone, making storytellers of us all.

2

The Teller

> *Every man is a special kind of artist, and in his originating activity, his play or work, he is doing more than expressing himself, he is manifesting the form which our common life should take in its unfolding.*
>
> *—Jacob Burckhardt*

And now what of the storyteller?

Each of you is a special kind of artist, and your storytelling is part of the form our common life is taking today —in its unfolding. You, too, are creating a part of this form, for storytelling is a creative art. You will use all the experience you have; you will build the richest possible background; you will use words put together in beauty, in truth; you will use your voice and all your gifts of expression to create the story for the eager listener to hear.

No song lives until it is sung and heard.

No story lives until it is told and heard.

The storyteller is the medium through whom the story comes to life, the transmitter, the reflector, the catcher of the spark between man and man, God and man.

Fritz Eichenberg reminds us:

> The normal child is born with every quality a creative human being needs. He has imagination—freedom to rise above earth-bound rationality. He has perception, grasping the essence of a thing seen for the first time. He has insight—feeling the vibration of human emotions before they become visible. He has enthusiasm—applying himself freshly and eagerly to each new task. He has spontaneity—reaching to life and its steadily changing aspects. The child is also able to concentrate on essentials without being side-tracked by the countless distractions of everyday life. All these qualities are the basic ingredients of creative man which we must try to preserve or recapture.

Imagination, perception, insight, enthusiasm, spontaneity, concentration—these are the qualities of any creative artist. Add to these the desire to share experience with listeners, sensitivity to the needs and moods of those listeners, sincere joy in the sharing process, and you have the makings of a good storyteller. A person of such quality and integrity would never tell mediocre or unworthy stories.

Anyone with sufficient desire and integrity can take the gifts with which he was born and develop them as experience widens opportunity. Anyone with a feel for sounds, for words, for those words put together in beauty and in truth may build a language and literary background. Any healthy person may become a vital, charming person. Anyone can learn how to use his voice, enunciate distinctly, develop skills of proper pitch and tempo in his speech. Anyone can become so interested in others that he loses himself in a total group experience. This is a path open to any of you who would become a good teller of tales. The heritage belongs to everyone, but the use you make of it, the development of the qualities for creative living, depends upon you, the desiring individual.

Your self and your experience are your resources to use, to enrich, to build with. You must treasure the quality of your experience for the experience itself. Lyman Bryson believes that we are in the throes of a cultural rebirth, with a revival of faith in creative living. He says in his book, *The Next America:*

> It is not like anything known before because it is on such a scale of participation that past standards do not apply. If it succeeds it will be the creation, by its own members, of a national community in which energy is more and more shifted from material and practical anxieties to the doing of things for the sake of greater human experience. . . . We shall be doing things for their own sake, which means for the developing experience they give, for the demands they make on personalities for greater power and sensitiveness. It is part of our recovered wisdom to know that we live not to pile up comforts or ornaments but for the quality of the experience itself.

You must realize the qualities with which you were born and learn to trust and use your own experience. Somehow education has struggled so hard to develop a conforming good citizen, that the "bending of the twig" has often stunted growth instead of nourishing it. The growing child must conform. So layers and layers of taboos, customs, acceptable behavior pile up, until all spontaneity, simplicity, directness is covered up. Imagination is stifled. There are some who refuse to conform. They dare to be concerned primarily with the joy of living, the quality of the experience itself, not primarily with the business of making a living. They expose themselves to art, to music, to the dance. Taste and appreciation grow. But exposure and appreciation are not enough. Awareness of the relationship of the arts to the business of living inevitably arouses the urge to create. These steps, however, are not only for the genius. This way of life is for everyone. Everything you do and make, everything you feel and think is worthy, is significant, if you live a creative life.

The heart of a child, the mind of a man, the spirit of an angel keep the channels open for creative living—not just for the genius but for you and you and you.

All your experience, then, for its own quality is your resource to use. Are you a homemaker? You must have loved beauty in many forms. You must have developed a good sense of humor to survive any active family! You must have developed genuine sympathy as the refuge and confidante of husband and child.

Are you a teacher? You must have developed all these and many other qualities: to speak clearly so that even those in the back of the room could hear, to enunciate distinctly, to give children a genuine delight in words.

Are you an executive or manager? You must have developed many of these same qualities and at the same time discovered how to organize your work, how to choose your materials, how to listen to people, how to select essentials.

You will use every aspect of those experiences in becoming a good storyteller—sensitiveness to beauty, enjoyment of humor, sympathetic feeling for others, ability to organize, ability to select essentials, speaking clearly—all these and many more are the qualities that go into the cauldron of life to simmer and simmer. Your whole self—mind, body and spirit disciplined by you—will make a good storyteller. It is important to know much about man's thinking and creative expression in music, literature, and art, but culture is not just an acquired familiarity with these. There must develop within you a constantly operating taste, a vibration to your own rhythm of conviction as part of the rhythm of the universe. Then your thinking and feeling give form—good form, right form—to that which you create. Only what we know through experience is ours with which to work. It is this realization and acceptance of such a way of living that will make of us all the creative artists essential for the good life, not only in our own time but in all time.

It is helpful to share the thinking of philosophers and teachers who are concerned with bringing about creative living. Stanwood Cobb in *New Horizons for the Child* assures us that creative people are the happiest people and gives an account of many school experiences that reveal the value of what he calls "a victorious attitude toward life." Natalie Cole in *Arts in the Classroom* actually takes you into her fifth-grade classroom in Los Angeles so that you dance and sing and draw with those children and see what happens in an atmosphere of freedom and encouragement.

John Dewey and Hughes Mearns not only have expounded
with conviction this whole concept culturally and philosophi-
cally, but also have given careful accounts of specific experi-
ments with both children and adults; see Dewey's *Art as Experience* and Mearns' *Creative Youth, Creative Power* and
Creative Adult. Viktor Lowenfeld compels honest thinking in
his book, *Creative and Mental Growth*.

To live creatively oneself, all the knowledge and understanding of how a human being grows and learns is of great value. No
one has ever made this quite so clear as Dr. L. Thomas Hopkins,
both in his lectures and in his writing, especially in *The Emerg-
ing Self*. It is a challenge to digest that exposition of growth
and to think through its implications for both living and learning. For concrete application, Chapters II and III in *Creative
School Music* by Dr. Hopkins and Lillian Fox discuss the nature and nurture of creativity in the learning process, especially
in music, but the implications belong to other areas as well.
For those who would like specific information, both physio-
logical and psychological, the books *The Child from Five to
Ten* and *Youth: The Child from Ten to Sixteen* by Arnold
Gesell and Frances Ilg are probably the best. They were written after years of observation, testing, and recording.

Although *The Here and Now Story Book* is not a book on
child development, Lucy Sprague Mitchell wrote the introduction from much first-hand experience with children in City and
Country School, New York, where she was especially concerned
with observing language patterns in relation to growth and
evolving interests of children from two to seven years old. Her
observation and description of the reactions, responses, interests of each age group are thought-provoking.

It is essential to understand the growth process, how actual
learning takes place, both for self-knowledge and self-develop-
ment as well as for the sharing of experience and the teaching
of children and young people. This means the fullest use and
development of your senses, your feelings, your intellect, and
your spirit.

Do you take your senses for granted? Or are you poignantly
alive to all the variety of experience they open to you when you

feel, taste, smell, see, and hear not just a cotton dress or a wood table, but velvet or an ancient Chinese teak table; not just meat balls or cabbage, but pomegranates and mangoes soaked in wine; not just a marigold or coffee, but a fresh wood violet and Soochang tea; not just a rock or a tree, but an emerald or a silver birch just turning golden in the fall; not just a sparrow's chirp or the sax of the boy next door, but a loon's call or the sound of the Budapest Quartet playing Beethoven. Our Christian, Protestant, Puritan heritage sometimes lays a heavy hand on sensual experience—full use of the senses—sometimes confusing it with sensuous experience chiefly associated with sex and all the taboos of our society. Such a book as Somerset Maugham's *The Moon and Sixpence,* based on the life of the artist Gauguin, reveals how an artist's expression in color comes from his profound sense responsiveness; John Cowper Powys' *In Defense of Sensuality* makes possible a wonderful rediscovery of what it can mean to respond to all the senses.

How do you look at a stone?

How would you test the texture of an oriental rug? With your cheek, as an experienced merchant does?

How do you feel glass? With your tongue, as a child does?

How do you like herbs or unusual flavors?

How do you react to the harmonic the violin player occasionally draws from his violin? Do you shrink from that high delicate pitch or do you respond to it?

Do the first hepaticas in the spring smell different on a rainy day?

New meanings from men's words put together in beauty, in truth, will emerge as you let your senses come alive and trust the full extent of your response. You can talk better about what you really know from first-hand experience.

Of greater significance perhaps is the development of your intellect and your emotions. The study of philosophy, history, sociology, anthropology, psychology is an individual matter—the more you learn, the richer you are and become.

But if you never went to college or if your college courses in these areas bored you because they seemed to pass on only cumulative facts or records without making you aware of the relationship of these facts to you and your life, don't run away from all books in these fields. Read a biography of a person whose way of life intrigues you—Schweitzer, Edith Cavell, Toscanini, Picasso, Beethoven, Gershwin, Bronson Alcott or Louisa, Sarah Orne Jewett, Samuel Clemens, Henry Ford, Thomas Edison, or St. Exupery. Some identification takes place—this could have been me. So you are part of the experience.

Or an historical novel may recreate a period or place for you with new, vital human experience. Or you may gain more from a general penetrating analysis of history such as Spengler's *Decline of the West* or Toynbee's *Study of History.*

Some reading in the special areas of sociology and anthropology may open many doors for you. Margaret Mead's books and those of Ruth Benedict are not merely scientific treatises. They open doors to valuable human understanding. So, too, do the psychologists, even down to the modern followers of Jung.

Always conscious of the fact that it is the whole person who is growing and creating, the thinking that a philosopher evokes and the spiritual awareness that comes from every religious experience must find their places in this building of background. To study Plato, Kant, Hegel, Nietzsche may be just intellectual exercise. It took Ouspensky's *Tertium Organum,* added to Aristotle and Bacon, to fire me into seeing relationships, but it could be something wholly different for you. Do not be afraid to dig down to the roots. Real thinking and awakening of the spirit requires digging—digging hard and with no fear, no reservations. It is probably the most exciting adventuring life offers.

This cultivation of the spirit is essential to the making of any artist, small or great. We have said one of the reasons for storytelling is to inspire, "to put spirit into." From spirit comes spirit. The nature lover says he finds his cathedral in the woods. The physician or social worker finds his solution in service to others. The minister, the priest, turns to his Bible, to prayer, to meditation. It is important to read and know the Bible. The Jewish Old Testament and the Christian Bible, consisting of that Old Testament and a new one inspired by the life of Jesus Christ on earth, give a wonderful record of the moral and spiritual growth of man, an amazing interpretation of the power of love and unselfish living in records, prophecies, dramas, poems, precepts, legends, stories, parables, sermons, letters, and prayers. For most of us in the Western world, this Bible is a great source book. Some may well use all the riches of books of other great religions: The Koran, the Sayings of Confucius, the Upanishads. *Small Rain* and *This is the Way*, contain excerpts chosen by Jessie Orton Jones which reveal basic spiritual truths in the Christian religion and other religions of the world. The illustrations in these two books by Elizabeth Orton Jones are truly childlike in understanding—but there is no age level for the spirit's understanding, is there?

Ruth Smith's *Tree of Life* opens the doors of several religions. *Every Day a Prayer* by Margueritte Bro is more than a book for daily meditation and prayer, for it is written by a person of great spiritual stature who culls from the writings of all religions, from poets and artists of the world. It can open many doors that some of us do not encounter in our ordinary routine of living. Every artist draws on nature and man, but also on God. For he who would inspire must himself be inspired.

But, to confine ourselves now to our special art, the art of storytelling—since the teller deals in words, it is important to have a feeling for language as well as some understanding of the language used; to become aware of and rooted in our literary heritage, especially folklore; and to share in the meaning and value of the closely related arts of music, art, poetry, the dance, and drama. A list of books in each of these areas—not a full bibliography in any sense of the word, but books which may be helpful for building background and understanding—will be found on pages 169-176.

Any good storyteller must have a feeling for language, and a fine feeling for words, nuances of meaning as well as of sound. It is interesting to note the increase in books for young people as well as adults that are concerned with the development of communication through language. The writings of Hayakawa, Laird, Pei, Piaget and others will be helpful. Your medium of expression is words, the spoken language. So your vocabulary must be rich and varied. The dictionary is your friend. A wide acquaintance with words actually means wider range of thought and imagination. It is amazing how limited many people are in their vocabularies. Five adjectives suffice to describe the gamut of emotions. Everything from a leaf to a great singer is "lovely"! Does such paucity of expression indicate meager capacity for appreciation as well? A wide command of words is also likely to make you more at home with the language of great writers. You will be able to interpret what they have told or written far better if their words are familiar to you. Enrich your vocabulary and enjoy words. Play with them as a musician plays with sounds or as an artist plays with color. Your medium becomes increasingly flexible as you work with it and enjoy it.

We can learn much from children here, for children play with sounds, with words. They enjoy words often as much for the sound as for the meaning, sometimes more. Poetry is meant to be heard—hence it is a wonderful medium for developing enjoyment of word sounds and meanings. Words have overtones and undertones. The writings of James Joyce and Gertrude Stein are not meaningless. They require from the reader a keen awareness of sound as well as of sense. If you think you do not understand what these writers say, read a page aloud and see how the totality of sounds illuminates the meaning. In fact, it takes both sound and meaning to establish significant communication. You enjoy a story and want to tell it, not only because of what it says, but also because of how it is told, what words have been chosen, how they sound and how they are put together. Words—all the words there are—are yours to put together in beauty, joy, and truth.

To have a sensitive ear, to know and love great literature—from folk tales and myths to Plato, Shakespeare, and the good writers of today—is essential to building your critical judgment. It is good, therefore, to read some critical evaluation of great literature, Bacon, Ruskin, Pater and Carlyle, as well as John Cowper Powys, Virginia Woolf, Sir Arthur Quiller-Couch, Edmund Wilson, Joseph Wood Krutch.

One finds one's own path in this building of background. Having discovered John Cowper Powys, it was inevitable that

I would read everything he wrote, so his *Enjoyment of Literature* took me a step farther. Virginia Woolf became not only my friend in *A Room of One's Own,* but also a guide to many new ways of appreciation in *The Common Reader.* Some others have been helpful to me and may well be to you. Robert P. Tristram Coffin has opened many doors to understanding and appreciation of poetry in *On the Green Carpet.* He takes his readers back to sources of creative living, to sources of the art of writing, and to the special art of writing poetry. For better understanding of Shakespeare's amazing genius, read Coffin's chapter on the yeomanly Shakespeare and the books of Marchette Chute, especially her *Shakespeare of London, Introduction to Shakespeare,* and *Stories from Shakespeare.* Her telling of the stories of all the plays in the original folio is a wonderful new resource for storytellers.

Wide familiarity with good and great literature is essential to every good storyteller, familiarity not only with the stories themselves, plot, characterization, place, mood, but also with the style of writing, the words chosen, and the way they are put together. A long process? Yes, that's the fun. It takes eagerness, enthusiasm, desire to learn, to become, to share. You keep finding more resources, your taste improves, your judgment grows, your capacities enlarge, your skill and artistry develop. This goes on all your life.

Added to a wide familiarity with many forms of literature and the special areas that seem to belong to you, every story-teller needs knowledge of our folk heritage. Such books as Bulfinch's *Age of Fable,* Gayley's *Classic Myths,* Fiske's *Myths and Mythmakers,* Dasents' *Popular Tales from the North,* Curtin's *Myths and Folklore of Ireland,* Frazer's *The Golden Bough,* Malory's *Morte d'Arthur,* and Botkin's *Treasury of American Folklore* should be not just resources you know about, but resources you know intimately.

Storytelling belongs to everyone who is young in heart and has a listening ear, but most of you who are reading this book are probably more concerned with telling stories to children. So a fuller knowledge of childen's literature is absolutely essential. An inspiring book to read is Paul Hazard's *Books, Chil-*

dren and Men. The insight of this French philosopher into the place of literature in the pattern of human growth is sensitive, illuminating. The Horn Book Company, which published it, has been responsible for so much light on our path. Bertha Mahoney Miller and Elinor Whitney, its past editors, in their *Realms of Gold* and their fine editing of Volume I of the Horn Book Papers, Newbery Medal Books, and Volume II, Horn Book Papers, Caldecott Medal Books, are rich contributors to our understanding. The wonderful leader of so much of the best in the growth of children's libraries in our country, Anne Carroll Moore, has written *My Roads to Childhood.* Her fine judgment is revealed in all we know of her own work in the New York Public Library. Her three volumes of critical comment on children's literature in the *Three Owls,* is continued in a "Three Owls'" notebook section of The Horn Book. This is the only magazine devoted solely to children's books and authors. It is as valuable as it is enjoyable. Lillian Smith in *The Unreluctant Years* and Dorothy Neal White in *About Books for Children* also show fine critical literary judgment as well as sensitive understanding of children.

The close relationship of all the arts is clearly evident. The richer your background and experience in music, drama, dancing, art, the richer your understanding and expression in your own art medium. General books such as Hendrik Wilhelm Van Loon's *The Arts,* with his special *joie de vivre* and wide appreciation, and Lewis Mumford's thoughtful *The Arts in Revival* give excellent general background.

Music and literature are so closely related, especially folk music and folklore, that music seems to be most closely related to our art of storytelling. Therefore, I am recommending some fine books to provide a background in music appreciation as well as many good song collections. Everything said about folk music applies to folklore and vice versa. Perhaps when you read it, you realized that only a musician could have written *Jean Christophe,* but if you have not done so, go the step farther with Romain Rolland in his *Essays in Music.* Then follow with James Mursell's *Education for Musical Growth,* Howard McKinney's *Music and Man,* William Newman's *Understand-*

ing Music, as well as the books of the two critics who have become well known to many of us through radio and TV, Deems
Taylor and Olin Downes. John Tasker Howard probably gives
the richest background for American music in *Our American
Music: Three Hundred Years of It.* Frank Luther's *Americans
and Their Songs* is one of the most complete records of our
country's songs. Beatrice Krone and I have developed this
whole idea of literature and music as keys to human understanding and as a basis for creative learning and expression in
Literature and Music as Resources for the Social Studies.

Not only do all these critics and scholars introduce music but
also musicians—especially the great artists and accounts of how
they achieved the heights in their performance. Practice? Of
course, to the point where the technique is never anything one
is aware of, but is rather a very part of one's being. There is
complete assimilation. Actually there is little practicing ever
done immediately before performance.

Perfect knowledge of the piece to be performed? Yes, such
knowledge and familiarity that there is a strong sense of kinship
with this piece of life which is being transmitted to others.

Assurance? Yes, because the music, the story is also yours
and you are happy, even proud to be sharing it. Yehudi Menu-
hin tells of how he relives in his mind's eye any concerto during
those hours before performance—in his feeling, his thinking,
his imagination. So fingers, mind, heart, spirit, the whole person
is in perfect tune and becomes the perfect medium for sharing.
All this is applicable to your own storytelling. Repeated performance of what you live with means that the story, the music
is part of you; the sharing, a living experience.

The Music Appreciation Readers of Hazel Kinscella are valuable in giving folk background and feeling in both music and
story. So, too, are many of the fine song collections. The Proven-
son's imaginative and charming illustrations enhance collections as *The Fireside Book of Folk Songs* and *The Fireside
Book of Favorite American Songs.* The Lomaxs' *Folk Song
U.S.A.,* Burl Ives' *Song Book,* Carl Sandburg's *Song Bag,* Jean
Ritchie's *Swapping Song Book* are all in the folk tradition and
again are *musts*—not just to know, but to live with, so that you

know them as friends. Opal Wheeler gives backgrounds of many songs we love, where they came from or how they were written in *Sing for America, Sing in Praise.*

The Recreation Association of Delaware, Ohio, has gathered hundreds and hundreds of folksongs and other songs and published them in many small, inexpensive paper-covered booklets, such as *Songs for the Open Road, Songs of Many Nations, Lift Every Voice.*

Max and Beatrice Krone believe that singing together is one of the greatest means of happy living. Their many collections of songs in their book, *A World in Tune,* arrangements of many songs from *Early Greek Music* to *Songs from Many Lands* are excellent. There are three collections which also give descants with the songs. Descants are built on the overtones one hears, a good means for developing the listening ear and for adding to understanding from the sounds themselves and their overtones. Words as well as tones have overtones. This is one way to build with all that we hear.

Most of the basic music series used in schools today have excellent selections from the folk music of America and the whole wide world. These are also good to build with.

Art, architecture, drama, dancing are closely related arts. Herbert Read's *Education Through Art,* Neutra's *Survival Through Design,* and Hazel Robertson's *Children's Theatre* all open new avenues of understanding, how to bring alive all the means for good creative expression.

There is not much literature concerned only with storytelling. *The Art of Storytelling* by Marie Shedlock, the English storyteller, is invaluable. In our own country, a distinguished storyteller is Ruth Sawyer. Her book, *The Way of a Story Teller,* is the best help I know. It lives because it is her own life story. From her rich living and telling you learn much about the history of this folk art, and about ways to develop your own art. She includes a group of stories she loves to tell.

So, making a good storyteller is like making a good forest or garden or home or person. It is a way of life, in which a channel is opened through which may pour all the background, experi-

ence, awareness, skill, artistry you possess and can develop. And
each of you will develop in your own individual way, despite
all these common resources from which to draw.

There is a river up near Castleton, Vermont, which sang a
song that says this clearly. You can find it in *The Blue Cat of
Castle Town* by Catherine Coblentz, the story of the blue cat
born only once in a blue moon, who will find his own hearth
place only if he can find a human being who can hear *and* learn
the river's song. But it is a song that everyone must learn who
would live the creative life, with storytelling as part of it.

> Sing your own song.
> Sing your own song.
> Out of yesterday song comes,
> It goes into tomorrow.
> Sing your own song.
>
> With your life fashion beauty.
> This, too, is the song.
> Riches will pass and power,
> Beauty remains.
> Sing your own song.
>
> All that is worth doing, do well.
> Sing your own song.
> Certain and round be the measure
> Every line graceful and true.
> Time is the mold, the weaver, the carver,
> Time and the workman together.
> Sing your own song.
> Sing well, sing well.
>
> —Catherine Cate Coblentz, *The Blue Cat of Castle Town*

3

The Telling

When you meet your friend on the roadside or in the marketplace, let the spirit in you move your lips and direct your
tongue.
Let the voice within your voice speak to the ear of his ear;
For his soul will keep the truth of your heart, as the taste of the
wine is remembered
When the colour is forgotten and the vessel is no more.*

F REQUENTLY when someone speaks of hearing a
story, he will use a figure of speech, saying of the
teller, "He spins a yarn," or "He weaves a tale." The spinner
takes many small bits of wool and spins them into a strong

* Reprinted from *The Prophet* by Kahlil Gibran with permission of the
publisher, Alfred A. Knopf, Inc. Copyright 1923 by Kahlil Gibran, renewal
copyright 1921 by Administrators C.T.A. of Kahlil Gibran Estate, and Mary
G. Gibran.

length of yarn. A weaver does more. He lays a good warp and then weaves the yarn in and out of it, his woof, into a pattern he wishes to create. The result is beautiful to see, as he knew it would be because he has chosen good yarn and suitable colors and has given much thought to what he is creating and who is going to use and enjoy it. The weaver himself enjoys the weaving.

So also does the good storyteller enjoy telling his story. You, too, take all the strands needed to tell a story and weave them into a pattern for your listeners to enjoy. There are many factors in this experience which will open the doors to humor or beauty or self-understanding or wonder in the hearts and minds of your listeners.

1. The story you tell must belong to you. You must like it. You must enjoy it. You must want to tell it.

2. You must know the story so well that it is part of you. There can be no possibility of forgetting.

3. You will use all the heritage that is yours for the taking and all the individual rich background you have built for yourself.

4. You will tell the story simply, directly, sincerely with freedom and ease and good use of your body.

5. You will trust the medium you use—words.

6. You will develop the instrument you use—your voice—so that it has correct pitch, good timbre, and appropriate strength.

7. You will pace your telling skillfully, changing the tempo as needed and using pauses effectively.

8. You will have good rapport with your listeners so that you can create with them a living experience.

First of all then, the story you choose to tell must be one you yourself like to live with, one you enjoy so much you want others to enjoy it too. Then you will tell it almost as if there were a compulsion to do so. Inevitably such a story will be a worth-while story, one that has stood the test of time, of many retellings including your own. No good storyteller will waste his time or that of his listeners with anything that is cheap or mediocre or stereotyped. It may be funny, it may be serious, it may be right out of everyday life, it may recreate the past, it may teach a lesson or entertain, it may give you insight or lift your spirits, but it must be a story worth living with.

— But not all stories, even good ones, belong to each of us. And no one tells a story well that is not part of himself. The listening children will always know whether this is your story, or just another one learned for the occasion. You can't fool them. When it is yours and the communication is good, they say, "She's the best storyteller there is," "She made it up herself," "She took us right there, didn't she?" "I love that story just like you do."

An eight-year-old boy was looking at an exhibit of books in his school one day. He kept breaking away from his group to look at books intended for older children, saying, "Sissy stuff, nothing ever happens, sissy stuff. 'She' wants you to know every word. That's not it. Something has to happen so you can hardly wait to find out what comes next." He picked up a story of *Pecos Bill and Lightning*. He read a bit and chuckled. "This is good. Say, did you ever tell a story? This would be a good one. What a guy! You don't have to know every word to get right in there and go with him. I'd like to tell this one so you could get in and go too. Gosh!"

That was his kind of story. It might be yours or it might not. Responses differ widely. Different types of stories evoke different feelings and understandings.

For instance, the British sense of humor differs from the American sense of humor. There is not more or less of it, but it is different. Its approach is often indirect, whereas the American approach is direct and forthright. It often has an element of fantasy or of whimsy, but American humor is down to earth, often slapstick. So *Winnie the Pooh* may not seem very funny or even childlike to you. Don't try to tell it. But you may have a large funny bone (American born and bred). Be grateful if you have much to do with children, for most of them have one, too. How often one hears, "Tell us a funny story." Tell the *Man Who Lost His Head* (he really did and what adventures he had before "Boula-boula-boula-boula-bang!" he found it). Tell some of the everyday adventures of Eddie or Ellen Tibbetts or Henry and Beezus or Herbert or Homer, those typical American children who get into typically American funny situations in *Eddie and Gardenia, Ellen Tibbetts, Henry and Beezus, Herbert, More Fun with Herbert, Homer Price.*

If you never liked *Alice in Wonderland* and do not see "what it is all about anyway," don't think you have to tell it because it is a children's classic. If you don't like to "mess around in boats," maybe neither the fanciful *Wind in the Willows* (beautiful as it is to many) or the realistic *Swallows and Amazons* (adventurous as it is to many) are good stories for you to choose.

If you do not like animals who talk like human beings, don't try to tell the *Story of Dr. Dolittle* and Gub Gub and all his animal friends; or of Freddy, the brilliant pig detective of farmer Bean's farmyard whose adventures are told in many books from *Freddy Goes to Florida* to *Freddy and the Flying Saucer Plans;* or of Minty and Louisa, whose talk Nellie could understand when she wore the golden horseshoe pin which used to belong to grandmother in the book *The Magic Pin.* But if you do know animals who talk to you and like them too, then it will be easy for you to make Rat and Mole and Gub Gub and Freddy and Minty and Louisa dear friends to all your listeners. You and they may meet the Piper at the Gates of Dawn or help save the life of a sick baby.

Do you believe in fairies? Then *Piskey Folk, Peter Pan, The Elves and the Shoemaker, The Leprechaun of Bayou Luce* or the *Fairy Tales* of Hans Christian Andersen or Charles Perrault or James Stephens, with all their chancy stories, will come easily from your tongue. But if you don't have much to do with the little people and think "that's all nonsense," just leave them alone or to those whose kin they are. So often it is said that an Irishman is a born storyteller. Certain it is that many are. Sure and if you do not know a leprechaun and have never a drop of Irish blood in you, the Irish fairy tales and legends may not be yours to tell. But read and reread Padraic Colum, William Butler Yeats, Seumas MacManus, James Stephens, if not for the myths or legends or fairy stories themselves, then for the lilt of the telling. The English language comes from the tongue of a gifted Irishman with a lilt and rhythm and beauty that everyone should know. You are likely to grow to enjoy it. And it may be that some of the fairy lore will begin to possess you, for through increasing acquaintance we all change and grow in capacity to know and to appreciate many things not of our own kind.

But perhaps you always ask, "Is it true?" "Did it really happen?" Then you will love little Martin, the shoemaker's son who met Mr. Lincoln on the steps of the White House in *Martin and Abraham Lincoln;* or Laura in *Little House in the Big Woods;* or Johan who became Johnny in *Johnny Texas;* or Johnny and Paul Revere in *Johnny Tremaine* or Daniel Boone in *On Indian Trails with Daniel Boone* or the Venable family in *Tree of Freedom* or Captain John Smith in *This Dear Bought Land.* These real people out of the past come alive as you tell their stories to eager listeners who also want a true story.

Begin where you are. Don't worry about what you do not react to, even if you wish you did or think you ought to. Tell what you do respond to, what you enjoy, what you care about, but always keeping your mind and heart open as you read and reread and listen to all kinds of stories. Constant exposure to that which is good and of wide range will increase your interests, develop your taste, cultivate your appreciation and ultimately affect both what you choose to tell and how you tell it.

The growing person will want to become familiar with all kinds of stories: myths, legends, hero tales, epics, sagas, fables, parables, folk tales, fairy tales old and new, realistic stories of the past and of the present, animal stories, mysterious stories, funny stories, imaginative stories, beautiful stories, and stories of spiritual insight. But you will only tell some of them. The variety of what you choose may increase as your experience increases. Take time to live with those that contain wheat, for it is wheat, not chaff, that nourishes. In a good threshing job the chaff falls to the ground, but time is so precious there is not much time to spend with the chaff. The stories you remember are more likely to be those that are wheat.

The content, the form, and the style of writing of stories both old and new all affect your reaction to them, so sensitive are human beings to each of these elements. All must meet in right balance for you if you are to like the story. You may like the idea of a story or the plot but not the way it is written. Irwin

Shapiro's *How Old Stormalong Captured the Mocha Dick* moves more rapidly than Anne Malcolmson's *Mr. Stormalong* and so, for many, lends itself better to telling. So you may choose one version of a story in preference to another, or adapt one of your own from several sources. You have to trust your own responses—more and more as your experience and skills grow.

As you steep yourself in stories old and new, these responses will increase both in number and in kind, but always you will tell best what you like best. Because storytelling then is such an individual matter, it is good to make and continuously build a list of stories you like best. This is your bank, your resource from which to draw.

Having chosen a story you like, you must know your story well if your listeners are to "get right in there and go with you." Does this mean you must memorize every word? Once in a while, but not often. You would scarcely change a word in a short story such as *Millions of Cats* or *The Noisy Book*, and they are easy to remember as they are. But a word-conscious speaker is not a good storyteller. Important as the words are, it is not just words but the way they are put together that creates the succession of events that build up to the climax, which carries your listeners "right in there with you."

If you are a visual-minded person, you may see your story as a succession of pictures. If you are more motor-minded, you are more likely to think of it as a succession of incidents. If you are audio-minded, you may hear the conversation and sounds that make such happenings come alive. Whatever pattern is your way, the plot line must be clear in your mind. Each incident you tell must be relevant to the main action of the story.

As Isak Dinesen said in one of her *Last Tales*, "The story itself does not slacken its speed to occupy itself with the mien or bearing of its characters, but goes on." This does not mean you need not know those characters well. You must care what happens to each one in order that your listeners may care. Only when you care what happens does the story really have meaning for you.

John had been reading *Tom Sawyer* and *Huckleberry Finn*.

Some days you weren't sure whether he was in Hannibal, Missouri, down by the river or in his own town by the lake. One night his father asked him a question. It was obvious that John had not heard and was really far away at the moment. His father said, "Do you like Tom and Huck?"

"Like?" said John. "I run around with both of them in my mind all the time."

But Joey didn't find Tom and Huck to his liking at all. All Joey's gang thought they did not like to read, to be read to, or to hear stories. One day Joey admitted he had read *Tom Sawyer*.

"Did you like that story, Joey? Didn't you like all Tom's adventures?" asked his teacher, feeling sure here must be some common ground.

"Like them?" he answered. "It was OK for him."

"But didn't you feel you were doing things with him?"

"Me? Not at all. As I said, it was OK for him."

If the story is to live for you, you must care about the characters and what happens, and always the main action must keep going. This means, of course, that you know the story so well that there is absolutely no possibility of your forgetting. Actually you must not just *know* it, you must *be* it.

Rushing in from school, Jeanie said, "Mommy, you have to go hear the lady tonight. She told us a story about a mouse today and mommy, she was a mouse! You have to go see what she is tonight. Whatever it is, she'll be it."

So *be* your story, that is, live in it. If it is a short folk story or a story in the folk idiom, memorize it and tell it just as it is. Most folk stories have been told so many times that all extraneous words have been chiseled away. In retelling other stories in your own words, keep the essential flavor, often using some of the exact words or phrases of the author. He may have worked weeks to get just the exact word or phrase to convey his meaning. The style of his writing may be appropriate to the nature of the story. This may be one of the reasons you respond to it. Now because your listeners evoke a story from you differently at different times and under different circumstances, you may change the story a bit to fit different audiences but you must never violate the essential nature of the story itself. But, always, if your listeners are to "get in there and go with you," you yourself must live in it.

To help those listeners "get in there" you will also need to use the rich heritage that is yours. You are in the great tradition and it is important to open the doors of children's minds and hearts to courage, beauty, goodness, wonder. You will also use all the specific background you have been building through your experience, your reading, your listening, your understanding. Your feeling for this English language you use, a rich language built up through the years from Celtic, Angle, Saxon, Scandinavian, French, Latin, and Greek sources is important to the way you speak, the way you use words. Your familiarity with literature, mythology, folk heritage, fiction, poetry builds your interest, your appreciation, your taste, your ability to recreate. Specifically in storytelling, you will use all that you can discover related to its value, its function, at home, at school, in life today. Marie Shedlock, Ruth Sawyer, and Lucy Sprague Mitchell will be invaluable friends.

Sometimes it may help to give a short background for the story you are telling, to set the stage a little, not with real props but with some information about the time and locale of the story or about the author. Sometimes it is interesting to tell where you first heard or found the story. I first heard the story of Pecos Bill told by a tall, lean cowhand under the Texas stars with all the ranch cowhands sitting around their campfire. Anything that will get your audience into the atmosphere or mood of the story is valuable to a listening situation.

Then tell your story simply, directly, sincerely, using few gestures. Storytelling is not dramatization. It is shared vital experience in which words are the means of communication. There are no specific gestures anyone can teach you to use in expressing joy or sorrow or anger. Your face will show what you feel. If you would naturally use gestures to express joy or sorrow or anger, use them. If you are free and wholly at ease in your story, your body will take care of itself. This is why it is often easier to tell stories while standing rather than sitting down. You may need to move around a bit "to get in there with him," and to take your listeners with you. Your behavior also depends on the size of your audience. You do things differently with a small group by the open fire than you do in a room or a hall with fifty or one hundred or two hundred people.

What you do must be your natural way of expressing yourself, must be characteristic of the story, and must fit your audience. You and the story are the constant factors, the audience the changing one, but always you belong to each other. Actually you may not tell a story exactly the same way twice because each audience draws it forth from you in slightly different form. It all depends not only on what you have to weave with but for whom you are weaving. There was Elinor who said, "Mother, you have to go meet the story lady and get acquainted with her well enough so you can invite her here for dinner. She belongs to us." The good storyteller and her listeners belong to each other.

The medium you use is words, so trust these words and your way of using them. No props are needed—no books, no pictures shown by turning pages as the story goes along—*not while you are telling your story*. What confusion this may make for a child—listening to the story, following you and your words, and having to glance at a picture at the same time to see what someone else thought this dramatic moment looked like. It is good to look at pictures, at illustrations for stories, but not *at* the moment of listening to the story. Gary over here can't see the bear, so you walk over to let Gary look. Barbara couldn't see the bird, so you walk all around to let her look. What has happened to the story? Trust the moments of telling for their own sake—look at pictures another time but don't expect children to do several things at the same time. Even many adults are not too skillful at doing several things at the same time! Also the listener may have a picture in his own mind very different from that of the illustrator, which may be just as valuable for him, or more so. This is not to minimize the wonder of beautiful illustrations which can and should give children great pleasure, but at the proper time, not while they are caught up in the vital experience of living a story being told in words.

Trust the words. They are your medium as tones are the

musician's as strands of yarn are the weaver's. You must have a feel for them, for many of them, the sound as well as the sense. You must enjoy them but also respect, even fear them on occasion. Mighty words! Such power they give you! It is a great trust—this use of the spoken word to light the fire of a kindred spirit of 6 or 16 or 60. Listen, listen, listen to the words you speak, to the words others speak. Listen to children, to babies and their wonderful sounds, to meaningless monosyllables, to just single words, to sentences, to paragraphs, to speeches. Feel the joy of the experimenter, the deep satisfaction of the scholar finding right words to enable others to understand clearly what he has discovered and must communicate. Play with them, experiment with them, build your own thoughts, your own dreams. To help recapture an appreciation for sound, repeat the nonsense refrain of folk songs or ballads. Pay special attention to those words in which the sound suggests the sense, such as squeal—sque-e-eal, howl—how-ow-ow-owl, squawk—squaw-aw-aw-awk. These are used most effectively in *The Bojabi Tree* to make come alive those noisy, hungry animals waiting on the river bank for news about the fruit. The repetition of certain sounds in a succession of active or descriptive words is most effective. Again in *The Bojabi Tree*, they splashed, spluttered, splanked, all *sp* sounds. And later they plunged, pounded, punched, all *p* sounds. Listen to sounds and observe the effect upon your listeners. Experiment widely with words and their sound effects. Experiment, too, with words for fine nuances of meaning, finding *the* one word which expresses exactly—not nearly—but exactly what you wish to say.

It is essential to know many words, to build a rich vocabulary. The dictionary and a thesaurus should be your best friends, the kind you like to live with. We use the English language, a colorful language of many words. The impact of some of those powerful Anglo-Saxon one-syllable words is tremendous. The music of the multi-syllabic word built on Greek meanings and patterns evokes another response.

The more at home you are with a great variety of words, the more at home you will be with the writing of great authors who choose and use their words with precision. Since you are both creator and mediator, facility with words is not just a valuable asset, it is a necessity.

It is important to speak clearly and distinctly, to enunciate the words so that they may be easily grasped by the listener. Perhaps a word about dialects is appropriate here. Those variations in pronunciation that develop everywhere—the Scotch burr, the Irish brogue, the Oxford English, the midwestern twang, the southern drawl, all variations of spoken English—are colorful, but not always easy to imitate. Few northerners can do justice to Uncle Remus and Br'er Rabbit and Br'er Fox. Few Americans can read Robbie Burns well. And none but the Irish have not only a brogue but a special lilt and cadence of word, phrase, and voice. Some few are good imitators. They have very good ears and great skill in reproducing what they hear. If this gift is yours, make the most of it. If not, don't try telling stories in a language pattern not comfortably your own. A storyteller is at his best in his own speech pattern. If your speech patterns are very different from those of your listeners, you can work with your pronunciation and inflection to make it easier for everyone to understand you.

The words of any given story must fit the story, must be appropriate to the characters, the mood, the time, the place of the action. They must also be understandable by the audience. This may be one reason the folk tale, with its simpler universal words, speaks easily to listeners of all ages. However, one never talks down to children or rewrites a great story in words of one syllable "so they will understand." If the story is not understandable, the listeners can well wait until they are old enough in experience to "take that one." Children's oral and recognition vocabulary is very large, probably 5000 words or more by the age of six, and the modern mass media are steadily enlarging it. Any six-year-old in this day of television knows what a "category" is, but this word is on no basic word list. Most children reach up, not down, so do not limit your choice of words. What children don't know today, they will know tomorrow, and context, too, carries meaning. So all the words there are, put together in known and newly devised patterns, are the warp and woof of which stories are woven.

The musician plays his tones on an instrument—a harp, piano, violin, or flute—or sings the tones using his own voice as instrument. So, too, does the storyteller speak his words, sing his tones using his own voice as instrument. The human voice is a wonderful instrument with vocal chords in the throat, a huge sound box below, reaching all the way down to the diaphragm, and a smaller sound box or resonance chamber above, within the bony structure of the skull. It takes proper use of all of these to produce a good sound for others to hear.

A pleasing, carrying voice uses all these component parts fully, being concerned with both the pitch and resonance. Pitch is very important to listening ears. A high-pitched voice is usually thin, often strident, capable of setting listeners' nerves on edge. Listen to your own voice. Is it in the median range? For a woman this is likely to be fairly near "F" above middle "C"; for a man about an octave lower. If it is too high, practice lowering it by talking to yourself. Say a sentence in a high voice, listening to yourself as if you were a third person, and see what the effect is. Then bring it to a pitch that is pleasant to listen to. The narrative part of your story is best told in your natural speaking voice. Cultivate that at a pitch which is pleasing to hear.

The voice should be resonant, not flat. It should be produced by an open throat, not a tight throat. You have heard people say, "He has a throaty voice." He just has not opened his sound boxes and the throat itself is probably constricted. The bones of the jaws, nostrils, even eyesockets vibrate when you speak. You know how skillfully teachers of the deaf work with children whom they are teaching to speak, placing the child's finger along the nostril to feel what happens and helping him to try to reproduce the vibration he feels, to make a pleasing sound. You can do this, too. Place your fingers on the upper jaw and below the eyes and on the nostrils, and hum. Hum as hard as you can until you feel the vibration of all those bones which hold the sound cavity within. Say "e" until you feel the vibration for this sound is a head tone. Make sure that you are using your upper resonance chamber fully.

All the exercises that a singer does to develop a pleasing, resonant, flexible voice are also valuable for developing a good voice for storytelling. Vocalize up three tones and down, up five tones and down, up the eight tones of the octave and down. Begin on "Middle C" going up and down, then move to "C sharp" to "D," to "D sharp," to "E," to "F." Do the same thing in reverse order.

Sound the vowels clearly and distinctly, *a, e, i, o, u,* exaggerating the lip movements as you say them, or sing them on different pitches. Do it slowly, then very rapidly. Notice that *a, i, o, u,* are open sounds which reverberate from the chest sound box. They are chest tones. *E* is a head tone, using the head as its sounding board.

Now sound all these vowels with the consonants *m, b, n, d* and *l,* in front of the vowels in turn. Notice what the lips do in *ma, me, mi, mo, mu,* and *ba, be, bi, bo, bu;* what the teeth and lips do in *na, ne, ni, no, nu* and *da, de, di, do, du;* and what the tongue does in *la, li, lo, lu.* Then open the throat wide to an *ah* sound, making sure there is no constriction. Then bring the lips into a rounded closing sound *oo,* but with the same open throat.

Practice these sounds with all the consonants, using exaggerated mouth movements to perfect them. Watch *k* so that your voice does not drop to the back of your throat. Let *r* vibrate, but not rumble or become guttural. The *s* should be sibilant but not hissing, the *th* clean but not thick.

If you come from certain parts of the South and find that your short *a* is really two sounds so that "Ann" sounds like "A-un," practice a brisk short *a* until you can say "Ann" in one syllable. Many people slur words or drop down into their throats last syllables at the ends of words or sentences. With a little attention and care, this speech pattern can be improved so that all listeners can understand the teller. Work so that your pronunciation and voice quality will be easy to understand and pleasing to hear. Listen to your own voice. Make a tape recording of a story. Then listen to it. Don't say, "I don't sound like that. I know I don't." But you do. There it is. And you know exactly what you have to work with, what you have to work on —pitch, resonance, vowel sounds, consonant sounds.

Now move from sounds to words—short ones, long ones— speak them clearly, distinctly, softly, loudly, with a low pitch with a high pitch. Listen to them, say them again with different accents or different sounds and with varying emotions back of them. Then try sentences, perhaps beginning with a familiar Mother Goose rhyme and going on to other remembered poetry or a psalm or a prayer you know well. New meaning will emerge from old words as you speak them with the new awareness which comes from better use of your voice.

Beside pitch and quality of tone or sound, there is also strength of sound, loudness or softness. The straight narrative parts of a story are best told in your natural speaking voice with good carrying tone. But in a tender or eerie moment, the voice must become soft but the control must be so exact, the vibration kept so right that even a whisper can be heard at the back of the room. In a stormy, tempestuous, exciting moment your voice grows loud, even louder, easily heard but never rasping or harsh to the listener's ear. This control of the voice is not ventriloquism, actually throwing the voice sound to a given place. It is made possible by developing a flexible instrument that has a wide range not only of pitch but of strength so that, whether soft or loud, it can be heard all over the room. This does not mean yelling to produce a loud sound. It means strengthening the volume with controlled modulation so that the voice may carry.

One of the most important factors in developing this well-modulated, resonant speaking voice is breath control. Your whole chest is the base of your sound production. This is your lower resonance chamber. You must fill the lungs with air all the way down to the diaphragm to produce clear, resonant sounds and hold them as long as need be. Find out whether you use only half of your lungs in breathing. If so, practice filling the whole lung. Place your hands at your waistline, middle fingertips meeting in back. Take a deep breath. Does this force the fingers apart? It should. Practice taking deep breaths until it does. Try panting. Try laughing not only with a ha-ha-ha! but with a ho-ho-ho! from the belly. Good breathing and breath control is the very foundation upon which fine sound production rests. Deep, regular breathing also has many good effects upon a human being. Tenseness anywhere in the body is always a handicap in performance. Breathing deeply for a few minutes before beginning to tell your story will not only relax you but give you the best foundation for effective sound production with that instrument of yours, the voice.

Every language has not only its specific words but also its characteristic inflections. This rising and falling of the voice, the lift or drop at the end of a sentence, has a great deal to do with the measure of the listeners' understanding and pleasure. There is a cadence in spoken phrases, sentences, just as there is in musical phrases. This should not be exaggerated, but pleasantly developed in a natural way characteristic of your own manner of speaking.

As in music, the sounds in a story are arranged in a special rhythmic pattern. So timing is of great importance in telling a good story well. A moderate pace is good for the narrative portion, a relaxed walk. But there are those quiet moments, tender, gentle, sometimes eerie. You drop your voice—you really lower it, not drop it—and you slow your tempo to a slow walk. Sometimes, at the very high dramatic moment of the story, the whole impact is heightened by a slow pace, giving time for the listeners' emotional identification as well as for intellectual comprehension. This may even become a very slow walk with a pause in each step.

Or when the action becomes lively it may be effective to quicken your pace to a brisk walk. The action may become so swift and exciting that you almost break into a run. Just don't stay there too long and take everyone's breath away!

This whole rhythmic pattern of timing is one of the most effective ways in which you build contrasts. For instance, in the story of Old Stormalong, the first time he tries to capture the whale, the whole crew is noisy and races to the place where the whale is, but he fools them and gets away. Stormalong and the crew fail. Now Stormalong does not enjoy failure so he tries many other kinds of work but without success, due chiefly to his lack of patience. When he goes back to the sea and again wants to capture that whale, he changes his whole technique. The first time there is a loud, noisy chase. The second time is a quiet, easy stealing up on the creature. The storyteller changes his technique in pitch and pace accordingly to fit the contrasting procedures.

Sometimes a pause, just before a word or a sentence with a new or climaxing idea, is effective. Again in Stormalong at the end: "Always he wears"—a long pause as the whole audience almost has to say it with you—"a ten-gallon hat."

Sometimes pauses are part of the structure of the story. Sometimes they help your listeners to realize you are there, inside the story place or time. The Irish call these runs, a moment or two for the listeners to catch their breath or to get into the mood of the story a little more fully. This may even be a bit of description of "the rolling hills" or "the sky with never a cloud to alter its blueness." Or it may be a refrain, pure nonsense such as "Wing wong waddle, To my jack straw straddle," or a repetition of rhythmic words such as "hundreds of cats, thousands of cats, millions and billions and trillions of cats," which recur several times in the story *Millions of Cats*. Because little children's response is so largely motor, they often move their heads or hand, and if they are free in their reactions, soon say such a refrain with you. This kind of participation is highly desirable in a mutual experience, so you pause before the next recurrence and your delighted audience is one with you in the telling. Obviously, this should never be done to the point of running away with the story. The teller must always be in control and always be the teller. The use of different kinds of pauses, actual silence, a bit of running-along action or description, a refrain has much to do with effectiveness in your telling.

Some stories are better read aloud, and there are many times when it is good to read a story. A story read aloud is probably not as effective as a story told, for the reader is more limited even though he may choose any story he pleases. A good storyteller is more free. A good reader does many of the same things a good storyteller does, modulating his voice, changing tempo, building up to his climax, and watching the effect upon his listeners. The way certain authors use words and phrases may be one of the chief reasons for enjoyment of the story. Because it is almost impossible to memorize and retain all the cadences, it is better to read the ringing, swinging prose of Meridel Le Seuer's tall tales of Davy Crockett and Johnny Appleseed, or the beautiful rhythmic prose of Padraic Colum's versions of the Norse legends in *Children of Odin* or Greek myths in *The Golden Fleece*. Colum does not tell his myths and legends in Irish, but only an Irishman with his gifts could have told them in such rich, moving, rhythmic English. See what it means to read these aloud.

CHANTICLEER

Meridel Le Sueur

And coming through the snow-covered trees, through the Christmas night, tall, muscular and fleet, Davy Crockett swung out of the wilderness into his own cabin clearing, into the cries and the arms of his family.

"I got the dynamite," he shouted above the din. "Ain't I the yaller blossom of the forest, the flower of gum swamp? I knowed it was Christmas Eve so I jumped on Death Hug's back, whistled up a hurricane, grabbed hold of a streak o' lightnin', greased it with rattlesnake oil, and it let me down in my own clearing in nothing flat."

"Shut up, you wind bag of brag." Polly was mad now he was safe. "We heard you were dead. We heard you were buried."

"Why," cried Davy Crockett, swinging her up in his arms, "I knowed that was a whopper of a lie the minute I heerd it!"

They all looked dismayed and then they all began to laugh and the hounds laughed and the little fiddler came out of the snow laughing in his long beard and they all went into the warm cabin. Robbie punched up the fire to warm the greatest hunter in Kentucky or Tennessee, the ring-tailed roarer, Davy Crockett.

He looked at his family and gave out a big laugh so the rafter shook. "Keep me in salt to keep me from spilin'. Give me food and I'll be easy and ready for a fight, a shoot, a sail, or a turner, or a twister. Tune up there, fiddler, I'm a roarin' to go!"

LITTLE BROTHER OF THE WILDERNESS

Meridel Le Sueur

But Johnny Appleseed was not lonely. He walked back and forth across the country like a shuttler tending his apple trees. He went into the wilderness, out of the wilderness. He was in the snake and the buffalo country, into the tall grass and the short grass country, through the forests, down the rivers.

With him walked the animals, and above him flew his friends the birds, and deep down in the tall grass and the short grass, the tiny eyes of quails saw him. Worms and snails moved out of the way of his toes. All the crawling, creeping, stinging things watched Johnny Appleseed going by, wearing the morning and the evening light, reading the sky, with a hoe instead of a gun.

They all said, "There goes Johnny Appleseed, going back for seed, or going West to plant them, with one pants' leg blue and the other red, his cup, the palm of his hand."

THE GOLDEN FLEECE

Padraic Colum

And now with sail spread wide the Argo went on, and the heroes rested at the oars. The wind grew stronger. It became a great blast, and for nine days and nine nights the ship was driven fearfully along.

The blast drove them into the Gulf of Libya, from whence there is no return for ships. On each side of the gulf there are rocks and shoals, and the sea runs toward the limitless sand. On the top of a mighty tide the Argo was lifted and she was flung high up on the desert sands.

A flood tide such as might not come again for long left the Argonauts on the empty Libyan land. And when they came forth and saw that vast level of sand stretching like a mist away into the distance, a deadly fear came over each of them. No spring of water could they descry; no path; no herdsman's cabin; over all that vast land there was silence and dead calm. And one said to the other: "What land is this? Whither have we come? Would that the tempest had overwhelmed us, or would that we had lost the ship and our lives between the Clashing Rocks at the time when we were making our way into the Sea of Pontus."

There is a place for reading some stories aloud as well as for telling them, but always you must live the story so that you can make it live for others. Padraic Colum once described a man who stood in a corner of a brilliantly lighted room in a situation not conducive to good telling or good listening to a story. The man used few gestures, spoke simply but sincerely. Soon everyone around him, including Colum, was completely unaware of his surroundings. What had happened? The listeners were living the story with him. This is what must happen when you weave a tale. You must so enter into the story with your listeners that they open their hearts and minds even as you opened yours to a full identification with the characters. You and they care as much what happens to the characters as if they were yourselves. Good weaving of your tale builds a genuine rapport with your listeners. And in like manner, good rapport with them makes you better in your weaving.

Choosing a story that belongs to you, that you enjoy; knowing the story so well you are completely at ease in it, with no possibility of forgetting; using all the heritage and background you have—knowledge of times and places, of people and relationships, and appreciation of man's need and skill to express his understandings in literature; telling the story simply, directly, sincerely; knowing well the medium you use—words, sensing their power with fine nuances and wide range of meaning; using your voice skillfully with careful concern for pitch, timbre, quality and strength so that it is pleasing to your listeners; pacing the tale to exactly the right tempo for each situation; pausing for effect when desirable, whether actually keeping silent or introducing a run or nonsense refrain; feeling close rapport with your listeners because you belong to each other; these are the elements that make telling a story an experience in which your listener "will keep the truth of your heart, as the taste of the wine is remembered when the colour is forgotten and the vessel is no more."

> No, it'll not do just to read the good old tales out of a book
> You've got to tell 'em to make 'em go right.
>
> —Richard Chase, *Grandfather Tales*

4

What Makes a Story Good to Tell

A tale, a yarn, a story
It is a wondrous thing
To live in rags or glory
Or in a fairy ring.

WHAT makes a story live?
What makes this story one you want children to live with, that you know they, too, will enjoy?

How do you know what is wheat, not chaff?

How can you be sure this is a cut diamond, not just a piece of white glass cut in imitation?

50

There are some generally accepted criteria. First of all, the story will have a good plot with something of interest to resolve. The incidents chosen to unfold this plot must be selected carefully, all of them relevant to the main action. For very young children a story may be episodic, with little evidence of cause and effect, but even the episodes chosen must be related, must fit the central character. The plot may develop by different means—conflict, contrast, repetition—but the main action must go on uninterruptedly. The plot line must be so clear that anyone wanting to tell the story can easily recognize and follow it in the telling.

The characters must be true to what they are supposed to be. They must be real enough so that you care what happens to them. Paper dolls, "wooden Indians," stereotypes are not worthy characters. If the characters are to live in you, they must live in the story. Both teller and listener must not only want to identify with the main character or characters of a story, but also be able to do so easily, naturally. The character may be someone out of the past, someone from a far country, someone you might easily know in your own community, but he must be real enough so that you want to live with him. Or he may be an imaginary character, a creation of fantasy. But for you to enjoy these creatures of imagination, they must be created from the stuff of imagination that has some universal, common appeal. What happens to these characters, whether real or imaginary, must seem possible and probable in terms of the situation they are in. They cannot be illogical or irrelevant, or listeners will instantly reject them.

The background must be authentic—in place, in time, in this world or out of it. Laura's log cabin home in *Little House in the Big Woods* is a real log cabin in the Wisconsin woods of a hundred years ago; Kati's uncle's farm in *The Good Master* is a real farm in Hungary; the Vermont village in *The Blue Cat* is true Vermont; so is the rabbit hole down which Alice went in *Alice in Wonderland*. The setting must give validity to the story.

The mood, the atmosphere of the story must be just right to make the story live. This depends not only on what is chosen for the story but also the style in which the story is written.

Homer's problem with the doughnut machine in *Homer Price* could be that of any American boy, so characteristic is the situation. *Pecos Bill* could have evolved only from a Texas ranch, *Paul Bunyan* only from a lumberjack's life in the North woods. It's really Halloween when *The Blue-Nosed Witch* comes down to join the "Trick or Treat" children. You feel the loneliness of the lighthouse in *Fog Magic* or *The Light at Tern Rock* or *Celia's Lighthouse*. The steady, even flow of the year's cycle on a farm is essential to one's caring for and understanding Peter in *Mountain Born* and *A Place for Peter*. All the grandeur of Mt. Fuji and the challenge it offers to those who would climb it is present in the story of *Fujio* and his eagerness to climb the mountain as his father does. The thick growth, the noisy monkeys take you right into a jungle river in *Picken's Great Adventure*. Any story that takes place in a given locale must give the sense and the feel of that place; if in a given period of time, it must give the characteristic atmosphere of that era; if at sea one must feel the sea; if at night one must feel the night. The setting must be authentic, the atmosphere must be characteristic to make the story ring true.

The style of the writing, both the words chosen and the way they are put together in sentences and paragraphs, must be appropriate to the nature of the story. Short, declarative sentences are best for direct action. Longer involved sentences are only appropriate to more complicated situations. The vocabulary must fit the story and fit the audience for whom it is intended. The rhythm and flow of the sentences must carry the listener along naturally at the pace of the story, in the mood of the story.

If all these factors, plot, characters, setting, mood, atmosphere, appropriate literary style combine harmoniously, the story is likely to be a story that lives. If these meet harmoniously for many readers, this quality of universality makes it a worthwhile story that may live for many listeners, in many places, and for a long time.

But a comic strip often has a good plot and characters in whom you are interested. If a boy reads the story of Robinson

Crusoe in a series of comic strips, will the story live for him as it does if he reads the book?

Surely there is something beyond plot, good characterization, authentic creation of setting and mood, something due to more than good literary style that makes a story live for you, live in you. The story that so lives on in you has a certain psychological plus factor that makes it become part of you.

It is not easy to define this "X" quality, this plus element. It might be easier to consider some of the characteristics of the story that has this plus factor which make it live for so many who listen to it. Such a story must meet the hearer at some point in his own experience. Only when this is true, is the listener able to identify with the story. All listeners bring to all stories their own experience. They identify with any story at the point where it hooks on to some meaningful or treasured experience of their own. Once in, they live in the story.

For instance, in *The Bojabi Tree* most children expect the tortoise to be slow but faithful. In *Little Lamb*, children enjoy having little lamb get his answer from a "Baa-baa black sheep," a familiar animal to most children. In the Noisy books, all children feel as one with Muffin when he cannot see anything because his eyes are bandaged, but he can hear everything. So can they.

In the second place, a good story not only meets you at some point of your experience but makes you want to go on from here to there, often equipping you for the going. It may take you on by widening your horizons or lengthening your point of view or deepening your understanding or lifting your spirit. Such stories as *Li Lun, Lad of Courage* or *Burrito* or *The Singing Shoemaker* widen your horizons to China, Mexico, and Greece. Such stories as *It Looks Like This, Bright April, Minute Man of the Sea* lengthen your point of view. Such stories as *The Hundred Dresses, The Blue Cat*, and, *And Now Miguel* deepen your understanding of people, of life. Such stories as *Cheerful, Little Wu and the Watermelons, The Carpet of Flowers, Hidden Treasure of Glaston* lift your spirit. The information about the time of the Middle Ages in England or early days of New England; of the place in Greece or Mexico; of the characters, adolescent Miguel or crippled Hugh add to your understanding and ability to move on in the experience of the story, even to stay with it beyond the point to which the story itself may bring you. There is a fourth dimension.

In the third place, a good story with whose characters and action you so identify will give you a sense of the relationship of this experience to total experience—this little piece of the universe and the universe. When you feel such a relationship, the story goes on and on, in and through you. This is what John felt when he said of Tom and Huck, "Why, I run around with them in the back of my head all the time."

In the story of the *Little Wild Horse*, Peter tames a wild horse and brings him to their ranch. No mention is made of Peter's getting a saddle but children invariably go right on to the time Peter must get the saddle, so truly do they participate in the joy of Peter's being skillful enough to tame and bring home that little gray horse.

So the story that is worth telling, worth living with may be a realistic story, a tale of fantasy, a funny story, a tall tale, but it will be universal in appeal because it meets many children at some point in their experience, takes them on from that point, and gives them a vivid sense of the relationship of this experience to all experience. You live in such a story so truly that it becomes part of you and you of it. It comes from the stream of life to become part of you and through you returns to the stream of life.

This universality, this inevitable dramatic impact upon the listener or reader is true of all great literature—so it is natural that it should be true of the story worth telling to children, to anyone.

Your goals in telling the story and the nature of your audience will affect your choice of story—therefore, you must know a wide range of stories. In one sense a good story is ageless, but you choose different stories for varying age groups because of the difference in children's response. One storyteller groups listeners into four stages of characteristic response and so groups stories into these four categories:

Rhythmic
Realistic
Imaginative
Heroic

These may overlap, and some stories could belong in more than one category. This classification could not be used literally —saying the rhythmic period includes children 4 to 7, the realistic 7 to 9, the imaginative 9 to 11, the heroic 11 to 14 and up— because realistic and imaginary stories appeal to all ages. But it indicates a pattern of growth.

Younger children's responses are largely motor. They may respond to the story with moving hands and heads. They love repetition; they love a recurring refrain or word pattern and may say it with you as it recurs. The young child is interested in himself, his movements, and everything around him that moves: animals, toys, wagons, automobiles, trucks, tractors, trains, busses, boats, airplanes. What he understands and is interested in is based on first-hand experience and analogies to that experience. So young children like stories of children like themselves, stories of animals they know or have seen, and stories of all the things that go. This does not mean all stories for younger children should be confined to the here and now, but remember that their enjoyment and understandings come from their place and time sense. This does not eliminate imaginative stories, but it does mean that both you and the children know when a story is "out of this world."

Lucy Sprague Mitchell discusses in considerable detail the responses and the language patterns of younger children in her introduction to *The Here and Now Story Book*. She also gives invaluable help in how to develop skill in building stories from immediate environment. This book is an important resource for all those who are concerned with young children. It also contains many excellent here-and-now stories such as *The Fog Boat Story* and *How the Engine Learned the Knowing Song*.

Because of their limited experience, very little children are not too concerned with cause and effect and are often quite content with a string of episodes which may be related but not necessarily sequential. *Peter's Long Walk, The Long Hike, Wu and Lu and Li* are charming episodic adventure stories.

In *The Buttons Go Walking*, the Button family, including all the children and their parents, have fun together. Sal's loss of her first tooth is every child's experience so every five- or six-year-old lives the whole of *One Morning in Maine* with Sal. Because Madeline received so much attention after her operation for appendicitis, not only all the little girls in the Paris convent where she was in school, but all who hear the story *Madeline* feel almost enough pain to warrant an immediate operation. *Ola* lives in Norway, but his adventures at the coming of spring can be those of any sensitive child anywhere.

Ping's tardiness is likewise so universal an experience that many children identify with this little Chinese duck as fully as they might with a child in hearing *The Story about Ping*. *Angus and the Ducks* is very dear to every child who wants to see what is just beyond the hedge or fence or barrier of any sort. And what child does not? Peter Rabbit and Jemima Puddleduck and Squirrel Nutkin may be animals in the garden but their predicaments are those of many an active child in *The Story of Peter Rabbit, The Story of Jemima Puddleduck, The Story of Squirrel Nutkin*.

Mike Mulligan's steam shovel Mary Ann was almost a person to Mike. How children love their adventures in *Mike Mulligan and His Steam Shovel* or those of the train in *Choo Choo*, and the little red train and streamlined train in *Two Little Trains*. The experience of being important, of being needed, and of doing your job adequately is the basis of the satisfaction the story of *Little Toot* brings.

Young children also like cumulative stories such as *Chicken Little, Ask Mr. Bear, The Camel Who Took a Walk, The Bumblebee's Secret*. At the first repetition of the part or refrain that recurs over and over, there may be just a smile of recognition. At the next repetition, some may say it with you. Eventually all may do so.

"Say it again."

"Tell it again."

"Chicken Little, the sky is falling,"—over and over and over again.

"Hundreds of cats, thousands of cats,"—over and over and over again.

"Run, run, run, as fast as you can; You can't catch me, I'm the gingerbread man,"—over and over and over again.

The Animals Came First is a beautiful Christmas story in cumulative pattern as it brings all the animals in the stable to the gentle Mary singing a lullaby to her baby on that first Christmas, so long ago, so long ago.

There are many cumulative songs children love for the same reason they love a cumulative story: "Old MacDonald Had a Farm," "This Old Man He Played One," "The Tree in the Wood," "The Twelve Days of Christmas." A good way to get a group of children into a happy listening mood may be to sing together one of those songs. Both stories and songs lend themselves to dramatization, often a good experience to follow hearing a story.

The wonderful word nonsense of *Mr. Upstairs, Mr. Downstairs* and of *The Vegetabull* is great fun for a little child. And *Georgie*, the friendly little ghost and *Brownies, Hush! Three Policemen* and *The Loudest Noise in the World* take a bit of imagination. *Petunia* and *The Cow Who Fell in the Canal* and *The Day the Cow Sneezed* take imagination, a sense of humor, a sense of curiosity, a desire for adventure, a feeling that "anything could happen" (and does). These are the possessions of most children before adults begin to build the layer of repressions and taboos. Children are not mistaken when they revel in these stories and rightfully claim them as their own.

The stories for the very young have a strong rhythmic appeal and a strong realistic appeal. As children's knowledge increases, the content of the realistic story, a real plot with cause and effect of the successive situations becomes important. So everyday adventures such as those of Mul Chand in the East Indian marketplace in *A Cap for Mul Chand;* or of *Lokoshi* the Eskimo boy; or of *Eagle Feather,* in this story of an Indian boy of today; or of *Yonie Wondernose,* left with the responsibility of looking after their Pennsylvania farm; or of Gar, who really helped his brother win the song contest in a *Song for Gar;* or of Johnny in *The Biggest Bear* when he went to search for a big bear so he could have a bear skin on his barn as all his neighbors did—all these probable and possible experiences are interesting to share. They could have happened long ago as they did to *John Billington, Friend of Squanto* or Davy Crockett in *Old Whirlwind* or Nepsie in *Aunt Flora* or the riders in *Riding the Pony Express* or William Tell and his son in *The Apple and the Arrow.*

You may well understand eager little Jenny Linsky's desire to belong, in *The Cat Club,* and *Susanna the Pioneer Cow*'s helpfulness or you may revel in those silly penguins in *Mr. Popper's Penguins* or you may sympathize with all the small creatures of *Rabbit Hill* for the love of animals is strong in the heart of nearly every growing child.

The characters may be any people, the content in or out of this world, but the action must be lively. "Tell an adventure story and make it good" they say to you. The eerie, the spooky, has tremendous appeal. Could this be because of the many mystery and suspense dramas given on television and radio, or because of the tremendous scientific progress that has been made in exploring the unknown? Perhaps some of both. The ghost or mystery story used to belong to Halloween. Now it is requested every day. If the mass-media environment changes children's interests, the storyteller who keeps close to his audience knows and accepts these changes as they come.

But some people say folk tales are the chief resource for the storyteller. Certainly they constitute one of the large resources. The content which comes from experience at a simpler stage of man's existence is universal experience, easily understandable by the child. In his own growth he is repeating this same type of experience. The form is a disciplined form, of which we spoke earlier. It is usually an *A-B-A* pattern. *A* is the introduction which sets time or place, or both.

"Once upon a time there was an old King."

"Once in faraway times, there was an old man and his wife who lived in a little house in the deep forest."

"It was a long time ago in the state of Texas."

Then follows *B*, the main theme and its development, the introduction of the characters and their problems. Then follows action in logical sequence, each incident happening as a result of what has gone before, building up to a climax. The conflict is resolved and the characters sent on their way. Sometimes this ending, the final *A*, like a musical coda, returns to the introduction and repeats much of it.

This *A-B-A* pattern is a basic one in many art forms. *B* is the long section that is developed by elaboration, contrast, and repetition to the high dramatic moment of climax. The action must be logical and reasonable, the successive events inevitable, each following from the other. Each part of the story prepares for what comes next. Irrelevant characters or happenings which may often enrich or make more complex a written story do not belong in a told story. They distract. The teller must hew to the line—his plot line. His characters must be consistent in behavior and action. Actually this simplifies making the story your own for telling. So steep yourself in folklore and folk music. Its distilled essence of life, its disciplined form, its balanced pattern, its basic rhythm will become part of the fibre of your being. Familiarity with this rich heritage gives the kind of security you feel when you build a house with a firm foundation.

Folk tales are not just for young children or just for children —not at all. Since they are from the people, they are for the people. In the truest sense they are ageless, as every good story is really ageless. But the content, the cumulative form, the length may mean some stories, such as *The Three Bears* and *The Gingerbread Man*, are more appealing to young children. *The Three Bears* is characteristic of the young child's "satiable curtiosity," as Kipling called it. *The Gingerbread Man* is based on the universal love of some form of the game of tag, the best runner always being the one who cannot be caught. But *Jack the Giant Killer, Cinderella, Little Red Riding Hood, Hansel and Gretel* introduce far more mature problems in human living— real hunger, selfishness, cruelty to stepchildren—problems which only become real as the child grows older and has wider experience of life.

Perhaps because of a revival in all the arts as important in the living of all people; perhaps because anthropology and psychology have grown so rapidly and have helped us understand something of man's origin and development; perhaps because literary criticism and musicology make us more keenly aware of our debt to the past; or probably because of *all* these influences, there is more folklore being published today than ever before. Folklore is no longer found only in archives and museums or only in the minds and hearts of a few remaining oldsters. It can be found now in beautiful books easily available to children, young people, and adults, rich resources for all storytellers.

Many picture tales from many countries have been collected in the Picture Tale Series, to be enjoyed by all children. They come from Russia, Mexico, Scandinavia, France, India, China, and other lands. You will find many a good story to tell in these collections. A recent selection from many of these individual collections has been made by Eulalie Steinmetz Ross in *The Buried Treasure and Other Picture Tales*. Individual authors and author illustrators have put down well-known folk and fairy tales in separate books. Keigwin's translation of *The Ugly Duckling*, one of Hans Christian Andersen's fairy tales, is a good version for telling. Children will also enjoy looking at this beautiful edition, illustrated by Johannes Larsen. Virginia Lee Burton has a delightful version of *The Emperor's New Clothes*, enhanced by her pictures. Children show such astonishment and delight when they realize that there are no clothes!

Hans Fischer's *Traveling Musicians* is another charming version of the Bremen Musicians. His illustrations add to the pleasure which the story gives. Margaret Wise Brown's *The Little Brass Band* is a good story to tell or to read and is often enjoyed more because it reminds children of the Bremen band.

The artist Marcia Brown has retold several of the famous old tales, adding to the beauty of her books with illustrations that catch the characteristic flavor and locale of each story. There are *Dick Whittington and His Cat, Cinderella, Puss in Boots, Stone Soup, The Flying Carpet*, and others.

Different versions of the same story or same type of story occur in various parts of the world. Realizing this helps build children's sense of kinship with others. In building better world understanding it is important to become aware of human like-nesses, seeing that differences make for variety and interest and need not cause dislike. It is an exciting adventure for a group of young people to start collecting creation stories from every possible source, peddler stories (songs, too—there are so many good ones), and many others. *Pito's House* is a Mexican version of the crowded house story; Rose Dobbs' *No Room* is another version. *The Cow in the House* (see page 87) is still another version.

Most of us first come to know Cinderella through the French fairy tales of Perrault. Marcia Brown has told the story in one of her beautiful books, described above. Padraic Colum's *Girl Who Sat by the Ashes* is another version. Eleanor Farjeon has a long retelling that is almost a novel, *The Glass Slipper*. You may know other versions from other countries, too, for the story is a common one. Every girl longs for a fairy godmother and her own prince charming.

Our own country has its characteristic folklore, too. Because we are a young nation we still have a tendency to think of every-thing and everybody American as big, bigger, biggest or good, better, best. So our folk heroes are huge fellows with inordinate powers, a strange mixture of reality and imagination. Paul may have been a good lumberjack once in the Maine or Wisconsin or Minnesota or Oregon woods (anyone in all four of those states can show you the log cabin where he was born). Someone tells how good he was. The next person says, "Oh, if he was that good, I can make him a little better." The next one does like-wise and the next and the next, until he has to skate around the skillet to grease it for his flapjacks. The sky is the limit for a good storyteller.

So Paul Bunyan is the greatest lumberjack that ever was; Pecos Bill, the cowboy who invented everything a cowboy wears or does; Mike Fink, the greatest captain on the Old Mis-sissippi's wild waters; Old Stormalong, the four-fathom tall sailor who finally did capture a white whale. To lure more people westward, ever westward, sometimes pioneers like Davy Crockett and Daniel Boone told such tall tales that no one knows exactly what is legendary and what is real in the stories of their lives.

In his illuminating article, "The Long Hunter and the Tall Tale," William O. Steele says:

> The tall tale was an American weapon, a necessary and inevitable one. It expressed the frontiersman's exuberance, his joy of living, the optimism that was to carry him over every obstacle from one ocean to the other. It enabled him to submerge his fears for the future in that optimism and to minimize his present difficulties and discomforts. And it allowed him to speak out his love for the wilderness and all it stood for—its hope and promise, its beauty and calm, its ferocity and its savage challenge.
>
> —*The Horn Book*, February, 1958

America is folklore.

The Frank C. Brown Collection of North Carolina Folklore in seven volumes under the general editorship of Newma J. White, published by Duke University Press, is a rich resource of folk ballads, folk songs, games, rhymes, customs, and the like. It is also evidence of the great interest in folk material of all sorts and of the importance of making it available to singers, storytellers, and teachers. Tall heroes built a tall America and are still building it. The Lone Ranger and Space Man may well become the folk hero of the future. Folk tales have come from the people and always will, for man loves to tell stories. Through them he voices not only his way of life, his needs, his achievements, but also his ambitions and his dreams. No wonder folk stories are to tell.

The bibliography (see page 163) includes many collections from all over the world which should be a rich resource for every storyteller. Oxford University Press is bringing to America a series of collections of folk and fairy tales, well worth knowing, from England, Scotland, Ireland, Wales, France, and other countries. It will be good to watch for new collections as they appear. There is not space to discuss in detail the many fine collections of folk tales. Use the bibliography carefully and continuously. Your own reading will determine which stories will prove the most meaningful to you, depending on your background, temperament, interests, and needs.

There are often occasions for telling fables. Best known to us are *Aesop's Fables* and those of La Fontaine. Margaret Wise Brown has told seventeen of La Fontaine's fables in especially interesting versions, particularly good for telling.

Occasionally, a musician is inspired by an old folk tale to write a musical composition. In Serge Prokofieff's delightful version of *Peter and the Wolf*, he not only tells the story but gives the instrument and musical phrase used to represent each character in his composition. Ruth Seeger in *Let's Build a Railroad* uses narrative and songs in a delightful combination, excellent for telling and inviting audience participation.

Because of the effectiveness of the form of most folk tales, many modern authors tell stories in the folk idiom. Among some of the more beloved stories of this type are *Millions of Cats* by Wanda Gág, *The Camel Who Took a Walk* by Jack Tworkov, *Five Chinese Brothers* by Claire Bishop, *The Tailor's Trick* by Rosalys Hall, *Hinkeldinkel* by Frank Jupo, and *The Loudest Noise in the World* by Benjamin Elkins.

Closely akin to the folk tale is the fairy tale, always appealing to the child whose imagination is becoming lively. "There has never been a better teller of tales than Hans Andersen," we have often said. His fairy tales appeal to us because they meet us so directly and help us accept ourselves as we are (*The Ugly Duckling* or *Little Match Girl*). Or they may help us see others as they are, even when those others do not truly see themselves as they are (*The Emperor's New Clothes*).

One of the most sensitive appreciations of Hans Christian Andersen is that by Paul Hazard in the third chapter of *Books, Children and Men*. This is what the great storyteller (perhaps many a storyteller) means in the life of a growing child.

> The teller of tales stands at his window. He listens to the swallows and the storks that have returned to Denmark for the fine summer days. He listens to his friend the wind. Or, he mingles with the crowd and listens once more to what the gingerbread merchant is relating, to what the old eel fisherman is telling. He makes use of everything. He tells them again in his own way, these stories that provoke a smile or a tear. He gives them a lyrical style, dramatic and always simple, a style of which he alone is master. He adorns them with brighter and more delicate colors; and, lending them wings, he

sends them to the very limits of the world. But he fills them also with intense feeling and therein, without doubt, added to all the other qualities, lies the final attainment which explains their great power.

The children are not mistaken. In these beautiful tales they find not only pleasure, but the law of their being and the feeling of the great role they have to fill. They themselves have been subjected to sorrow. They sense evil confusedly around them, in them; but this vivid suffering is only transitory and not enough to trouble their serenity. Their mission is to bring to the world a renewal of faith and hope. What would become of the human spirit if it were not refreshed by this confident young strength? The new generation arrives to make the world beautiful once more. Everything grows green again. Life finds its reasons for enduring. Andersen, imbuing his tales with an invincible belief in a better future, communes with the soul of children, harmonizes himself with their deep nature, allies himself with their mission. He upholds, with them and through them, the ideal forces which save humanity from perishing.

—Paul Hazard, *Books, Children and Men*

As discussed in the first chapter, fairy tales are not always differentiated from folk tales, but, a fairy tale in the truest sense of the word, is composed by an individual in contrast to the traditional tale evolved from the folk and handed down from one generation to another. In music there are folk songs and composed songs. But the line in both literature and music is not too clearly drawn. Many an author and composer uses folk or fairy material as a resource from which to start his tale or composition. And some people use the words interchangeably or together as one phrase (folk and fairy tales). The bibliography on page 185 contains many of the best of folk and fairy tales now available in English from every country of the world. Here, too, you will want to know them well to determine which are to be especially yours.

And there are charming modern fairy tales to delight those with growing imaginations. Other children beside Alice go through a window into another world in Dan Wickenden's *The Amazing Vacation* or the children of *Half Magic*, and *Magic by the Lake* by Edward Eager. Animals have amazing personalities in *The Hobbit*, *The Lobster Books*, *The Wind in the Willows*, *Stuart Little*, *Charlotte's Web*, and all the Freddy books. And there are little people today, very little people, very tiny people. Do you know *The Borrowers?* If you ever miss one earring (not two, just one), or a bobby pin or a hairpin, it is just those Borrowers who made away with them. Undoubtedly, *Peter Pan* started much of children's flying, but *Mary Poppins* and *Miss Pickerell* are keeping it up. Fairy tales old and new have a very real place in the hearts of many children. So, too, they must find their place in a good storyteller's heart.

Perhaps because we live in a scientific age and facts seem so important, perhaps because the social order places a strong emphasis upon realism in all the arts, the realistic story is an appealing type of story for all ages. Such books must be true to the essence of art in offering to children knowledge of life and the sharing of great emotions, in arousing vibrations of heart and mind and body which may endure all their lives. Jane Moffat and Rufus M. and all those Moffats have such fun together, fun not dependent upon gadgets or things that cost money. This is a good family with whom to become acquainted in *The Moffats, Rufus M.*, and *The Middle Moffat*. So, too, is that Larsson family over in Sweden. What fun to go with them on *The Saucepan Journey* or share in *Little O's* mischievous adventures. You, too, may discover with little Johan, who became *Johnny Texas* in America, that life in Texas can be "exciting and good like fresh bread and butter when you are hungry."

Robin lived in England a long time ago. His father had to go off to the wars, his mother had to serve as a queen's lady-in-waiting, and he was to begin his training for knighthood as a page boy. Through good fortune it is Brother John who finds Robin alone and unable to walk. It is a long road back to health, but Brother John is there all the way, even teaching Robin to swim to strengthen his withered leg. Then comes the day of the siege of the castle where they are staying. Robin swims the moat to find the small door in the opposite wall and get word to relief forces. There are walls about everyone's life, and there is a door in every wall if you have the courage to swim across and find it. Even with handicaps you can get through the door, as Robin did in *The Door in the Wall*.

Children can identify with real children whether there is joy or whether there is sorrow, for they take life as it is. Due to war and poverty today, there are many broken homes, many homes in which a father or older brother returns from war experiences very different from the man the family used to know. So it was with Marly's family in *Miracles on Maple Hill*. Marly remembered how often mother had told of those miracles on grandmother's farm and insisted it might help Dad to go there now that he was home again and had changed so much. More than one miracle happened after the first maple sap started dripping into those buckets on Maple Hill.

A seventh-grade boy was talking with a storyteller one afternoon about what he liked. He was one of the two older boys who kept on coming to the story hour. "I like your stories," he said. "I don't know any folks I can talk things over with, but I find out a lot in stories. Gosh, I live quite big this year."

"Big?" she asked.

"Yeah, bigger than just me, you know. That's because so many stories are better than they used to be."

"Better? In what way?"

"They're more like it really is. The hero isn't always good or always right. The team doesn't always win. Some of the people get what they deserve, not just what they want. And say, want to know something? We can take it straight. I know. I ain't got folks but I got my stories."

There is always place for the realistic story, but perhaps today's social order means more children "can take it straight." Out of the past, out of the present, alone, with friends, in a family group, the real children of stories are not discouraged by the truth, but face it squarely. Through knowing them, living children also face truth and know the meaning of life, as this boy was doing. The story may reach goals far beyond the more obvious ones the storyteller may have had in mind. No wonder you must "trust the words."

A good story of a dog or a horse, even a wild animal, is a real story that has great appeal to children. Perhaps this appeal is strongest at that age when the child, in his first awareness of his own personality, his own individuality, his singularity, thinks that no one understands him. So he loves his dog, his horse, his bird with a fierce devotion. Charlton Ogburn has caught this experience with poignancy in *The White Falcon*. No wonder so many boys who hear it say, "That's me." Every child who hears *Lassie Come Home* trudges with that collie dog all those long miles back home from Scotland to England, so close is the kinship one feels. He who knows what it is to have a dog share all one's living, one's working, listens eagerly to *Big Red*, that setter in the Pennsylvania hills.

Perhaps one reason *Robinson Crusoe* appeals even today to so many children is that in this period of finding one's self, one's individual nature, abilities, and capacities the desire to prove adequate is almost overpowering. This may be one of the reasons (excitement and adventure play their share, of course) why the *Black Stallion* is so beloved. After the shipwreck, Alec had to make friends with the powerful black stallion and find food for himself and the horse, if both were to live. In *Desert Stallion*, a little Arab boy saves the life of a wild desert stallion to the point where they belong to each other.

Undoubtedly watching, knowing animals and their way of life helps children understand their own ways, their own life cycle. Therefore, authors who tell of wild animals from first-hand experience make a powerful appeal to an eager child, sensitive to the world around him. The Georges do just this in *Meph the Skunk, Vision the Mink, Vulpes the Red Fox, Bubo the Great Horned Owl, Dipper of Copper Creek*. George Cory Franklin does it, too, in *Tricky* and *Tuffy* and *Monte* and all his "true" stories of foxes, bears, and other wild animals of the Southwest.

In the free world today childhood is a stage of being, important in and of itself. The child is not a miniature adult, nor is he a being just on the way to becoming an adult. Each experience of life has inherent as well as relative value. There is, therefore, a self-acceptance for many, an enjoyment of each step of the way, since the end of the journey is not yet clear or of great moment. So the realistic story is often his own story, his own kind of story. He feels it, he knows it, he lives it in and of and through his being. Profound understanding of this new or different (and changing) concept of the child will build in you a keener awareness of the kind of story in which he and you belong. The real story, the true story offers him a clear-cut opportunity for identification.

But in his growing stature of both mind and body, he begins to realize how much he must know of what has gone before in order to understand the here and now, of how far he must project himself outside his immediate center of living to be secure in that center. So begins vicarious learning, stretching of the imagination back in time, away in space, in and out of this world. The space story of today may be essentially a fairy story in twentieth-century form. The realistic and imaginative are perhaps entwined in a new relationship. It may not be either/or for this type or that type, but both/and for all who accept the terms of life as they are today. This only challenges the storyteller to widen his range.

One means of identification that leads to increased self-understanding and growth is to become acquainted with great people, what they have done and why; and how you are what you are because of what they did; with people who have interests like your own who may not be great but are, to some measure, successful. The early hero tale recognized this. It is not just the thrill of Ulysses' adventures, but the chance to identify with this hero that still makes the *Iliad* and *Odyssey* great stories to live with. Each nation immortalizes its heroes: Moses, Genghis Khan, Agamemnon, Pericles, Caesar, Charlemagne, Marco Polo, Columbus, Sir Francis Drake, De Soto, Cortez, John Smith, George Washington, Thomas Jefferson, Robert E. Lee, Abraham Lincoln. Tell their stories so your children may know what blood courses in their veins.

No hero could possibly mean as much to some small boys as America's great baseball heroes, so you tell the moving life story of Lou Gehrig or other heroes of the plate. Maybe some of your boys are going to become scientists, and no one could be as thrilling to know as Galileo, George Washington Carver, or Albert Einstein. Maybe some of your girls are sure they want to be nurses, so they are eager to learn about Florence Nightingale, Clara Barton, or Edith Cavell. Maybe—not maybe but surely—many are going to conquer space by flying and will want to know how Charles Lindbergh or Amelia Earheart did it.

It is a short step, or possibly few steps, from the hero close to an interest or immediate need to the hero who is great in terms of man's development. The hero of baseball may lead to the great soul who delivered his people or who freed the slaves; to epics from Greece or India or Hungary, *The Odyssey, The Ramayana, The White Stag;* to ballads of heroes, *Song of Roland, Song of Robin Hood;* to historic fiction, *The Waters Prevailed* (Gilbraltar in days of the Stone Age), *The Golden Conquest* (Cortez' conquest of Mexico), *Little House in the Big Woods* (pioneer Wisconsin), *Adam of the Road* (medieval England), *The Courage of Sarah Noble* (early Connecticut), *Away Goes Sally* (early Maine), *Henry's Lincoln* (the Lincoln-Douglas debates); to life stories of athletic heroes or scientists or nurses or all the great men of history, *The Story of Jim Thorpe, The Story of Christy Mathewson, Albert Einstein, George Washington Carver, The Curies, The Story of Amelia Earheart, We, Riding the Wind, Christopher Columbus, Marco Polo, George Washington, Lafayette, Robert E. Lee, Abraham Lincoln, Mahatma Gandhi, Sun Yat Sen, Wilfrid Grenfell, Albert Schweitzer.*

The opportunity to identify with a hero is one of the most valuable experiences every growing human being cherishes. A good storyteller, therefore, opens wide the gates to such experience for herself and for her listeners. Some of the myths, legends, epics, and sagas may seem more difficult to tell than the folk or fairy tale. They demand a different quality, a different pacing. Some people fit this stately mood and tell them well. Give yourself opportunity and time to grow and develop this skill. Some of the simpler versions of the Greek and Norse myths which are good to begin with are Dorothy Hosford's *Thunder of the Gods* (Norse) or *Songs of the Volsungs* (Norse) or Catherine Sellew's *Adventures with the Gods* (Greek), *Adventures with the Heroes* (Norse). Olivia Coolidge's *Greek Myths, Legends of the North* are particularly good versions for telling to slightly older children.

Although the Padraic Colum versions, such as *The Golden Fleece* and *Heroes Before Achilles* and *Children of Odin,* are distinguished, they are better for most people to read aloud. The famous Hungarian epic of the discovery of this land flowing with milk and honey is beautifully told by Kate Seredy in *The White Stag*. If there is any East Indian background or interest developed from social studies, stories of any of the five brothers from the *Mahabharata* or the hero Rama in the *Ramayana* can be thrilling to tell.

Many hero tales are told in metrical form as in a ballad or story poem. The troubadours, minstrels, and minnesingers of the Middle Ages frequently told and sang their stories in such forms. Often the metrical form is used as a basis of a prose story: Robin Hood's tale grew from the old ballad about the generous outlaw of Sherwood Forest in merrie old England; Roland's story grew from the *Song of Roland* in medieval Europe.

There are modern ballads and story poems with exciting tales to tell: Browning's *How They Brought the News from Aix to Ghent*, Longfellow's *Paul Revere's Ride*, Nathan's *Dunkirk*. Parker's *100 Story Poems*, Untermeyer's *The Magic Circle*, Cole's *Story Poems New and Old* are rich collections of such ballads and story poems to tell, to read aloud, to chant or sing together.

Now in this atomic age children inevitably reflect the fears, uncertainty, and insecurity of their elders. But if this civilization —more specifically our own culture—is to survive, its children need cogent reasons for faith in the "on-goingness" of life, in themselves and in their capacities and abilities to do what is valid and good. What is faith in an age when most of man's gifts are being used to create instruments of destruction? But life does continue and will continue, and children will live and renew it as it renews them. Stories of spiritual significance, therefore, have a unique role in our time—stories that stress integrity, sensitivity to that which is good, concern for others, awareness of beauty, a sense of humor. These are the values that help the child grow from an "I-centered" human being to an "other-centered" human being. He moves from interest to tolerance, from tolerance to sympathy, from sympathy to empathy. This growth demands persistence, courage, loyalty.

In *Little Wu and the Watermelons*, Wu's hard work to earn money to buy for his mother something beautiful such as he sees other mothers have enables him not only to buy the earrings but to bring good fortune to the whole family. It is the persistence of José Maria in *A Carpet of Flowers* that brings not only the blue flowers for the eyes in the flower carpet for the Virgin of Guadelupe but also makes possible the miracle of his recovering his sight.

In *Li Lun, Lad of Courage*, it takes real spirit for Li Lun to go far from his home, carrying in his hand only a few grains of rice which he must grow to convince his father he is not afraid. It takes a special kind of courage for the son of a chieftain of an island in the South Pacific to prove to his father he is not afraid of water. It took both courage and persistence for the pioneers, moving westward, ever westward, opening up this land, of whom there are thrilling stories such as that of the Venable family in *The Tree of Freedom, Children of the Covered Wagon, On Indian Trails with Daniel Boone,* and many others.

Little children may discover that unselfishness and thoughtfulness of others is a good way of life in stories such as *A Little Oven* and *A Kiss Is Round*. Older children will find it in stories such as *Stepsister Sally* and *Adopted Jane, The Hundred Dresses, Su Mei's Golden Year* (modern China), *Hill Doctor* (southern mountains), or *Thirty-One Brothers and Sisters* (a Zulu family in Africa).

Fine family feeling characterizes *Little Red House* and *The Buttons Go Walking*, both for younger children; *The Moffatts, All-of-a-Kind Family, Mostly the Meldons, Miracles on Maple Hill, Golden Name Day* are for slightly older children.

Sensitivity to the beauty all around us in nature, in other people, in the things man makes is ever aroused in stories such as *Wind in the Willows* (awe and wonder and enjoyment in the River Bank and Wild Wood), *Rabbit Hill* (little animals), *A Little Boy Lost* (South America), *The Good Master* (Hungarian farm), *The Boy Knight of Rheims* (the days of building the great cathedral), and *Golden Conquest* (Cortez and Montezuma).

Perhaps funny stories were never so important as they are now in this time of tension. Humor grows from that long-range point of view that sees things in relationship and can then be amused when things get out of relationship. Something grows a little too big, something else grows not quite big enough, or other things get into odd juxtaposition—then "it is to laugh." It is important to find stories that have this fine basic humor, not humor that is created at the expense of the other fellow, but humor that stems from this deep sense of relationship. It takes profound awareness on your part to develop your own sense of humor and be able to tell a humorous story well. Dr. Seuss has wonderful nonsense in his rhythmic stories *And to Think That I Saw It on Mulberry Street, Horton Hatches the Egg, The 500 Hats of Bartholomew Cubbins,* and many others. *Ferdinand,* the bull who loved to smell flowers, and *The Man Who Lost His Head,* who really did, that fine fall day and had amazing adventures in his search until he woke up, are ageless funny stories. There is wonderful nonsense in *Mr. Popper's Penguins* and *My Father's Dragon.* All the fun of the kind of mischief children get into is genuinely caught in the *Eddie* books, *Henry and Beezus, Fun with Herbert, Homer Price.* Many of our tall tales are full of humor because of their incongruities: *When the Mississippi Was Wild, Daniel Boone's Echo, Ol' Paul, Pecos Bill and Lightning, Tony Beaver, Young Mike Fink, Old Stormalong.* Even a story-teller with a keen sense of humor must have a certain kind of skill to tell a funny story, a certain objectivity, often with tongue in cheek, sometimes with, sometimes without a twinkle in the eye. The rewards are worth any amount of effort. Even if you think you do not have a keen sense of humor, remember it can be cultivated. The Irish may be born with more of it than most, but they do not have a corner on it. Everyone can plant a tiny seed, which if watered, nourished, and cherished will grow— even into quite a large tree, fairly adequate to meet the needs of your children and yourself.

And don't forget those special, hard-to-put-in-any-category stories such as *Stuart Little, The Hobbit, The Borrowers.* They may be limited in appeal to special children. But there are an amazing number of special children.

One day a nine-year-old boy asked his teacher if she thought he needed to go to a psychiatrist. A little alarmed, she said, "Why, no. What made you ask that?"

"My mother said so, because my favorite book is *Stuart Little*. I'd love a mouse for a brother. I'd even like to be one."

Of course this happens to those with imagination—imagination needed for all creativity, even the next step in scientific or social research. It must be recognized, cherished, and developed. It is essential, not irrelevant, to our time. Actual survival of our civilization may depend more than we realize upon the values and concerns in the hearts and minds of today's children. There is no limit to what a story may mean in the life of a child today and tomorrow and tomorrow.

Basic as are these values to sound growth, many of you have special immediate interests as teachers, librarians, social workers needing specific stories that follow the cycle of the seasons, the year's holidays or stories for Sunday school or a special camp or playground situation.

If you are following the seasons, there are poems for the whole year through in *Sing a Song of Seasons*. Or begin with Addison Webb's *Book of Seasons*. Or tell the story of the beautiful island near the Maine coast in *The Little Island*. And therein lies a discovery, for it is not just a story of the external happenings characteristic of each season. It is a story of faith— a good way to begin to find out that faith is believing what you do not know until you can find out.

"Spring comes on forever." Very young children are happy to share it in *Spring Is Here* or to discover they, too, are a part of it all when the sun burns their noses, as happens to *Little Red Nose*. Or take them venturing with *The Deer in the Snow* to discover first signs of spring.

Then as "Sumer is icumin in," little children will enjoy *On a Summer Day* and *The Lovely Summer*. Third graders will enjoy going with Bob on *Bob's Summer Sleigh Ride*. It is exciting for older children to find out what happened *When the Sun Danced*.

As the leaves begin to turn, little children enjoy *Now It's Fall*, *Johnny Maple Leaf*, *Autumn Harvest*. *Harvest Feast* really has a feast of stories appropriate for the fall season for slightly older children.

When all the leaves have fallen from the trees and in many places a blanket of snow covers the earth, the younger ones say with you *I Like Winter* or enjoy *White Snow, Bright Snow.* Those a little older may enjoy a trip to the farm where there are *Pancakes for Breakfast* or may find out how animals live in winter in *Go with the Sun.* There is real winter adventure, too, written long ago in *Snow Over Bethlehem*—that is in Bethlehem, Pennsylvania—or in our own time in *Snow Bound in Hidden Valley* or through the terrible South Dakota blizzard in *Prairie School.*

Holidays loom large in all our lives but perhaps especially so while we are in school. For the New Year there is *Patrick's Golden Slippers,* with its background of the annual mummer's-day parade in Philadelphia on New Year's Day. Children a little older will enjoy going back to the time of the pilgrims *When the New Year Came in March.*

If you dearly loved to make valentines, you will enjoy telling of Appolonia's struggle to make just the right valentine in *Appolonia's Valentine.* Valentine's day in Hungary is charmingly portrayed in one chapter of *The Good Master,* a fine story by itself. Many children wonder how we came to celebrate this day. *The Story of Valentine* tells the story of the Roman philosopher Valentine and of how the children he befriended showed their love for him when he was imprisoned for his faith. If you teach junior high school boys and girls, this may be just the right time to tell a good romance such as *Sarah* or *Sandy.*

February, too, is important as a month of many birthdays—Abraham Lincoln's is on the twelfth day. There are a number of tender stories of Abraham Lincoln and children. Martin, the troubled small son of a shoemaker met Abraham Lincoln on the White House steps and took a nail out of his shoe. *Martin and Abraham Lincoln* is a moving story. *Lincoln's Little Correspondent* is an amusing story of the little girl who wrote Lincoln about his homely face and suggested he grow a beard. *Henry's Lincoln* gives a vivid sense of how Lincoln affected people in this story of the day of the Lincoln-Douglas debate. Older children find *The Perfect Tribute* a moving story of the Gettysburg address. Life stories such as those by the d'Aulaires and Genevieve

Foster, each called *Abraham Lincoln,* give true pictures of this great man.

So, too, do their life stories of *George Washington*—far more valuable to tell than the improbable cherry tree legend. In *Silver for General Washington,* the struggle of the army at Valley Forge takes on new dimensions. These stories are good to tell on or near February 22.

An Irish folk tale of Yeats or Stephens or MacManus or the tale of *Molly the Rogue* will add local color to St. Patrick's Day with its shamrocks and wearin' of the green.

As spring brings new life over all the countryside, the Easter celebration both as a religious holiday and as a holiday symbolic of the renewal of life is a joyful one for children. If you loved a look-inside Easter egg, you will enjoy telling *The Look-Inside Easter Egg. Tell Me Little Boy* and *The Easter Bunny That Overslept* are delicate Easter fantasies. *A Tale for Easter* is an exquisitely simple story of pre-Easter preparations and the fun of Easter morning. The charming old Pennsylvania Dutch custom of making an egg tree may inspire your children to make one too, after hearing it described in *The Egg Tree.*

Younger children will realize that the Fourth of July is not just a day on which to shoot fireworks, but has a deep meaning for all Americans if you tell *The Fourth of July Story.* For older children this may be just the right time to tell a story of Thomas Jefferson, adapting it from *Thomas Jefferson, Champion of the People* by Judson, or *Thomas Jefferson* by Lisitzky, or another life story of your choice.

Younger children and all who are interested in discovery days will feel they know that little fair-haired boy of Genoa who always hung around the waterfront when they hear *The Columbus Story.* We celebrate his birthday on October 12. Those slightly older will feel they were with him on his first voyage as they hear *Ship Boy with Columbus.* And the older group will share the sailing experiences vividly with a lad near their own age in *He Went With Christopher Columbus.* If you would help them know the man, tell *Columbus Sails* or *Son of Columbus.* In story, you and your children can relive Columbus' great sea adventures and discoveries.

October ends with a holiday increasingly beloved by all children, Halloween. Originally a religious observation of All Soul's Eve or All Hallows Day, it has evolved to a day associated with ghosts, witches, and all things eerie and spooky. Tiny children will enjoy Sylvie and her *Pumpkin Moonshine*. *The Blue-Nosed Witch* has great adventure when she comes down and joins a tricks-or-treat group of children on Hallowe'en. There are many other stories in *Spooks, Spirits and Shadowy Shapes, Ghosts, Ghosts, Ghosts,* or *Ghosts and Goblins*.

The harvest season really culminates in Thanksgiving. Stories such as *The First Thanksgiving* or *The Thanksgiving Story* are not only interesting but informative—telling children how this celebration originated in the Pilgrim colony long ago.

Then Christmas crowns the year. Christmas stories are truly ageless, but the *Animals Came First* or *Lullaby*, the story of why a pussy-cat always washes his face, or *Pedro, the Angel of Olvera Street,* a charming story of a Mexican posada, have great appeal for young children. *Christmas on the Mayflower* has true historic interest. *Maggie Rose* reveals a small girl's sense of responsibility, a sense of family feeling as well as that of neighborliness in this story of how a hitherto indigent family rises to meet an emergency. *The Fairy Doll* and *The Magic Christmas Tree* are for the imaginative ones, especially girls. Mrs. Seymour gives vivid realistic pictures of Christmas in various countries in *Arne and the Christmas Star* (Norway), *Kaatje and the Christmas Compass* (Netherlands), and several others. Perhaps the choicest collection of Christmas stories (there are many good anthologies) is *The Long Christmas* with a story for each of the twelve nights from Christmas to Twelfth Night.

The bibliography on page 163 gives almost complete lists of most of the best books related to each of the important holidays and may help you find just those most suitable for your special needs.

Perhaps you are a Sunday school teacher. You and the parents want your children to know the Bible, yet the full Bible is too long. There are excellent children's Bibles, some of which keep the King James version, some of which retell the most beloved stories of both Old and New Testament. *The Book of Books,* the

Junior Bible each select essential portions of the Bible. *The Small Child's Bible,* the *Children's Bible, The Lord Is My Shepherd* all retell the great stories. Each of these is not only a beautiful book for a growing child to live with, but a rich resource for telling the wonderful stories of Abraham, Samuel, Joshua, David, Jesus, and his friends.

Often children feel that ancient Palestine was not a real country with real people like ourselves. The adventures of *Ethan the Shepherd Boy* on the night the star shone so brightly and the baby Jesus was born in Bethlehem of Judea, and little *Anne of Bethany* who met the Holy Family when they were fleeing into Egypt will make children feel these children were real like themselves, sometimes lonely, sometimes afraid.

Some of the people who lived unselfish lives dedicated to the service of others have been made saints. Their life stories have deep meaning for children. You may want to tell of some of these: St. Francis in *Song of St. Francis* or *God's Troubadour,* St. Christopher in *Christopher the Giant* or St. Bernard in *Bernard and His Dogs,* or others in *Ten Saints.* Joseph Gaer makes the founders of the world's great religions such as Buddha, Mahomet, and Jesus Christ come alive in *Young Heroes of the Living Religions.*

The choice is wide, as wide as life itself and all living for the growing storyteller who would open doors for children. You may be using this oldest, least formal teaching device to increase children's knowledge or to impart ethical values or to cultivate standards. You may be using this direct means of communication by the spoken word primarily to entertain a group of children; or to develop their growth and understanding of the spoken word; or to develop their spiritual awareness, love of beauty, sense of humor; or to broaden their reading interests; or to develop a realization and appreciation of the development of myths, legends, fables, parables, folklore, fairy tales, ballads as keys to understanding mankind and man's growth through the ages; or to do what all great literature does—to give readers and listeners the opportunity for identification so that they may understand themselves better, conquer their fears, be courageous enough to accept themselves as they are and release their dreams and creativity so that they may make their unique contribution to the on-going stream of life. Or the end result of this "coming together of the lamp and the lighter, the seed and the sower," as Edward Yeomans used to describe storytelling, may be something far beyond any of those goals.

Whoever you are, wherever you are, whatever you need, stories are a rich resource for you to use in building your house of life.

What stories will you choose to tell?

Those that belong to you as a person and that fit your needs and interests, those that belong to your listeners and that fit their needs and interests. It is good to remember that whatever is in the mind's eye is always there as a resource. So fill your mind's eye with poetry, music, pictures, stories of every kind from the whole wide earth. The stories you learn and live are always yours and your listener's stories too for their learning and living, for stories are an extension of life, rich experience coming out of the stream of life, through you and your listeners and returning to the stream of life.

They are not just to inform, but they often impart knowledge.

They are not just to entertain, but they may give pleasure.

They are not just to enrich vocabulary, but they may give awareness of the power of the spoken word.

They are not just to give knowledge of the literary forms in which man has expressed himself, but they may enable one to understand man's development better through those forms.

They are not just to illumine, but they may reveal beauty and truth.

They are not just to explain man to himself, but they may enable him to accept life as it is and live it more abundantly.

They are not just to arouse curiosity, but they may keep alive the wonder without which man cannot live—for "when we begin to wonder, things begin to happen."

No wonder your children want to hear stories—and need to!

Some Good Stories to Tell

Stories

THE PEDDLER AND HIS CAPS

Once upon a time there was a peddler who sold caps. On top of his head he wore his old brown cap. On top of the brown cap he put his yellow caps. On top of the yellow caps he put his blue caps. On top of the blue caps he put his green caps. And on the very top he put his red caps. Then he would go down to a village, walking up one street and down another, calling, "Caps for sale! Caps for sale!"

One day nobody wanted to buy a cap, not even a red one. "Well," thought the peddler, "this will be a good day to just take a rest."

So he walked off to the edge of the village, where he found a large tree. He settled himself down by the tree, balancing all the caps against the trunk of the tree and went sound asleep.

He slept a long time. When he woke up, the first thing he did was to feel for his caps. All he could find was his old brown cap. He looked in front of him.

No caps.

He looked to the left of him.

No caps.

He looked to the right of him.

No caps.

He walked all around behind the tree.

No caps.

Then, he looked up in the tree.

There he saw monkeys and every monkey had a cap on.

"You monkeys you," he shouted shaking his finger at them, "you give me back my caps." But the monkeys only shook their fingers back at him and shouted, "Tsk, Tsk, Tsk!"

"You monkeys, you," he shouted, shaking the finger of his other hand at them," you give me back my caps." But the monkeys only shook their fingers back at him and shouted, "Tsk, Tsk, Tsk!"

"You monkeys, you," he shouted as he stamped his right foot, "you give me back my caps."

But the monkeys only shouted back at him, "Tsk, Tsk, Tsk!"

"You monkeys, you," he pleaded as he stamped his left foot, "give me back my caps." But the monkeys only answered back, "Tsk, Tsk, Tsk!"

Then the peddler was so angry he took his old brown cap off and threw it on the ground.

Every monkey took his cap off and threw it on the ground. So the peddler gathered all his caps together again. On top of his head he put his old brown cap. On top of the brown cap he put his yellow caps. On top of the yellow caps, he put his blue caps. On top of the blue caps he put his green caps. And on the very top he put his red caps.

Then he went back to the village, up one street and down another, calling, "Caps for sale! Caps for sale!"

The form of this story is almost perfect. It is interesting to notice how like a music form it is. First there is an introduction. Then the main problem or theme is given. This is developed by contrast and repetition. It is finally resolved and finished with a coda which is practically a repetition of the introduction. I use it with children of all ages and frequently with older children, even college students in creative writing for the study of form.

It lends itself naturally to action: walking, sleeping, looking around, shaking your fingers, stamping your feet, throwing down the cap, putting back the caps, walking.

Inevitably there must be a long pause after the last "No caps," just before he looks up in the tree.

In the final recapitulation of the caps, the children are usually so excited they want to tell how he put them back. Often I wait just before saying, "Red" and they are so a part of the experience, we all say "Red!" together.

It is, of course, a wonderful story to dramatize. But if there is a large group of children, this may be difficult.

But they can all stand up (even on their chairs if it seems all right to do this) and become the monkeys in the trees while the peddler begs for the return of his caps. Not one bit of instruction is needed. They *are* the monkeys and respond eagerly the moment the peddler starts shouting for the return of his caps.

THE DRUM THAT SAVED LAMBKIN

Once upon a time there was a wee, wee lamb. One day he thought he would go to see his Granny. "I shall have a fine time." he said. "I shall have such good things to eat when I get there. I am as happy as I can be."

As he was going along the road he met a wolf. Now a wolf likes to eat little lambs. So the wolf said: "Lambkin! Lambkin! I'm going to eat you."

But Lambkin skipped around on his little legs and said: "To Granny's house I go, Where I shall fatter grow, Then you can eat me *so!*"

The wolf likes fat lambs, so he let Lambkin go.

By and by Lambkin met a tiger. The tiger also likes to eat little lambs. So he called out, "Lambkin! Lambkin! I'm going to eat you."

But Lambkin jumped about on his little legs and said, "To Granny's house I go, Where I shall fatter grow, Then you can eat me *so!*"

The tiger likes fat lambs, so he let Lambkin go on to his Granny's. At last Lambkin got to his Granny's house.

"Oh, Granny dear!" he called to her.

"I told Wolf and Tiger that I would get fat. Please put me into your corn bin."

So his Granny put him into the corn bin. He stayed in the corn bin and ate, and ate, and ate. He grew so fat that he could hardly walk.

"How fat you are now, Lambkin!" said his Granny. "You must go right home."

"Oh, no!" answered Lambkin. "The tiger will eat me up."

"But you must go home, Lambkin," said his Granny.

"Well then," said Lambkin, "I will tell you what to do for me. You must take a goat skin and make me a little drum. Then I can sit inside it and roll home."

So his Granny made him a little drum of skins.

When the drum was ready, Lambkin got into it and curled up. Then he began to roll along the road to his home. Soon he met the tiger. The tiger called out, "Drumkin! Drumkin! Have you seen Lambkin?"

The lambkin, in his soft little nest, called back, "Lost in the forest, And so are you! On, little drum, Tum-*pa!* Tum-too!"

The tiger was very angry. "Now I shall have no fat lambkin to eat," he said. "Why didn't I eat him when I had him?"

But the little lambkin rolled along in his drum. He laughed to himself and sang, "Tum-pa, tum-too! Tum-pa, tum-too!"

At last Lambkin met the wolf who said, "Drumkin! Drumkin! Have you seen Lambkin?"

Lambkin, in his soft nest, called back, "Lost in the forest, And so are you! On, little drum, Tum-pa! Tum-too!"

Now the wolf was very wise. He knew Lambkin's voice. So the wolf called out: "Lambkin! Lambkin! Come out of that Drumkin!"

"Come and make me," called Lambkin.

Then the wolf ran after the lambkin. But the drum rolled faster and soon rolled away from him. The last thing the wolf heard was Lambkin singing, "Lost in the forest, And so are you! On, little drum, Tum-pa! Tum-poo!"

—A folk tale of India

THE BUN

Once upon a time there was an old man, and one day he wanted something nice to eat, so he said to his wife: "My dear, please make me a bun." But she answered: "What am I to make it of? We have no flour." "What nonsense," he said, "of course, we have!" You've only got to scrape the sides of the bin and sweep its floor and you'll get plenty!"

So his wife took a feather brush and scraped the sides and swept the floor of the bin and got a little flour together. Then she kneaded the dough with cream, rolled out the bun and spread it over with butter and put it in the oven.

And the bun turned out simply splendid! She took it out of the oven and put it on the window sill to get cold. And there the bun lay and lay, and he began to feel lonely, so he just took and rolled off! From the window sill he rolled down on to the bench on to the floor, and over the floor to the door. Then he rolled right over the threshold into the lobby, out of the lobby on to the front doorsteps, and down the steps right out of doors, and rolled straight along the road into the field.

Suddenly he met a hare and the hare said to him: "Mr. Bun, Mr. Bun, I shall eat you up!"

"No you shan't, Mr. Hare, for I'll sing you a song." And he started singing: "I'm Mr. Bun, I'm Mr. Bun. I was scraped from the sides and swept from the floor of the bin, I was kneaded with cream and fried in butter, and was put to cool on the window sill, but I got away from gaffer and I got away from granine, and I shan't find it hard to get away from you!" And when he had finished his song he went on rolling farther, and was out of sight before Mr. Hare had time to look.

And he went on rolling, when suddenly he met a wolf, and the wolf said to him: "Mr. Bun, Mr. Bun, I shall eat you up!" "No you shan't Mr. Wolf, for I'll sing you a song." And he started singing: "I'm Mr. Bun, I'm Mr. Bun. I was scraped from the sides and swept from the floor of the bin, I was kneaded with cream and fried in butter, and was put to cool on the window sill, but I got away from gaffer and I got away from granine and I got away from Mr. Hare, and I think I'll find it easy enough to get away from you!"

And he went on rolling farther, when suddenly he met a bear.

And the bear said to him: "Mr. Bun, Mr. Bun, I shall eat you up!" "Indeed you shall not, you old crooked-paws, you couldn't if you tried." And he started singing: "For I'm Mr. Bun, I'm Mr. Bun. I was scraped from the sides and swept from the floor of the bin, I was kneaded with cream and fried in butter, and was put to cool on the window sill, but I got away from gaffer, and I got away from granine, I got away from Mr. Hare and got away from Mr. Wolf— Goodbye, Bruin!"

And he went on rolling farther, when suddenly he met a fox, and the fox said to him: "How do you do, Mr. Bun, how pretty you are and how well-baked you are!" And Mr. Bun was pleased at being praised and he started singing: "I'm Mr. Bun, I'm Mr. Bun. I was scraped from the sides and swept from the floor of the bin, I was kneaded with cream and fried in butter, and was put to cool on the window sill, but I got away from gaffer and I got away from granine, I got away from Mr. Hare and got away from Mr. Wolf, I got away from Bruin and I'll get away from you!"

"That's a fine song," said the fox, "please sing it to me again, but come and sit on my nose, I've got so deaf lately."

So Mr. Bun jumped up on Mr. Fox's nose and sang his song again. And the fox said: "Thank you Mr. Bun, but please sing it just once again. And come sit on my tongue, then I shall hear still better." And Mr. Fox put out his tongue and Mr. Bun jumped on to it, and Mr. Fox just closed his mouth and ate Mr. Bun up.

—Valery Carrick (translated by Nevill Forbes),
Picture Tales from the Russian

THE LITTLE HOUSE

Once upon a time a jar rolled off a peasant's cart and was left lying in the middle of a field. And a little mouse came running along and saw the jar lying there, and thought what a nice house it would make, and began to wonder who lived there.

And the little mouse said: "Little house, little house, who lives in the little house?"

And nobody answered. Then the little mouse looked in, and found no one there!" "Well then," he said, "I shall live here myself." So he settled himself in the jar.

Then a frog came hopping along and said: "Little house, little house, who lives in the little house?"

"I, Mr. Mouse, I live in the little house, and what sort of animal are you?"

"I am Mr. Frog."

"Come inside, then, and let's live together."

"Very well, let's."

So the frog crept into the jar, and they began to live together. Then a hare came running over the field.

"Little house, little house," says he, "who lives in the little house?"

"Mr. Frog and Mr. Mouse, and who are you?"

"I am Mr. Hare who runs over the hills. May I come in, too?"

"Yes, you may; come and live here, there's plenty of room."

Then a fox came running past and said: "Little house, little house, who lives in the little house?"

"Mr. Hare, Mr. Frog, and Mr. Mouse. And what is your name?"

"They call me Mr. Fox."

"Very well then, come and live with us."

"Right you are!"

So the fox got into the jar too, and all four began to live together. And they went on living there, when suddenly a bear came along out of the forest and said: "Little house, little house, who lives in the little house?"

"Mr. Fox, Mr. Hare, Mr. Frog and Mr. Mouse; and who are you?"

"I am Mr. Bear-Squash-you-all-flat." And the bear sat down on the jar and squashed it flat.

—Valery Carrick (translated by Nevill Forbes),
Picture Tales from the Russian

A COW IN THE HOUSE

Mabel Watts

Once there was a poor farmer and his wife, and they lived in a little red house. Now this house had only two tiny rooms, and one dinky little porch sitting on the side.

But the farmer and his wife thought their house was quite cozy and comfortable. They thought it was just about the right size until one morning when the farmer's wife decided to roll out some noodles to put in the soup.

Now the noodles were extra long, and the kitchen was extra short. And there the trouble began.

"If we only could buy a larger house," said the farmer's wife.

And she fussed. And she fretted. And she complained the whole morning long.

"But we have no money to buy a larger house," declared the farmer. And away he went to tell his troubles to Grandpa Wiseman.

"If you will do exactly as I tell you," said Grandpa Wiseman, "then everything will turn out just right."

"Indeed I will," said the farmer. "What shall I do?"

"First," said the old man, "you must take your hen into the house."

So the farmer went home, and he took his hen into the house.

Now the hen had never been inside the house before, and she had no idea how to behave!

All day long the farmer and his wife kept coaxing her out of the wood box. They kept shooing her away from the table. They kept shaking her out of their laps.

But there she was back again, quick as a wink!

At last the farmer could stand it no longer. And away he went to see Grandpa Wiseman again.

The old man said, "Now you must take your goat into the house."

"But you don't know my goat," said the farmer. "She is a very tricky customer!"

"Still," said Grandpa Wiseman, "you promised to take my advice. Remember?"

Yes, the farmer remembered that very well. And he went back home and took his goat into the house.

The goat could scarcely believe her good fortune. Getting into the house like this was a great adventure, and she made the most of it.

She chewed up the window curtains. She jumped on the bed. And she butted the furniture around.

Besides, the hen and the goat did not get along very well together. So back went the farmer to tell Grandpa Wiseman about it.

"The hen and the goat are lonesome," declared the old man. "They need company. So now you must go home and take your pig into the house!"

"Oh, no," said the farmer. "Not the pig, surely!"

"Yes," said Grandpa Wiseman. "The pig!"

The pig took up an awful lot of room, and he was more trouble than the goat and the hen put together.

Everywhere the farmer went to put his feet, there was the pig.

Everywhere the farmer's wife went to put something down, there was the pig.

Cackle, cackle, said the hen. Maa, maa, said the goat. Oink, oink, said the pig.

The farmer and his wife couldn't get a word in edgewise. They couldn't take a step one way or the other without bumping into one of the animals.

Furthermore, the hen and the goat and the pig did not get along very well together. So back went the farmer to tell Grandpa Wiseman about it.

"The hen and the goat and the pig are lonesome for the cow," said the old man. "You must take her into the house, too!"

So the farmer went back home again. And he squeezed his cow into the house.

The bewildered cow couldn't make head nor tail of things. And the minute she got into the house, down she sat, right square in the doorway.

Now it was difficult for the farmer and his wife to get in or out of the door to do their chores.

And what with the hen and the goat and the pig taking up all the rest of the room, there was nothing for the farmer and his wife to do but sit and twiddle their thumbs!

At last the farmer climbed out through the window. And away he went to see Grandpa Wiseman again.

"How are you getting along now?" asked the old man.

"Well," said the farmer quietly, "we're a little bit crowded, and that's the truth. Still, it could be worse!"

"And how could it be any worse?" asked Grandpa Wiseman, with a twinkle in his eye.

"Suppose my cousin should come and stay with us," said the farmer. "And his wife, and his ten children, all steps and stairs. And their dog, and their cat."

"Ha! Ha!" laughed the old man. "Things would really be higgledy-piggledy then, wouldn't they?"

"Yes, indeed," said the farmer, "things can always get a little bit worse!"

"Now we're getting somewhere with this problem," said Grandpa Wiseman. "Run along home now, and push the cow out of the house!"

"By all means," said the farmer. And he could hardly wait to get home to do as he was told.

Ah, that was simply wonderful, having the cow out of the way.

And the farmer hurried off to tell the old man about it.

"Fine!" said Grandpa Wiseman. "Now drive the pig back into the pigpen."

"Yes, indeed!" said the farmer. And he lost no time in doing as the old man told him.

"And does your house seem any larger now?" Grandpa Wiseman asked the farmer.

"Oh yes," was the answer. "We have lots and lots of room now!"

"Fine!" said the old man. "Now it is time to turn out the goat!"

Soon the goat was out in the yard again. And the house had never seemed so large before.

"We are beginning to rattle around like peas in a pod," the farmer told Grandpa Wiseman.

"In that case," he was told, "you can turn the hen loose."

Now the little red house was just the right size for the farmer and his wife.

"I wouldn't want a larger house now," declared the farmer's wife. "Not for all the world!"

And away she went to the kitchen to roll out some noodles.

The noodles were extra long, and the kitchen was extra short. Still, there was plenty of room in that little red house.

"It's all in knowing how to make the best of things," said the farmer. "And that's the truth!"

THE BOJABI TREE

Edith Rickert

ROBIN RAT

In the land of All-the-Beasts there was a GREAT HUNGER. Some of the animals who were so HUNGRY were

Tabby Tiger
  Bruno Bear
    Katy Crocodile
     Robin Rat
      Pinky Pig
       Giddy Goat
        Tommy Tortoise

and many more—more than you could ever count in a year.

They ran around the wood, here and there and everywhere, eating roots and twigs and any old scraps they could find. But still they were HUNGRY.

One day they came to a Big Tree full of fruit. But they could not eat it, for they did not know what it was.

They sat down in a circle round the tree, and said, "What can we do?"

When they had thought a while, they said, "Let us send Robin Rat up the river to Leo, our King, and ask him what the fruit is and whether we may eat it."

Robin Rat was young and spry. He scuttled up the tree and brought down one of its fruits to show King Leo.

It was a delicious looking fruit! It looked like an APPLEORANGE-PLUMPEARBANANA but it smelled like a BANANAPEARPLUM-ORANGEAPPLE.

Then Robin Rat scuttled down to the river bank and climbed into his little canoe.

All the day and all the day he paddled and paddled and PADDLED up the river.

And the Great Red Sun dropped behind the trees.

Then he found King Leo on the bank, all ready to receive visitors. He was wearing his crown tipped on the back of his head because he felt happy. He smiled at Robin Rat as pleasant as you please, and asked him to stay to supper.

After supper they curled up and went to sleep. There was nothing else to do, you see. For this is the way it looked in the GREAT WOOD.

In the morning King Leo said politely, "What can I do for you, my small friend?"

Then Robin Rat answered, "Please tell us, King Leo, what is the name of this tree and whether we may eat the fruit of it. We are all SO HUNGRY!"

King Leo looked at the fruit that was like an APPLEORANGE-PEARPLUMBANANA and he sniffed at the fruit that was like a BANANAPLUMPEARORANGEAPPLE.

Then he said, "It is a good fruit. You may eat it. The name of the tree is BOJABI."

Then Robin Rat hung his cap over his right ear and climbed into his little canoe.

All the day and all the day he paddled down the great river.

And all the way he was thinking how much he could eat of that DELICIOUS fruit.

And at night he came home.

All the Beasts were waiting for him on the shore. He came up, whisking his paddle this way and that way through the water, just to show how well he could do it.

"What is it, Robin Rat?" said All the Beasts. "Tell us the name!" they roared and howled and grunted and whined and shrieked and squealed, each in his own PARTICULAR voice.

"Oh!" said Robin Rat. "I knew it a while ago, but now I have clean forgotten it."

Then All the Beasts stepped into the water and upset Robin Rat's little canoe.

They SPLASHED and they SPLUTTERED and they SP-L-ANKED Robin Rat. Squeaksqueaksqueaksqueaksqueak!

Nobody heard a word more from *him* that day.

PINKY PIG

But now All the Beasts were HUNGRIER STILL.

They sat in a circle round the tree and thought a while.

Then they said, "Let us send Pinky Pig to King Leo to ask the name of the tree. But Pinky Pig, DO NOT FORGET IT!"

Pinky Pig trotted away home—trip trap, trip trap, trip trap.

He put on his best blue coat and buttoned it up, though it squeezed him a little.

Then he trotted—trip trap, trip trap, trip trap—down to his little rowboat and took his oars to row up the big river.

All the day and all the day he rowed and he rowed and he ROWED up the big river.

And the Great Red Sun dropped behind the trees.

Then he found King Leo on the bank, all ready to receive visitors. His crown was a little crooked because he had put it on in a hurry when he saw Pinky Pig coming.

He smiled politely but he did not invite Pinky Pig to stay to supper.

"What can I do for you, my plump friend?" he asked.

Pinky Pig showed him the fruit that looked like an APPLE-ORANGEPEARPLUMBANANA and smelled like a BANANA-PLUMPEARORANGEAPPLE, and said, "Please, King Leo, we must know the name of this tree or we cannot eat the fruit. Please be so kind as to tell us."

Then King Leo said, "I have told Robin Rat. I will tell you. The name of the tree is BOJABI! Do not forget it."

Pinky Pig trotted back to his rowboat—trip trap, trip trap, trip trap.

All the night and all the night he rowed—he rowed—and he ro-o-owed until the oars—dropped-from-his-hands—and the big river took the boat down itself.

Pinky Pig curled up under the seat. And this is the sound that came from the boat: H-r-r-r-umph h-h-r-r-r-umph h-h-h-r-r-r-r-UM-MPH!

In the morning Pinky Pig sat up and rubbed his eyes. He was at home. All the Beasts stood on the river bank looking at him. "What is it, Pinky Pig? Tell us the name!" they whistled and snarled and squealed and shrieked and whined and grunted and howled and roared, each in his own PARTICULAR voice.

"I know it," said Pinky Pig. Then he yawned.

"I knew it last night," he said, "but-ah-ah-I-must-have-been-asleep, and-ah-for-got-ten it." That is the way he talked when he was yawning.

Then All the Beasts jumped into the water and smashed Pinky Pig's boat and his oars.

They PLUNGED about and PUNCHED poor Pinky Pig and POUNDED him until he went plop—plop—into the water.

SQue-e-e-e-e-e-E-E-E-E-E-E-AL!

He ran home with the water running off him and making little puddles here and there.

Nobody heard a word more from *him* that day.

GIDDY GOAT

But now All the Beasts were HUNGRIER and HUNGRIER. They could have eaten nails if there had been any nails in the Great Wood.

They sat in a circle round the tree and thought a while.

Then they said, "Giddy Goat is older than Pinky Pig, and wiser than Robin Rat. Let us send him to King Leo to ask the name of the tree so that we may eat the fruit of it before we starve. But Giddy Goat, DO NOT FORGET IT!"

"A-rashum!" said Giddy Goat. He was afraid of catching cold. Away he ran—kerlipp, ker-lipp—to his house to get a big woolly muffler to wear on the river. He wrapped it three times round his neck and tucked it neatly under his beard.

Then he ran—ker-lipp, ker-lipp—down to his little sailboat on the river.

All the day and all the day he sailed and he sailed and he SAILED up the big river.

And the Great Red Sun dropped behind the trees.

Then he found King Leo on the bank, *not* ready to receive visitors. His crown was on straight and he looked very CROSS.

"Whatdoyouwant?" he snapped—just like that.

"A-rashum!" said Giddy Goat. "I beg your Majesty's pardon. I have a cold coming on."

He showed King Leo the fruit that looked like an APPLE-ORANGEPEARPLUMBANANA and smelled like a BANANA-PLUMPEARORANGEAPPLE, and said, "If you would be so very kind, King Leo, to tell us the name of this tree, so that we may know whether we may eat the fruit of it."

Then King Leo said, "I have told Robin Rat. I have told Pinky Pig. I will tell you. But I will not tell ANYBODY ELSE. The name is BOJABI. DO NOT FORGET IT!"

"A-rash-oo!" said Giddy Goat and he skipped away—ker-lipp, ker-lipp—to his sailboat.

All the night and all the night he sailed and he sailed and he SAILED.

All the way he was remembering the name, and he remembered it very well.

He sailed so fast that he got home in the early, early morning. And all the way when he wasn't remembering the name, he was sneezing: "A-tchoo! A-rashum! A-tchoo!"

All the Beasts were waiting for him—rows and rows of them. Those in the back rows looked over the shoulders of those in the front rows, or climbed on their backs.

They pushed and jostled one another until they had upset Giddy Goat's sailboat. Ker-splash!—he went into the river.

Such a sight as he was when they pulled him out. His long hair was full of water. His beard was full of water. His eyes were full of water. His beautiful new muffler was full of water.

When the animals crowded round him to ask the name of the tree, he shook himself so that the water flew in their faces, and ran away home—ker-lipp, ker-lipp—with a most dreadful A-TCHOO!

His wife made him go to bed. And not one word could anyone get from him all that day but A-tchoo! A-rashum! A-tchoo!

Tommy Tortoise

By this time All the Beasts were so HUNGRY that they sat round the tree and cried. You see there was no one else who had a boat.

"What shall we do?" they wailed and howled and buzzed and grunted and groaned and sobbed and lamented, each in his own most PARTICULAR VOICE.

Then Tommy Tortoise, who had been lying asleep in the sun, opened one eye, and said, "What is all this fuss about? Haven't you found out the name of this tree YET?"

They said they had not and cried harder than ever.

"Oh well," said he, "if that's all, I'll go and get it for you."

"YOU!" snarled Tabby Tiger.

"You! You!" grunted Bruno Bear.

"You!" snapped Katy Crocodile, biting her word off short.

"You-u-u-u!" trumpeted Elizabeth Elephant.

"You! You! You!" chattered Mimi Monkey.

You never heard such a noise—not even at the circus—as there was when they all said this, each in his own PARTICULAR voice.

"Yes, me—I mean I," said Tommy Tortoise in his little, thin voice.

Then he crawled slowly home, trailing one foot after the other, as some boys do on their way to school.

He found his mother knitting stockings and rocking the baby.

"Hssh!" said Mrs. Tortoise. "He's just dropping off."

"Mother," said Tommy Tortoise. "How can I remember the name of that tree if I go up the river to get it?"

"Tommy," said Mrs. Tortoise, "do you remember how you used to go to school with all the other little tortoises and learn things?"

"Yes," said Tommy. "Nine times one makes nine, Nine times two makes eighteen, Nine times three makes twenty-seven—" He said the Nines table because anybody can say the Tens, and he wasn't sure about the Elevens.

"Hsh!" said Mrs. Tortoise. "That will do. You will wake the baby."

"But I will tell you how to remember." She whispered in his ear.

Then she said, "Now, Tommy, whatever happens to you, mind your manners. Remember to bow to King Leo and to speak to him so politely that he will know you have been well brought up."

"Yes, Mother," said Tommy Tortoise.

Then he put on his cap with the red tassel, and he went down to the river. He had no boat; so he had to swim.

All the day and all the day he swam and he swam and he SWAM.

When he was tired swimming, he would turn over on his shell and float with all his legs kicking in the water, just as the baby kicks in his bath.

And the Great Red Sun dropped behind the trees.

When Tommy Tortoise reached King Leo's home, King Leo was NOT curled up comfortably wearing his crown and ready to receive visitors. He was standing on the river bank waving his tail. His big head was waggling *this* way and *that* way, and he was not smiling AT ALL.

Before Tommy could speak a word, or even make his best bow, King Leo said: "R-R-R-R-R-R-R-R-R-R-R-R-R-R-R-R-R-R! S-s-cat! S-scamper! S-scat! S-skedaddle! I told Robin Rat. I told Pinky Pig. I told Giddy Goat. I WILL NOT TELL YOU that the name of the tree is bojabi. R-R-R-R-R-R-R-R-R-R-R-R-R-R-R-R!"

"Bojabi," whispers Tommy Tortoise to himself, and jumps—ker-lump—into the river again.

All the night and all the night he swam and he swam and he SWAM. But it was easy work to let the big river carry him on its back.

All the night and all the night he made up a little song and sang it, like this:

> "O Robin Rat, what shall we eat?
> Bojabi—bojabi—bojabi.
> O Pinky Pig, so fat and neat,
> Bojabi—bojabi—bojabi.
> O Giddy Goat, so fast and fleet,
> Bojabi—bojabi—bojabi.
> O Humpy Hippo, hard to beat,
> Bojabi—bojabi—bojabi.
> O Bruno Bear, with clumsy feet,
> Bojabi—bojabi—bojabi.
> O Katy Crocodile, here's a treat,
> Bojabi—bojabi—bojabi.
> O Tommy Tortoise, of Puddle Street,
> Bojabi—bojabi—bojabi.
> O All-the-Beasts, come quick and eat
> Bojabi—bojabi—bojabi."

And THAT was what his mother had told him to do.

All the Beasts were lying on the bank of the river. Far away they heard the little, thin voice of Tommy Tortoise singing his song. They pricked up their ears, looking *this* way and *that* way as they listened.

And presently Tommy Tortoise came crawling up through the mud.

"What is it?" they cried, each in his own PARTICULAR voice. You would have thought that all the circuses in the world were there.

"Bojabi," said Tommy Tortoise, and crawled away home without another word.

That night All the Beasts had bojabi for their supper.

But Tommy Tortoise had cream with his.

After that All the Beasts in that wood were never hungry. They could always eat bojabi.

They made Tommy Tortoise their king. "For," they said, "if he could remember the name of the bojabi tree, he can do anything."

As far as I know he is king of All the Beasts in the Great Wood to-day.

—Adapted from an African folk tale

JACOBLE TELLS THE TRUTH

Lisl Weil

Once there was old Jacob and little Jacoble—and they had seven little lambs to take care of. One fine day they were on their way home. The sun still shone brightly. The seven little lambs thought of the wonderful green grass they had eaten for lunch. Old Jacob was thinking of how thankful one must be for such a fine day. And little Jacoble . . . he did not know . . . what to think . . . until he thought a wonderful idea, and he cried, "Jacob, oh, Jacob! Do you know what I saw yesterday?" "I saw a green rabbit flying in the air and it was so big—bigger than an elephant!"

"Of course you saw that with your own eyes." said old Jacob.

"Of course I did," said Jacoble, and he was all proud.

"It's a good thing you really saw that big flying green rabbit. Because if you hadn't—" said old Jacob, "—that bridge we are going to go over is a very strange one. As soon as anyone who hasn't told the truth crosses it, the bridge breaks in two under his feet.

Then they walked on.

"Ja-cob," said Jacoble a little later. "You know that big green

flying rabbit I saw yesterday. . . . Well, it wasn't really flying, and
. . . it wasn't quite as big as an elephant. . . . But it was very big.
It was just about the size of a horse. Of a young horse!"

"Big as a horse?" asked old Jacob, as they came nearer and nearer
the bridge, and little Jacoble began not to feel so well.

"Jacob, oh Jacob," said Jacoble. "That big green rabbit I saw
yesterday— —I had something in my eye—so I couldn't see very
well. It wasn't such an awfully big rabbit after all. But it was green.
Yes, that's what it was—all green!"

Old Jacob didn't say a word. He just walked over the bridge. But
Jacoble didn't follow him. He was very frightened. Little Jacoble
just stood at the edge of the bridge. He had good reason to be
frightened. "Jacob," he said. "Oh, Jacob! You know that rabbit I
saw yesterday. It wasn't green. No, no. It was just a little brown
rabbit."

Then he didn't feel frightened any more . . . and he ran happily
over the bridge.

HOW THE ENGINE LEARNED THE KNOWING SONG

Lucy Sprague Mitchell

Once there was a new engine. He had a great big boiler; he had
a smoke stack; he had a bell; he had a whistle; he had a sand-dome;
he had a headlight; he had four big driving wheels; he had a cab.
But he was very sad, was this engine, for he didn't know how to use
any of his parts. All around him on the tracks were other engines,
puffing or whistling or ringing their bells and squirting steam. One
big engine moved his wheels slowly, softly muttering to himself,
"I'm going, I'm going, I'm going." Now the new engine knew this
was the end of the Knowing Song of Engines. He wanted desper-
ately to sing it. So he called out:

> "I want to go
> But I don't know how;
> I want to know,
> Please teach me now.
> Please somebody teach me how."

Now there were two men who had come just on purpose to teach
him how. And who do you suppose they were? The engineer and

the fireman! When the engineer heard the new engine call out, he asked, "What do you want, new engine?" And the engine answered:

"I want the sound
Of my wheels going round.
I want to stream
A jet of steam.
I want to puff
Smoke and stuff.
I want to ring
Ding, ding-a-ding.
I want to blow
My whistle so.
I want my light
To shine out bright.
I want to go ringing and singing the song,
The humming song of the engine coming,
The clear, near song of the engine here,
The knowing song of the engine going."

Now the engineer and the fireman were pleased when they heard what the new engine wanted. But the engineer said:

"All in good time, my engine,
Steady, steady,
'Til you're ready.
Learn to know
Before you go."

Then he said to the fireman, "First we must give our engine some water." So they put the end of a hose hanging from a big high-up tank right into a little tank under the engine's tender. The water filled up this little tank and then ran into the big boiler and filled that all up too. And while they were doing this the water kept saying:

"I am water from a stream
When I'm hot I turn to steam."

When the engine felt his boiler full of water he asked eagerly.

"Now I have water,
Now do I know
How I should go?"

But the fireman said:

"All in good time, my engine,
Steady, steady,
'Til you're ready.
Learn to know
Before you go."

Then he said to the engineer, "Now we must give our engine some coal." So they filled the tender with coal, and then under the boiler the fireman built a fire. Then the fireman began blowing and the coals began glowing. And as he built the fire, the fire said:

> "I am fire,
> The coal I eat
> To make the heat
> To turn the stream
> Into the steam."

When the engine felt the sleeping fire wake up and begin to live inside him and turn the water into steam he said eagerly:

> "Now I have water,
> Now I have coal,
> Now do I know
> How I should go?"

But the engineer said:

> "All in good time, my engine,
> Steady, steady,
> 'Til you're ready.
> Learn to know
> Before you go."

Then he said to the fireman, "We must oil our engine well." So they took oil cans with funny long noses and they oiled all the machinery, the piston-rods, the levers, the wheels, everything that moved or went round. And all the time the oil kept saying:

> "No creak,
> No squeak."

When the engine felt the oil smoothing all his machinery, he said eagerly:

> "Now I have water,
> Now I have coal,
> Now I am oiled,
> Now do I know
> How I should go?"

But the fireman said:

> "All in good time, my engine,
> Steady, steady,
> 'Til you're ready.
> Learn to know
> Before you go."

Then he said to the engineer, "We must give our engine some sand. So they took some sand and they filled the sand domes on top of the boiler so that he could send sand down through his two little pipes and sprinkle it in front of his wheels when the rails were slippery. And all the time the sand kept saying:

> "When ice drips,
> And wheel slips,
> I am sand
> Close at hand."

When the new engine felt his sand dome filled with sand he said eagerly:

> "Now I have water,
> Now I have coal,
> Now I am oiled,
> Now I have sand,
> Now do I know
> How I should go?"

But the engineer said:

> "All in good time, my engine,
> Steady, steady,
> 'Til you're ready.
> Learn to know
> Before you go."

Then he said to the fireman, "We must light our engine's headlight." So the fireman took a cloth and he wiped the curved mirror behind the light and polished the brass around it. Then he screwed in a big electric bulb and closed the little door in front of it. And then he turned a switch. All the time the light kept saying:

> "I'm the headlight shining bright
> Like a sunbeam through the night."

Now when the engine saw the great golden path of brightness streaming out ahead of him, he said eagerly:

> "Now I have water
> Now I have coal,
> Now I am oiled,
> Now I have sand,
> Now I make light,
> Now do I know
> How I should go?"

And the engineer said, "We will see if you are ready, my new engine." So he climbed into the cab and the fireman got in behind him. Then he said, "Engine, can you blow your whistle so?" And he pulled a handle which let the steam into the whistle and the engine whistled "Toot, toot, toot." Then he said, "Can you puff smoke and stuff?" And the engine puffed black smoke saying, "Puff, puff, puff, puff, puff." Then he said, "Engine, can you squirt a stream of steam?" And he opened a valve and the engine went, "Szszszszsz." Then he said, "Engine, can you sprinkle sand?" And he pulled a little handle and the sand trickled drip, drip, drip, drip down on the tracks in front of the engine's wheels. Then he said, "Engine, does your light shine out bright?" And he looked and there was a great golden flood of light on the track in front of him. Then he said, "Engine, can you make the sound of your wheels going round?" And he pulled another lever and the great wheels began to move. Then the engineer said:

> "Now is the time,
> Now is the time.
> Steady, steady,
> Now you're ready.

Blow whistle, ring bell, puff smoke, hiss steam, sprinkle sand, shine light, turn wheels!

> 'Tis time to be ringing and singing the song,
> The humming song of the engine coming,
> The clear, near song of the engine here,
> The knowing song of the engine going."

Then whistle blew, bell rang, smoke puffed, steam hissed, sand sprinkled, light shone and wheels turned like this:

> "Toot-toot, ding-a-ding, puff-puff,
> Szszszszsz, drip-drip, chug-chug."

That's the way the new engine sounded when he started on his first ride and didn't know how to do things very well. But that's not the way he sounded when he had learned to go really smooth and fast. Then it was that he learned *really* to sing "The Knowing Song of the Engine." He sang it better than anyone else for he became the fastest, the steadiest, the most knowing of all express engines. And this is the song he sang. You could hear it humming on the rails long before he came and hear it humming on the rails long after he had passed. Now listen to the song.

"I'm coming, I'm coming, I'm coming, I'm coming,
I'm coming, I'm coming, I'm coming, I'm coming,
I'm coming, I'm coming, I'm coming, I'm coming,
I'm Coming, I'm Coming, I'm Coming, I'm Coming,
I'M HERE, I'M HERE, I'M HERE, I'M HERE,
I'M HERE, I'M HERE, I'M HERE, I'M HERE.
I'm Going, I'm Going, I'm Going, I'm Going,
I'm going, I'm going, I'm going, I'm going,
I'm going, I'm going, I'm going, I'm going."

SERENA AND THE COOKIE LADY

Grace Klem

For years and years Mrs. Twigley had lived with her cat Serena in a white house. The house was little and old. So was Mrs. Twigley. Serena was younger, although she had had sixty-seven kittens and was now a grandmother.

Serena and Mrs. Twigley were the best of friends. They shared a fondness for many things—ice cream, a snug, spicy kitchen, a quiet country walk, a little doze by the fire.

Mrs. Twigley was a bright old lady of nice habits. When she was happy, she played cowboy songs on a banjo. When she was worried, she knitted furiously. And when she felt sad, she baked cookies to take her mind off her troubles.

Serena, for her part, was dignified and beautiful. She kept the mice away and she never got into mischief. At night she slept on an old-fashioned feathered hat in a striped hatbox that she had found one day in the attic.

Life was pleasant, in any case, for Serena. She liked the lively strum of the banjo, and the sharp click of the needles, and the good warm smell of baking.

Whenever Mrs. Twigley spoke, Serena listened thoughtfully and looked wise. Mrs. Twigley was sure that she was an extremely clever cat, although she had never proved it.

Serena and Mrs. Twigley lived happily together a long while before hard times set in. Perhaps Mrs. Twigley did not figure very well, or perhaps there had not been enough money in the first place. But the fact was that Mrs. Twigley and Serena found themselves growing poorer and poorer, though they were just as fond of ice cream as ever.

"Bother!" exclaimed Mrs. Twigley, knitting furiously, "money isn't important until there isn't any. Then it is very important indeed. I am afraid, Serena, that we shall have to sell this little old house and move away."

And she began to bake cookies.

She felt so sad that she baked a great many cookies. She baked so many that they filled the kitchen and the dining room, the front hall, and the back pantry. They overflowed into the parlor and up the stairs. There were chocolate cookies, ginger cookies, sugar cakes and bars, bumpy cookies, heart-shaped cookies, little pigs and stars.

When Mrs. Twigley stopped to catch her breath and look around, she was a little surprised.

"Dear me," she sighed, "we can't live on cookies!"

Serena sniffed and looked very wise. With that an idea struck Mrs. Twigley.

"Why not?" she said. "Why can't we live on cookies? They're the best cookies in the county, if I say it myself! We could put up a sign and sell them. Then we wouldn't have to leave this little old house. What a wonderful plan!"

Mrs. Twigley tied up the cookies in neat little packages. She hung a sign on the door:

HOMEMADE COOKIES FOR SALE

She put her few nickles and dimes and quarters in the milk-glass hen on the mantel, all ready to make change. Then Mrs. Twigley and Serena sat down to wait for customers.

They waited. And waited. And waited.

Nobody came. Mrs. Twigley, who didn't always figure very well, had forgotten that hardly anybody ever came down Huckleberry Lane past the little old house on the edge of the village, off the main highway. Only the milkman and the farmer down the road went by, and the farmer's children taking a short cut home from school.

Mrs. Twigley grew so sad that she started to bake cookies again. She made all the old favorites and invented new ones. When she stopped to look around she saw chocolate cookies, ginger cookies, sugar cakes and bars, bumpy cookies, heart-shaped cookies, little pigs and stars, and pinwheels and elephants, lions and moons, cocoanut kisses and sweet macaroons—as well as honey cookies, oatmeal cookies, raisin sticks and squares, spicy cookies, bell-shaped cookies, ducks, and chicks, and bears.

But she did not see Serena anywhere.

Mrs. Twigley called and called, but there was no answer. She looked upstairs and downstairs. She searched in the pantry and in the parlor. She went into the garden and called again. At last Mrs. Twigley heard a faint meow. It seemed to come from the big oak tree in the back yard.

Mrs. Twigley peered up into the branches. She could hardly believe her eyes. There, high above her, sat Serena!

"Dear me," gasped Mrs. Twigley, "how did you get way up there? How are you going to get down again?"

Serena looked more wise than worried.

Mrs. Twigley coaxed and coaxed but Serena stayed in the big oak tree.

After a while Peter Pippin, the farmer's boy, came short-cutting home from school.

"I'll fetch her for you, Mrs. Twigley," he said, and he climbed up the tree.

Peter had almost reached Serena when she walked calmly to the end of a rather thin branch. Peter couldn't catch her there, so he scrambled down the tree.

"I'm sorry, Mrs. Twigley," he said. "I'll have to go home and get my father's ladder. I'll be right back with it."

"Well, thank you kindly, Peter," said Mrs. Twigley "and take some cookies along with you."

Peter ran off, munching happily. Soon he returned with the ladder, and the farmer, and the hired man, and the farmer's wife, and the baby who was too young to leave at home, and the gray goose who always followed the baby.

By this time Serena had crawled back to a stronger branch, but she showed no signs of coming down.

Farmer Pippin set the ladder against the tree and started up. He had almost reached Serena when she climbed a little higher. The farmer went to the top of the ladder, but Serena was still out of reach. Farmer Pippin had to give up.

"Bother," said Mrs. Twigley, "I can't think what has gotten into that cat. She never made any trouble before. But thank you kindly, and have some cookies before you go."

The farmer and the hired man and the farmer's wife all agreed that they had never tasted such good cookies. Mrs. Pippin bought six bags because she had such a large family and no time for baking. Mrs. Twigley put the money in the milk-glass hen on the mantel.

Serena stayed in the oak tree. She meowed once in a while but she still looked more wise than worried. She stayed up in the oak tree all night.

Bright and early the next morning Mrs. Twigley called the village Police Department. The Chief of Police himself came around. When he saw where Serena was, he shook his head.

"Ma'am," he said, "we policemen have separated dogs in dog fights and we have chopped ducks out of the frozen lake. We pushed a cow off the railroad track, and once we caught a runaway horse. But this cat is up too high. We haven't any ladders. Maybe the Fire Department can help you."

The Chief of Police said good-by, and before he went he bought cookies. He was a fat man and he liked sweet things.

A little later in the morning the Fire Department arrived with engines and hook-and-ladders and trucks, with almost the whole town trailing after.

The firemen set to work quickly. They put up big ladders and climbed higher and higher on them. They had almost reached Serena when the village fire alarm rang. Down rushed the firemen and back onto their engines and hook-and-ladders and trucks. Away they went, leaving the cat in the oak tree. But before the people followed the firemen to the fire, most of them bought some of Mrs. Twigley's cookies.

Serena was crying now, loudly and sadly. Mrs. Twigley went into the kitchen and baked more cookies because she felt so worried about Serena.

More and more people came to the little old house. Some of them came to help and some came to look. When they smelled Mrs. Twigley's freshly baked homemade cookies they became very hungry. Everyone wanted to buy cookies.

There was such a pushing and scrambling that no one noticed Serena. No one saw her creep cautiously to the edge of a branch. No one saw her leap to the roof of the house, then to the top of a truck parked in the driveway, and then down to the ground.

After the excitement over the cookies quieted down and the milk-glass hen on the mantel was bulging with money, Mrs. Twigley hurried out and looked up into the oak tree.

Serena was not there. Mrs. Twigley looked all around the yard. Serena was nowhere in sight.

"Bother!" said Mrs. Twigley, "where is Serena?"

Mrs. Twigley looked in the garden. She searched in the parlor and in the pantry. She looked downstairs and upstairs.

At last Mrs. Twigley found Serena, fast asleep on the feathered hat in the striped hatbox.

Then Mrs. Twigley took the milk-glass hen off the mantel and sat down to count her money. There was enough to last for days! And besides, Mrs. Twigley had enough orders for cookies to keep her busy baking for weeks!

Now, all over the county, people know the way to Huckleberry Lane. They come for chocolate cookies, ginger cookies, sugar cakes and bars, bumpy cookies, heart-shaped cookies, little pigs and stars.

Mrs. Twigley and Serena will never have to leave the little old house. They have ice cream every day. Mrs. Twigley does not knit anymore because she is not worried. But every day, when she has finished baking cookies, she sits down and plays her banjo.

Serena sits beside her and listens.

"Sometimes, Serena," Mrs. Twigley observes, between cowboy songs, "I wonder if you didn't stay up in the big oak tree on purpose." Serena sniffs, but she looks very wise.

THE LITTLE OLD WOMAN WHO USED HER HEAD

Hope Newell

Once upon a time there was a Little Old Woman. She lived in a little yellow house wtih a blue door and two blue window boxes. In each of the window boxes there were yellow tulips.

All around her house was a neat blue fence. Inside the fence was the Little Old Woman's soup garden. She called it a soup garden because she raised vegetables in it, to cook in her soup. She raised carrots, potatoes, turnips, garlic, cabbages and onions.

The Little Old Woman was very poor. If she had not been so clever, she probably could not have made both ends meet. But she was a great one for using her head. She always said, "What is the good of having a head if you don't use it?"

So, as you will see, she managed to get along very well.

The Little Old Woman had only one blanket for her bed. It was a nice red flannel blanket, but it was full of holes.

"I must get a new blanket before winter comes," she said. "Or better yet, I might buy me a feather bed. How warm and cozy I would be in a feather bed on cold winter nights!"

But feather beds cost a lot of money, so the Little Old Woman bought a flock of geese instead. As she was driving them home from the market, she said to herself:

"These twelve geese will lay eggs for me all summer. Then when winter comes I will pluck their feathers and make myself a feather bed. What a clever Old Woman I am!"

When the Little Old Woman arrived home, she drove the geese into the yard and closed the gate. Then she ate her supper and went to bed.

The next morning she heard a great noise in the yard. When she opened the door the geese came running to her.

"Honk, honk!" said the big gander, flapping his wings.

"Honk, honk!" said all the other geese, flapping their wings. Everywhere she went, the twelve geese followed her, saying, "Honk, honk!" and flapping their wings.

"Dear me," said the Little Old Woman, "I do believe they want something to eat. I must buy them some corn."

So she went to the market and bought a bag of corn for the geese.

Every morning when she opened the door, the geese came running to her.

"Honk, honk!" they said, flapping their wings. Then she remembered to give them some corn. The geese ate so much corn that pretty soon the Little Old Woman had to buy another bag of corn. After a while, that bag was empty too, and she had to buy another bag of corn.

"These geese eat a lot of corn," she said, "but after all, they are growing bigger and bigger. Their feathers are growing thicker and thicker. They will make me a fine feather bed when winter comes."

By and by the nights began to grow cold. The red flannel blanket was so full of holes that it did not keep the Little Old Woman warm. She shivered all night long.

"Winter will soon be here," she thought. "It is high time I plucked the geese and made my feather bed."

The next morning she went out to pluck the geese.

"How warm and contented they look," said the Little Old Woman.

"They will be cold if I pluck their feathers. Maybe if I cut the holes out of the red blanket, it will be warm enough for me."

But when she fetched her scissors and cut the holes out of the red blanket, the holes were still there. In fact, they were bigger than ever.

"What am I to do?" she thought. "If I take their feathers the geese will be cold. If I do not take their feathers, I will be cold. I suppose I had better use my head."

And here is how the Little Old Woman used her head. First she tied a wet towel around her forehead. Then she sat down with her forefinger against her nose and shut her eyes.

She used her head and used her head and used her head. She used her head so long that it began to ache, but finally she knew what to do.

"The red blanket is no good to me," she said. "I will cut it into twelve pieces and make each of the geese a warm red coat. Then I can pluck their feathers to make me a feather bed."

The Little Old Woman set to work and made each of the geese a little red coat. On each coat she sewed three shiny brass buttons.

"Now I must pluck the geese and make my feather bed," said the Little Old Woman.

She took a basket and went out to pluck the geese. She plucked the big gander and put his feathers in the basket. She plucked the grey goose and put her feathers into the basket. Then she plucked the other geese and put their feathers into the basket.

When all the geese were plucked, the Little Old Woman put a little red coat on each goose and fastened it with the shiny brass buttons.

"How handsome the geese look," she said. "I was very clever to think of making the little red coats to keep them warm."

Then she carried the basket of feathers into the house and sewed them into a strong ticking to make a feather bed.

When the bed was all finished, the Little Old Woman said to herself:

"I shall sleep very warm this winter. How wise I was to buy a flock of geese to make a feather bed. It all comes of using my head."

One cold winter night, the Little Old Woman was out in the barn putting her geese to bed. She gave them some corn and took off their little red coats. Then she brushed each little coat with a whisk broom and carefully shook out the wrinkles.

As she was folding the coats in a neat pile, she thought:

"My poor geese must be very cold at night. I have my cozy fire and my feather bed. But they have not even a blanket to keep them warm."

After the geese had eaten their corn, they began to go to roost. "Honk, honk!" said the big gander, and he hopped up on the roost. "Honk, honk!" said the grey goose, and she hopped up on the roost.

Then the Little Old Woman closed the barn door and went into the house. When she went to bed, she lay awake worrying about the geese. After a while she said to herself:

"I cannot sleep a wink for thinking how cold the geese must be. I had better bring them in the house where it is warm."

So the Little Old Woman dressed herself and went out to the barn to fetch the geese. She shooed them off the roost and put on their little red coats. She picked up two geese, and tucking one under each arm, she carried them into the house.

Then she went out to the barn and picked up two more geese. She tucked one goose under each arm and carried them into the house.

When the Little Old Woman had brought all the geese into the house, she said to herself:

"Now I must get them ready for bed again."

She took off their little red coats and gave the geese some corn. Then she brushed each little coat with a whisk broom and carefully shook out all the wrinkles.

As she was folding the coats in a neat pile, she thought:

"It was very clever of me to bring the geese into the house. Now they will be warm, and I shall be able to sleep."

Then the Little Old Woman undressed herself again and went to bed.

After the geese had eaten their corn, they began to roost.

"Honk, honk!" said the gander, and he hopped up on the foot of the Little Old Woman's bed. "Honk, honk!" said the grey goose, and she hopped up on the foot of the Little Old Woman's bed. "Honk, honk!" said all the other geese, and they tried to hop up on the foot of the Little Old Woman's bed.

But it was not a very big bed, and there was not enough room for all the geese to roost. They began to fight. They pushed and shoved each other. They hissed and squawked and flapped their wings.

All night long the geese pushed and shoved each other. All night long they hissed and squawked and flapped their wings. They made so much noise that the Little Old Woman did not sleep a wink.

"This will never do," she said. "When they were in the barn, I did not sleep for thinking how cold they must be. When they are in the house, I cannot sleep because they make so much noise. Perhaps if I use my head, I shall know what to do."

The Little Old Woman tied a wet towel around her forehead. Then she sat down with her forefinger against her nose and shut her eyes.

She used her head and used her head, and after a while she knew what to do.

"I will move the roost into the house," she said. "The geese will have the cozy fire to keep them warm. Then I will move my bed out into the barn. My feather bed will keep me warm, and I will not be worrying about the geese. They will not keep me awake with their noise. I shall sleep very comfortably in the barn."

The Little Old Woman moved the roost into the house, and she moved her bed out into the barn.

When night came again, she brought the geese into the house. After she had fed them some corn, she took off their little red coats. Then they all hopped up on the roost, and the Little Old Woman went out to the barn to sleep.

Her feather bed kept her as warm as toast. She was not worried about the geese, because she knew that they were warm too. So she slept as sound as a top all night long.

All the year round the Little Old Woman used her head to find out what to do.

One evening she said to herself. "How time does fly! It seems only yesterday that I made my geese their little red coats and plucked their feathers to make my feather bed. Now it is fall again.

"I have used my head so much this year that I think I will give it a rest."

So the Little Old Woman sat down in her rocking-chair to rest her head.

"The nights are growing colder," she thought. "I had better sit closer to the fireplace."

She got up and moved her chair closer to the fireplace and sat down again. She folded her arms across her apron and put her feet on her little footstool.

"A fireplace is nice and warm," she said to herself. "I must gather some wood tomorrow so I can make a fire. My fireplace will be even warmer when I build a fire in it. And besides, a fire is so cozy to look at.

"The evenings will be very long now. I shall have plenty of time to sit by my fire and think. I shall think about pleasant things for that will rest my head.

"I shall think how warm my geese are in their little red jackets. I shall think how comfortable my rats are in their little box.

"I shall think how comfortable I am in my feather bed.

"It will be very pleasant to sit by my fire and think how contented and happy we are, and all because I used my head."

THE BLACK SOMBRERO

Nanda and *Lynd Ward*

This is the story of a cowboy named Johnson, and his cow pony called Pinto. He lived in the far-off western foothills. And he was the best roping and branding cowboy of that region.

Besides his pinto pony, Johnson owned a shiny guitar and a good, strong lariat for roping the cattle. But most important of all, he had a great black felt hat called a sombrero. It was his prize possession.

One day while Johnson was branding the calves of the Bar X ranch, a small wind blew down from the mountains. This was a very young and very mischievous wind.

"Whoosh!" he cried, when he saw Johnson's hat. "What fun it would be to whisk away this big black sombrero!" And with a gusty puff he snatched off the big hat.

Then he went racing down the valley, chuckling with glee.

"Holy Smoke!" shouted Johnson. "That wind has blown off my sombrero. Come along, old Pinto. We will have to follow that wind and find my hat."

So Johnson mounted his cow pony and started out south in the direction the wind had gone. As he rode along he made up a sad little song about his hat.

> "I once had a hat,
> A very fine hat,
> A wind came along
> And blew it away!
> Hi de ho,
> Hi de hay!
> That frisky young wind
> Just wanted to play."

Johnson rode for days and days. Every night he stopped at a grassy knoll to get some sleep. As he lay on the ground, using his saddle for a pillow, he would strum his guitar and hum the sad little song to his horse Pinto.

Finally, one day Johnson came to the great prairie. All he could see for miles and miles was rippling brown grass. But his sombrero was not in sight.

"Old Pinto," he said at last, "maybe one of the prairie dogs has seen my great black hat."

The pony nodded his head up and down in agreement. So Johnson went on toward the mounds that marked the entrance to the prairie dogs' homes.

One fat fellow was sunning himself on his doorstep as Johnson rode up.

"Pardner," the cowboy asked, "have you seen my great black sombrero blown by the wind?"

The prairie dog opened one sleepy eye. Then he yawned. "I don't know," he answered. "If your hat was a great round black thing, then it was here. And I really appreciated it very much. It kept my den underground nice and dry. When the long rains came, the water could not wash down the entrance because I put your hat over it. Many thanks."

"But where is it now?" asked the cowboy.

"That I don't know," replied the furry little animal. "For when the rains left, the wind returned and swept the hat away across the prairie to the south. But go see the rattlesnake. He lives among the group of barren rocks in the middle of the prairie."

So Johnson thanked the prairie dog and rode on toward the south.

Soon he stopped his cow pony and went to sleep. The next morning he mounted Pinto and continued on. By and by he came to the barren rocks.

The rattlesnake was coiled loosely around a large boulder. Despite his small eyes and wicked darting tongue, he was the wisest creature on the prairie.

"Pardner, have you seen my great black sombrero, blown by the wind?" asked Johnson.

"I don't know," said the snake in a rasping voice. "If your hat was a great round black thing, then it has been here. And I really appreciated it very much. It was quite damp with water. I had only to coil up in it to get a wonderful bath. It saved me a trip down to the prairie that morning. Many thanks."

"But where is it now?" asked Johnson.

"That I don't know," replied the snake. "The wind soon returned and swept the hat across the prairie toward the desert. But go on until you find the pack rat. He lives in the sagebrush on the edge of the desert. And he knows everything that goes on there."

So Johnson thanked the snake and rode south toward the desert.

He rode on and on through the brown prairie grass. It seemed to go on forever. But at last he saw the line of sagebrush on the edge of the desert. Johnson found the busy pack rat scurrying here and there, collecting nuts and any little shiny objects he might come across.

"Pardner," asked Johnson, when the little animal stopped for a moment, "have you seen my great black sombrero blown by the wind?"

Now the pack rat knew what a sombrero was. He had been around people enough to know a few things.

"Yes," the little rodent replied. "I found it where the wind left it in the brush."

"I couldn't use it so I traded it to the armadillo for some piñon nuts. He lives near the foothills. Just follow this line of brush until you come to a large barrel cactus. The armadillo's burrow is right next to it on the right."

So Johnson thanked the pack rat and rode on along the line of brush until he found the barrel cactus.

Looking around, he saw the armadillo just entering his burrow. He had nine creamy white bands encircling his dark gray armor.

"Say, Pardner," said Johnson, "do you have my great black sombrero? The pack rat told me he traded it to you."

"Yes," said the armadillo. "Come and look into my burrow and you will see it."

So Johnson dismounted and followed the armadillo to his burrow.

He peered down into the little underground room below.

"Holy Smoke!" said Johnson.

"There is an owl, a mother cottontail rabbit, and five baby cottontails down there. And the baby rabbits are sleeping in my hat!"

"Yes," said the armadillo quietly. "Since there aren't enough burrows to go around, I have boarders. The baby rabbits are so young, they have to have a warm snug nest to live in. So when I saw your hat I knew it was just the right thing."

"Well," said Johnson, "this is a problem. I do need my hat to keep the sun off my face. But the baby rabbits need it for a nest."

So Johnson sat down beside the burrow and thought. He thought and thought and thought and thought and thought and thought and thought.

"I've got it!" he shouted at last. "I can take the whole rabbit family with me back to the ranch. I will take care of them until the babies are grown. The grass is much better there and they will grow very fat. They won't need my sombrero when we reach the ranch."

"That's a good idea," agreed the armadillo. "My little burrow has really been quite crowded. But there is quite enough room for the owl and me."

So Johnson said goodbye and, taking up the small family of cottontails in his sombrero, he mounted his pony. Then he rode north over the prairie, past the sagebrush and barren rocks and on up into the valley, back to the ranch. As he rode along he sang the little song he had made up. But this time it was very gay.

> "I once had a hat,
> A very fine hat.
> The wind came along
> And blew it away!
> Hi de ho,
> Hi de hay.
> So I rode 'cross the prairie
> And found it one day."

THE FIVE CHINESE BROTHERS

Claire Huchet Bishop
and
Kurt Wiese

Once upon a time there were Five Chinese Brothers and they all looked exactly alike. They lived with their mother in a little house not far from the sea.

The First Chinese Brother could swallow the sea.

The Second Chinese Brother had an iron neck.

The Third Chinese Brother could stretch and stretch and stretch his legs.

The Fourth Chinese Brother could not be burned.

and

The Fifth Chinese Brother could hold his breath indefinitely.

Every morning the First Chinese Brother would go fishing, and whatever the weather, he would come back to the village with beautiful and rare fish which he had caught and could sell at the market for a very good price.

One day, as he was leaving the market place, a little boy stopped him and asked him if he could go fishing with him.

"No, it could not be done," said the First Chinese Brother.

But the little boy begged and begged and finally the First Chinese Brother consented. "Under one condition," said he, "and that is that you shall obey me promptly."

"Yes, yes," the little boy promised.

Early next morning, the First Chinese Brother and the little boy went down to the beach.

"Remember," said the First Chinese Brother, "you must obey me promptly. When I make a sign for you to come back, you must come at once."

"Yes, yes," the little boy promised.

Then the First Chinese Brother swallowed the sea.

And all the fish were left high and dry at the bottom of the sea. And all the treasures of the sea lay uncovered.

The little boy was delighted. He ran here and there stuffing his pockets with strange pebbles, extraordinary shells and fantastic algae.

Near the shore the First Chinese Brother gathered some fish while he kept holding the sea in his mouth. Presently he grew tired. It is very hard to hold the sea. So he made a sign with his hand for the little boy to come back. The little boy saw him but paid no attention.

The First Chinese Brother made great movements with his arms and that meant "Come back!" But did the little boy care? Not a bit and he ran further away.

Then the First Chinese Brother felt the sea swelling inside him and he made desperate gestures to call the little boy back. But the little boy made faces at him and fled as fast as he could.

The First Chinese Brother held the sea until he thought he was going to burst. All of a sudden the sea forced its way out of his mouth, went back to its bed . . . and the little boy disappeared.

When the First Chinese Brother returned to the village, alone, he was arrested, put in prison, tried and condemned to have his head cut off.

On the morning of the execution he said to the judge:

"Your Honor, will you allow me to go and bid my mother good-bye?"

"It is only fair," said the judge.

So the First Chinese Brother went home . . . and the Second Chinese Brother came back in his place.

All the people were assembled on the village square to witness the execution. The executioner took his sword and struck a mighty blow.

But the Second Chinese Brother got up and smiled. He was the one with the iron neck and they simply could not cut his head off. Everybody was angry and they decided that he should be drowned.

On the morning of the execution, the Second Chinese Brother said to the judge:

"Your Honor, will you allow me to go and bid my mother good-bye?"

"It is only fair," said the judge.

So the Second Chinese Brother went home . . . and the Third Chinese Brother came back in his place.

He was pushed on a boat which made for the open sea.

When they were far out on the ocean, the Third Chinese Brother was thrown overboard.

But he began to stretch and stretch and stretch his legs, way down to the bottom of the sea, and all the time his smiling face was bobbing up and down on the crest of the waves. He simply could not be drowned.

Everybody was very angry, and they all decided that he should be burned.

On the morning of the execution, the Third Chinese Brother said to the judge:

"Your Honor, will you allow me to go and bid my mother good-bye?"

"It is only fair," said the judge.

So the Third Chinese Brother went home . . . and the Fourth Chinese Brother came back in his place.

He was tied up to a stake. Fire was set to it and all the people stood around watching it. In the midst of the flames they heard him say:

"This is quite pleasant."

"Bring some more wood!" the people cried.

The fire roared higher.

"Now it is quite comfortable," said the Fourth Chinese Brother, for he was the one who could not be burned. Everybody was getting more and more angry every minute and they all decided to smother him.

On the morning of the execution, the Fourth Chinese Brother said to the judge:

"Your Honor, will you allow me to go and bid my mother good-bye?"

"It is only fair," said the judge.

So the Fourth Chinese Brother went home . . . and the Fifth Chinese Brother came back in his place. A large oven had been built on the village square and it had been all stuffed with whipped cream. The Fifth Chinese Brother was shovelled into the oven, right in the middle of the cream, the door was shut tight, and everybody sat around and waited.

They were not going to be tricked again! So they stayed there all night and even a little after dawn, just to make sure.

Then they opened the door and pulled him out. And he shook himself and said, "My! That was a good sleep!"

Everybody stared open-mouthed and round-eyed. But the judge stepped forward and said, "We have tried to get rid of you in every possible way and somehow it cannot be done. It must be that you are innocent."

"Yes, yes," shouted all the people. So they let him go and he went home.

and

The Five Chinese Brothers and their mother all lived together happily for many years.

WHY COWBOYS SING IN TEXAS

Henderson LeGrand

Everybody knows how cowboys sing, today, in Texas.

But there was a time when cowboys did not sing, in Texas. That was a lonely time. This book tells how song came to Texas. This is a story heard beside a campfire by the Rio Grande. The story of why cowboys sing, today, in Texas.

Today, cowboys sing, in Texas. They sing, "Yippee yi." And they sing, "Yippee yay." Everybody knows how cowboys sing, today, in Texas.

But it was not always so. Things were quiet, once, in Texas. Long ago, in the days when cowboys did not sing. Cowboys were silent then. And the most silent cowboy in all of Texas was Slim Jim Bean.

Once, in that old and silent time, Slim Jim was guarding a herd of cattle at night. It was a long, dark night. And Slim Jim Bean was lonely. I wish I could hear a little noise, he thought. Any kind of a little noise that would not frighten the cows. Slim Jim knew that if anything frightened the cows they would stampede. They would stampede and run all over Texas. It might take a month of Sundays to round them up again. Slim Jim thought of just the noise he would like to hear. It was a song he sang when he was a boy. He remembered the words. He remembered the tune. "I believe I could sing that song again," he said. "Just a little song should not frighten the cows." So Slim Jim opened his mouth and he sang. The song woke the cows. And they didn't like it. They couldn't stand that song. A big black cow stampeded. A little yellow cow stampeded. Big ones and little ones, spotted ones and plain ones—they all stampeded. They stampeded all over Texas.

Slim Jim and the other cowboys rode out to round up the cows. They rode through the mesquite with its long straight thorns. They rode through the Spanish dagger with its long sharp spikes. They rode through the cat's-claw with its long curved briers. And they rode through clumps of cactus with its long prickly needles. But the thorns did not hurt them. And the spikes did not hurt them. And the briers did not hurt them. And the needles did not hurt them. Because they wore leather cowboy chaps on their legs.

Slim Jim was the best rider and the best roper in all Texas. But it took him and the other cowboys half a month of Sundays to round up those cows. "Now, listen!" the other cowboys said to Slim Jim. "No more singing in Texas." And Slim Jim promised he would sing no more. He would sing no more, in Texas.

That night Slim Jim went out to guard the cows again. It was very quiet, and Slim Jim was lonely. He thought about his song. The song kept running through his mind. Slim Jim tried to keep his promise. He tried hard not to sing. But the song went round and round in his mind. It went round and round. It went round and round. Slim Jim couldn't hold back. He opened his mouth and he sang his song. And the cows didn't like it. A little tan cow stampeded. A big red cow stampeded. Big ones and little ones, spotted ones and plain ones —they all stampeded. They stampeded all over Texas.

Slim Jim and the other cowboys had to ride through all those thorny bushes again. This time it took them nearly a whole month of Sundays to round up these cows. "Now, listen!" the other cowboys said to Slim Jim. "There will be no more singing. No more singing in Texas."

"Boys," Slim Jim said, "I can't promise. It's lonely at night on this lone prairie. That song keeps running through my mind. It goes round and round. It goes round and round. And when that happens, I have to sing it." Then Slim Jim got on his horse and he said, "I can't promise not to sing. So I will go away. I will go far away. I will find a place where there are no cows to be frightened by my singing." And Slim Jim rode away.

On the tenth day Slim Jim came to a river. It was a very dry river. It was so dry that it was dusty. So Slim Jim knew it was the Rio Grande. Everyone in Texas knows the Rio Grande is the dustiest river in the world. There was a little water out in the middle. But not enough for the fish to swim in. They had to walk on the bottom. Slim Jim could see them walking around down there. "Hm," he said, "a tasty fish would make a fine supper." Slim Jim was a cowboy, not a fisherman. He had no fishhooks and he had no fishline. But Slim Jim saw something. He saw that there was only enough river to cover the smallest fish. The biggest ones were half out of water as they walked along the bottom. Slim Jim was a cowboy and he was a good roper. He was the best roper in all Texas. So he whirled his rope—and he roped a fish. Slim Jim camped on the river bank and cooked his fish. It was lonely there, beside the river. Slim Jim's song kept running through his mind. He opened his mouth and he sang. He sang that song. And his song did not frighten the fish in the Rio Grande. Not a single fish stampeded. "This is the place for me," Slim Jim said. "I shall stay here, and sing, and be a fisherman." So Slim Jim laid aside his leather cowboy chaps, because a fisherman would not need them. And he stayed beside the river. And he fished. And he sang.

But while Slim Jim fished and sang there was trouble in Texas. The other cowboys remembered Slim Jim's song. That song kept running through their minds. It went round and round. It went round and round. They just couldn't help it—they sang that song. And the cows didn't like it. They couldn't stand that song. A big brown cow stampeded. A little white cow stampeded. Big ones and littles ones, spotted ones and plain ones—they all stampeded. They stampeded all over Texas. The cowboys rode for a whole month of Sundays. But they couldn't get the cows rounded up again. Then up spoke Cactus Pete of the Pecos country. "Boys," he said, "we need help. Slim Jim Bean is the best cowboy in all Texas. We must get Slim Jim to help us round up those cows." The other cowboys agreed. So they rode out to find Slim Jim.

They rode all over Texas. They rode until they came to the Rio Grande River. And that was where they found Slim Jim, fishing. "Cows are stampeding all over Texas, Slim Jim," they told him. "We must get them rounded up again or Texas will be plumb ruined. You must help us round up those cows, Slim Jim." Slim turned away from the river. His voice rose loud and free. "Slim Jim will ride and round 'em up," he cried. "All you cowboys follow me." So Slim Jim rode to round up the cows. The cows that were stampeding all over Texas. He rode through all those thorny bushes. And Slim Jim felt the thorns. He felt them because he was not wearing his chaps. The leather cowboy chaps he laid aside when he became a fisherman. When he felt the mesquite thorns, Slim Jim shouted, "Yip!" When he felt the Spanish dagger spikes, Slim Jim shouted, "Yippee!" When he felt the cat's-claw briers, Slim Jim shouted, "Yi!" When he felt the cactus needles, Slim Jim shouted, "Yay!" And when he felt them all at the same time, Slim Jim shouted, "Yippee yi, yippee yay!"

Slim Jim rode through all the thorny bushes in Texas. And his voice rose loud and free, "Yippee yi, yippee yay!" Everywhere that Slim Jim rode, the cows heard him. The cows that were stampeding all over Texas. They liked those new sounds that Slim Jim made. They stopped running to listen to Slim Jim's yips and yippees and yis and yays.

Then up spoke Cactus Pete of the Pecos country. "Slim Jim," he said, "the cows like those yippee yi noises." The other cowboys all said, "Make those noises again, Slim Jim. The yippee yi noises. The noises the cows like." So Slim Jim did it. He made the noises again. And he made them again. He made a song out of those noises. Yippee yi, yippee yay—yippee. The other cowboys listened. They liked Slim Jim's new song. So they all joined in and sang. They sang Yippee yi, yippee yay—yippee. The cows liked the new song. The big cows liked it. The little cows liked it. Big ones and little ones, spotted ones and plain ones—they all stopped to listen. Then Slim Jim and the other cowboys rounded them up. And that was the end of the big stampede, in Texas.

And that is why cowboys sing, today, in Texas. They sing, "Yippee yi." And they sing, "Yippee yay." They sing Slim Jim's song, today, in Texas.

RAGMAN OF PARIS

Elizabeth Orton Jones

Ragman was going home with his funny old cart full of rags. It had been a busy day for Ragman because spring was coming and people wanted to get rid of their old winter clothes.

Ragman was very happy. He sang a little tune. It was one that Mimi knew very well. Mimi was Ragman's horse. She pulled his funny old cart. She wore a little red stocking cap on each of her ears to keep out the flies. And she wore bells on her heels, so that people could hear when Ragman was near and come with their rags to sell.

Yes, Mimi had heard Ragman sing that tune before. But it had been a long time ago. She was so happy to have spring here again and Ragman singing that she stopped in the middle of the street and began to giggle, the way some horses do, you know.

"Mimi!" said Ragman. "Have you the giggles again? Well, I'll just get down and walk around until you stop."

Ragman went into a little park. He saw a green shrub, the first green leaves of the year. He saw, also, a pile of nice old rags under the shrub. So he picked them up and carried them back to the cart. Mimi had stopped giggling.

"Silly Mimi!" said Ragman. "Let's be getting along now!"

Mimi began to trot. And, after Ragman had put the rags which he had found into his sack, he began to sing again.

But just as he came to the second verse of his song, he thought he saw his sack wiggling.

"Pooh!" said Ragman. "Sacks never do that!"

And he began to sing again. But just as he came to the third verse, he looked at his sack, and, sure enough, it was really wiggling! And something in the sack was saying:

"Let me out!"

Ragman opened his sack, and out popped the head of a little boy.

"Hello!" said the little boy. "Do we have to stay in this sack?"

"We?" asked Ragman. "Are there more of you?"

"Yes!" said a little voice from underneath.

Then Ragman pulled two little boys out of his sack. They really did look more like two bundles of rags than two little boys.

"Well, I never!" said Ragman. "Who are you?"

"We're Mich and Tobie," explained Mich, who was the elder.

"Mich and Tobie what?" asked Ragman. "Don't you belong to anyone?"

"No," they said.

"Well, then, you belong to me. I'm the ragman of Paris, so that Ragman is my name. And that's Mimi up there."

Mimi giggled ever so little and turned her ears backwards.

"I like Mimi!" said Tobie, who was not afraid any longer.

"You'll like Poufon, too," said Ragman. "He is the proudest cat in Paris. But most of all you'll like Madame Pouf, who is a very fat lady."

"Where do they live?" asked Mich and Tobie.

"They live in a little house not far away. I live there, too. And so do you, from now on," said Ragman.

As Mimi trotted along, pulling the funny old cart, Mich and Tobie thought how nice it would be to live in the house where Ragman lived, and Madame Pouf and Poufon.

Then, all of a sudden, Mimi turned into a little street. She stopped before an old house. In one window sat a very proud cat. In another window was the face of a jolly fat lady, very much surprised at what she saw in Ragman's cart.

When Ragman lifted Mich and Tobie down from the cart, they ran into the house to see Madame Pouf.

"Heavens above!" cried she, taking them into her arms. "What little ragamuffins! But Madame Pouf will fix you, never you mind!"

She led them into the kitchen where she filled three great copper pots, two with hot water and one with soup. She put Mich into one pot and Tobie into another. The soup she set on the stove to boil.

And while the boys were sitting in the copper pots, only their heads and shoulders out of water, and while the good-smelling soup was cooking on the stove, Madame Pouf began to count the petticoats she wore. Mich and Tobie had never seen so many.

"Now tell me," she said, "which one you like best."

Then she showed them one petticoat striped round and round with red and blue, and one striped crosswise with blue and green.

"Do you like any of those?" she asked.

"No," said Mich and Tobie.

Then she came to a plain red petticoat and a plain white petticoat, a plain green one, a plain yellow one, and a plain sort of lavender one.

"Do you like any of those?" asked Madame Pouf again.

"Oh, no!" said Mich and Tobie.

"Well!" sighed Madame Pouf. And she went on counting her petticoats. There was a white one spotted with greenish blue, and a red one spotted with bluish green. There was an orange one with purple spots and a black one with spots of every color.

"Like any of those?" she asked.

"No, we don't," said Mich and Tobie.

Then she came to a red petticoat with white daisies on it, then a green one with pink balloons on it, then a blue one with yellow rabbits on it every so often.

"Well?" asked Madame Pouf.

Mich said, "I'd like the blue one with yellow rabbits on it if the rabbits weren't yellow."

"Yes," said Tobie, "I'd like the rabbits to be pink."

Madame Pouf looked worried. "I haven't very many more," she said, shaking her head.

And then she whispered, "Heavens above!" as she went on counting the rest of her petticoats.

Madame Pouf came to a red checkered petticoat, and a black and white checkered one, and a petticoat checkered in purple and a petticoat checkered in blue.

"There!" said Mich and Tobie. "We like that one, checkered in blue!"

So Madame Pouf took it off and laid it on the floor. She lifted Mich and Tobie out of the copper pots, dried them on the table cloth, and laid them, side by side, upon the petticoat checkered in blue. Then she took a great pair of scissors and began to cut—snip, snip, snip—all around Tobie.

"Don't cut me by mistake!" said Tobie.

She only smiled and began to cut—snip, snip, snip—all around Mich. "Done!" said she, at last. "Up now!"

And up they sat. By this time the good-smelling soup was ready to eat. And as Mich and Tobie, each with a bowl of it, sipped the soup from two big spoons, Madame Pouf sewed up the pieces she had cut out of her blue checkered petticoat. She sewed them up the sides and down the arms, added a bit of red trimming, and soon they were ready—a shirt for Mich and a shirt for Tobie.

"Thank you, Madame Pouf!" they said, after putting on their shirts. "They just fit!"

And as they ran to show their new clothes to Ragman, Tobie said, "I like Madame Pouf, don't you?"

"Yes, I do!" said Mich.

Then followed happy days for Mich and Tobie as they had adventures all over Paris. The cobbler in the little blue cobbler's shop told them how his father was made cobbler to all France because he once made a king's shoe comfy. They discovered Poufon's green whisker and that he was a most special cat who could talk. They visited the baker, the milk shop, and the butcher to help Madame Pouf. One day a little boy in the bookstalls read them his favorite story. They watched the flower lady's stall one evening while she had supper and really made money for her.

The day of their picnic in Luxembourg Garden was climaxed by a ride in the goat cart. What fun! But they played so long they were locked in. Poufon used the last five words he could speak this year to tell Madame Pouf where they were. Somehow Ragman got inside the gates, no one ever knew how, and rescued them. Now that Poufon could no longer speak, people might think that he was an ordinary cat. So Ragman bought a little silver bell to hang around his neck. Ragman and Madame Pouf and Mich and Tobie knew he was no ordinary cat and now everybody knew, when Poufon came along that he was a very worthy cat.

One evening, when Ragman came home from his work, he said to Mich and Tobie, "Would you like to take a ride in my cart, just for fun?"

"Oh, yes!" said Mich and Tobie, climbing into the cart beside him.

"What is the difference between taking a regular, everyday ride and taking a ride just for fun?" asked Mich.

"Well," said Ragman, "if someone calls out, 'Why are you going so fast all round Paris in your funny old cart?' and I say, 'I've rags to sell!' or 'I'm going to find Mich and Tobie in the Luxembourg Garden!'—that is a regular, everyday ride. But if someone calls, 'Why are you going so fast all round Paris in your funny old cart?' and I say, 'Oh, just for fun!'—then that is a very different sort of ride!"

"It's the sort of ride we're having now," said Tobie. "I wish someone would call out to us!"

And someone did. It was the old cobbler who sat stitching and stitching in his little blue shop. He said, "Why are you going so fast . . ."

But before he could finish, Tobie said, "Just for fun, Cobbler! Good night!"

Then they passed the street-sweeper, who had found his broom, and who was sweeping the last street that day. He said, "Why are you going . . ."

"Just for fun!" cried Mich and Tobie together. "Good night, street-sweeper!"

A little farther along they saw their friend, the flower lady, pushing her cart home for the night. She called out, "Why are you . . ."

"Just for fun!" cried Mich and Tobie and Ragman. "Good night!"

And the funny old cart jogged merrily on, around and up, around and up, until they came to the top of Montmartre. That is a hill higher than all Paris. From its top they could see the whole city spread out before them, and all its little evening lights.

"This is a magic sort of place," said Ragman.

"Oh," said Mich and Tobie.

"No one has ever been able to count the lights of Paris," said Ragman. "Some are always coming on while others are going out. It's much more difficult than counting the stars, but more fun!"

"Let's try to count them!" said Tobie.

And they did.

Just for fun! Just for fun!

THE SING-SONG OF OLD MAN KANGAROO

Rudyard Kipling

Not always was the Kangaroo as now we do behold him, but a Different Animal with four short legs. He was grey and he was woolly, and his pride was inordinate: he danced on an outcrop in the middle of Australia, and he went to the Little God Nqa.

He went to Nqa at six before breakfast, saying, "Make me different from all other animals by five this afternoon." Up jumped Nqa from his seat on the sandflat and shouted, "Go away!" He was grey and he was woolly, and his pride was inordinate: he danced on a rockledge in the middle of Australia, and he went to the Middle God Nquing.

He went to Nquing at eight after breakfast, saying, "Make me different from all other animals; make me, also, wonderfully popular by five this afternoon." Up jumped Nquing from his burrow in the spinifex and shouted, "Go away!" He was grey and he was woolly, and his pride was inordinate: he danced on a sandbank in the middle of Australia, and he went to the Big God Nqong.

He went to Nqong at ten before dinner-time, saying, "Make me different from all other animals; make me popular and wonderfully run after by five this afternoon." Up jumped Nqong from his bath in the salt-pan and shouted, "Yes, I will!"

Nqong called Dingo—Yellow-Dog Dingo—always hungry, dusty in the sunshine, and showed him Kangaroo. Nqong said, "Dingo! Wake up, Dingo! Do you see that gentleman dancing on an ashpit? He wants to be popular and very truly run after. Dingo, make him so!"

Up jumped Dingo—Yellow-Dog Dingo—and said, "What, *that* cat-rabbit?" Off ran Dingo—Yellow-Dog Dingo—always hungry, grinning like a coal-scuttle,—ran after Kangaroo. Off went the proud Kangaroo on his four little legs like a bunny.

This, O Beloved of mine, ends the first part of the tale! He ran through the desert; he ran through the mountains; he ran through the salt-pans; he ran through the reed-beds; he ran through the blue gums; he ran through the spinifex; he ran till his front legs ached. He had to!

Still ran Dingo—Yellow-Dog Dingo—always hungry, grinning like a rat-trap, never getting nearer, never getting farther,—ran after Kangaroo. He had to!

Still ran Kangaroo—Old Man Kangaroo. He ran through the ti-trees; he ran through the mulga; he ran through the long grass; he ran through the short grass; he ran through the Tropics of Capricorn and Cancer; he ran till his hind legs ached. He had to! Still ran Dingo—Yellow-Dog Dingo—hungrier and hungrier, grinning like a horse collar, never getting nearer, never getting farther; and they came to the Wollgong River. Now, there wasn't any bridge, and there wasn't any ferry-boat, and Kangaroo didn't know how to get over; so he stood on his legs and hopped. He had to!

He hopped through the Flinders; he hopped through the Cinders; he hopped through the deserts in the middle of Australia. He hopped like a Kangaroo. First he hopped one yard; then he hopped three yards; then he hopped five yards; his legs growing longer. He hadn't any time for rest or refreshment, and he wanted them very much. Still ran Dingo—Yellow-Dog Dingo—very much bewildered, very much hungry, and wondering what in the world or out of it made Old Man Kangaroo hop. For he hopped like a cricket; like a pea in a saucepan; or a new rubber ball on a nursery floor.

He had to! He tucked up his front legs; he hopped on his hind legs; he stuck out his tail for a balance-weight behind him; and he hopped through the Darling Downs. He had to! Still ran Dingo—Tired-Dog Dingo—hungrier and hungrier, very much bewildered, and wondering when in the world or out of it would Old Man Kangaroo stop. Then came Nqong from his bath in the salt-pans, and said, "It's five o'clock." Down sat Dingo—Poor Dog Dingo—always hungry, dusky in the sunshine; hung out his tongue and howled. Down sat Kangaroo—Old Man Kangaroo—stuck out his tail like a milking-stool behind him, and said, "Thank goodness *that's* finished!" Then said Nqong, who is always a gentleman, "Why aren't you grateful to Yellow-Dog Dingo? Why don't you thank him for all he has done for you?" Then said Kangaroo—Tired Old Kangaroo—"He's chased me out of the homes of my childhood; he's chased me out of my regular meal-times; he's altered my shape so I'll never get it back; and he's played Old Scratch with my legs."

Then said Nqong, "Perhaps I'm mistaken, but didn't you ask me to make you different from all other animals, as well as to make you very truly sought after? And now it is five o'clock."

"Yes," said Kangaroo. "I wish that I hadn't. I thought you would do it by charms and incantations, but this is a practical joke." "Joke!" said Nqong from his bath in the blue gums. "Say that again and I'll whistle up Dingo and run your legs off."

"No," said the Kangaroo. "I must apologize. Legs are legs, and you needn't alter 'em so far as I am concerned. I only meant to explain to Your Lordliness that I've had nothing to eat since morning, and I'm very empty indeed."

"Yes," said Dingo—Yellow-Dog Dingo—"I am just in the same situation. I've made him different from all other animals; but what may I have for my tea?"

Then said Nqong from his bath in the salt-pan, "Come and ask me about it tomorrow, because I'm going to wash."

So they were left in the middle of Australia, Old Man Kangaroo and Yellow-Dog Dingo, and each said, "That's *your* fault."

THE EMPEROR'S NEW CLOTHES

Hans Christian Andersen

Many years ago, there was an Emperor, who was so excessively fond of new clothes, that he spent all his money in dress. He did not trouble himself in the least about his soldiers; nor did he care to go either to the theatre or the chase, except for the opportunities then afforded him for displaying his new clothes. He had a different suit for each hour of the day; and, as of any other king or emperor one is accustomed to say, "He is sitting in council," it was always said of him, "The Emperor is sitting in his wardrobe."

Time passed merrily in the large town which was his capital; strangers arrived every day at the court. One day, two rogues, calling themselves weavers, made their appearance. They gave out that they knew how to weave stuffs of the most beautiful colors and elaborate patterns, the clothes manufactured from which should have the wonderful property of remaining invisible to everyone who was unfit for the office he held, or who was extraordinarily simple in character.

"These must, indeed, be splendid clothes!" thought the Emperor. "Had I such a suit, I might at once find out what men in my realms are unfit for their office, and also be able to distinguish the wise from the foolish! This stuff must be woven for me immediately." And he caused large sums of money to be given to both the weavers in order that they might begin their work directly.

So the two pretended weavers set up two looms, and affected to work very busily, though in reality they did nothing at all. They asked for the most delicate silk and the purest gold thread; put both into their own knapsacks; and then continued their pretended work at the empty looms until late at night.

"I should like to know how the weavers are getting on with my cloth," said the Emperor to himself, after some little time had elapsed; he was, however, rather embarrassed, when he remembered that a simpleton, or one unfit for his office, would be unable to see the manufacture. To be sure, he thought he had nothing to risk in his own person; but yet, he would prefer sending somebody else to bring him intelligence about the weavers and their work, before he troubled himself in the affair. All the people throughout the city had heard of the wonderful property the cloth was to possess; and all were anxious to learn how wise, or how ignorant, their neighbors might prove to be.

"I will send my faithful old minister to the weavers," said the Emperor at last, after some deliberation. "He will be best able to see how the cloth looks; for he is a man of sense, and no one can be more suitable for his office than he is."

So the faithful old minister went into the hall, where the knaves were working with all their might at their empty looms. "What can be the meaning of this?" thought the old man, opening his eyes very wide. "I cannot discover the least bit of thread on the looms." However, he did not express his thoughts aloud.

The impostors requested him very courteously to be so good as to come nearer their looms; and then asked him whether the design pleased him, and whether the colors were not very beautiful, at the same time pointing to the empty frames. The poor old minister looked and looked, but he could not discover anything on the looms, for a very good reason, viz: there was nothing there. "What!" thought he again. "Is it possible that I am a simpleton? I have never thought so myself; and no one must know it now if I am so. Can it be, that I am unfit for my office? No, that must not be said either. I will never confess that I could not see the stuff."

"Well, Sir Minister!" said one of the knaves, still pretending to work. "You do not say whether the stuff pleases you."

"Oh, it is excellent!" replied the old minister looking at the loom through his spectacles. "This pattern, and the colors—yes, I will tell the Emperor without delay how very beautiful I think them."

"We shall be much obliged to you," said the impostors, and then they named the different colors and described the pattern of the pretended stuff. The old minister listened attentively to their words, in order that he might repeat them to the Emperor; and then the knaves asked for more silk and gold, saying that it was necessary to complete what they had begun. However, they put all that was given them into their knapsacks, and continued to work with as much apparent diligence as before at their empty looms.

The Emperor now sent another officer of his court to see how the men were getting on, and to ascertain whether the cloth would soon be ready. It was just the same with this gentleman as with the minister: he surveyed the looms on all sides, but could see nothing at all but the empty frames.

"Does not the stuff appear as beautiful to you as it did to my lord the minister?" asked the impostors of the Emperor's second ambassador, at the same time making the same gestures as before, and talking of the design and colors which were not there.

"I certainly am not stupid!" thought the messenger. "It must be that I am not fit for my good, profitable office! That is very odd; however, no one shall know anything about it." And accordingly he praised the stuff he could not see, and declared that he was delighted with both colors and patterns. "Indeed, please your Imperial

Majesty," said he to his sovereign when he returned, "the cloth which the weavers are preparing is extraordinarily magnificent."

The whole city was talking of the splendid cloth which the Emperor had ordered to be woven at his own expense.

And now the Emperor himself wished to see the costly manufacture, while it was still in the loom. Accompanied by a select number of officers of the court, among whom were the two honest men who had already admired the cloth, he went to the crafty impostors, who, as soon as they were aware of the Emperor's approach, went on working more diligently than ever, although they still did not pass a single thread through the looms.

"Is not the work absolutely magnificent?" said the two officers of the crown, already mentioned. "If your Majesty will only be pleased to look at it! What a splendid design! What glorious colors!" And at the same time they pointed to the empty frames, for they imagined that everyone else could see this exquisite piece of workmanship.

"How is this?" said the Emperor to himself. "I can see nothing! This is indeed a terrible affair! Am I a simpleton, or am I unfit to be an Emperor? That would be the worst thing that could happen —Oh! the cloth is charming," said he, aloud. "It has my complete approbation." And he smiled most graciously, and looked closely at the empty looms, for on no account would he say that he could not see what two of the officers of his court had praised so much. All his retinue now strained their eyes, hoping to discover something on the looms, but they could see no more than the others. Nevertheless, they all exclaimed, "Oh, how beautiful!" and advised his majesty to have some new clothes made from this splendid material for the approaching procession. "Magnificent! Charming! Excellent!" resounded on all sides, and everyone was uncommonly gay. The Emperor shared in the general satisfaction, and presented the impostors with the riband of an order of knighthood, to be worn in their button-holes, and the title of "Gentlemen Weavers."

The rogues sat up the whole of the night before the day on which the procession was to take place, and had sixteen lights burning, so that everyone might see how anxious they were to finish the Emperor's new suit. They pretended to roll the cloth off the looms, cut the air with their scissors, and sewed with needles without any thread in them. "See!" cried they, at last. "The Emperor's new clothes are ready!"

And now the Emperor, with all the grandees of his court, came to the weavers; and the rogues raised their arms, as if in the act of holding something up, saying, "Here are your Majesty's trousers! Here is the scarf! Here is the mantle! The whole suit is as light as a cobweb; one might fancy one has nothing at all on, when dressed in it; that, however, is the great virtue of this delicate cloth."

"Yes indeed!" said all the courtiers, although not one of them could see anything of this exquisite manufacture.

"If your Imperial Majesty will be graciously pleased to take off your clothes, we will fit on the new suit, in front of the looking glass."

The Emperor was accordingly undressed, and the rogues pretended to array him in his new suit; the Emperor turning round, from side to side, before the looking glass.

"How splendid his Majesty looks in his new clothes, and how well they fit!" everyone cried out. "What a design! What colors! These are indeed royal robes!"

"The canopy which is to be borne over your Majesty in the procession is waiting," announced the chief master of the ceremonies.

"I am quite ready," answered the Emperor. "Do my new clothes fit well?" asked he, turning himself round again before the looking glass, in order that he might appear to be examining his handsome suit.

The lords of the bedchamber, who were to carry his Majesty's train felt about on the ground, as if they were lifting up the ends of the mantle; and pretended to be carrying something; for they would by no means betray anything like simplicity, or unfitness for their office.

So now the Emperor walked under his high canopy in the midst of the procession, through the streets of his capital; and all the people standing by, and those at the windows, cried out, "Oh! How beautiful are our Emperor's new clothes! What a magnificent train there is to the mantle; and how gracefully the scarf hangs!" in short, no one would allow that he could not see these much-admired clothes; because, in doing so, he would have declared himself either a simpleton or unfit for his office. Certainly, none of the Emperor's various suits, had ever made so great an impression as these invisible ones.

"But the Emperor has nothing at all on!" said a little child.

"Listen to the voice of innocence!" exclaimed his father; and what the child had said was whispered from one to another.

"But he has nothing at all on!" at last cried out all the people.

The Emperor was vexed, for he knew that the people were right; but he thought the procession must go on now! And the lords of the bedchamber took greater pains than ever, to appear holding up a train, although, in reality, there was no train to hold.

—Translated by Mrs. Edgar Lucas

THE ANIMALS CAME FIRST

Jean-Louise Welch and *Ruth Carroll*

"Meow, meow. Where are all the rats tonight? I haven't found one in the courtyard. Maybe there will be some in the stable. Meow, meow."

The cat came into the stable. She stopped suddenly, cocked her head and listened. From the far corner of the stable came a low, new sound. There was also a faint glow of light.

The cat's whiskers twitched. "What can that be?"

The sound continued. It was sweet and soft. Not like a noise any of the animals who lived in the stable made.

"This is very strange. I'll go and ask the donkey if he knows what it is."

So the cat hurried to the donkey's stall. He was sound asleep.

"Now isn't that just like a donkey," thought the cat. "He's asleep while something so strange is going on right here in the stable. "Meow, meow. Wake up!"

The donkey twitched his ear, opened one eye and said sleepily, "What's the matter? Who is it? What do you want?"

"It is I, the cat. Wake up! Listen! What is that sound?"

The donkey was wide awake by now. He pricked up his long, grey ears and listened.

"Sure enough, there is a new sound. What can it be? Did you ask the dog?"

"No, I didn't see him," replied the cat. "Of course he would know. He keeps watch over the stable all night. I'll go and find him."

The cat turned to go.

"Wait," called the donkey. "Jump on my back and I will take you to find the dog. I want to find out what is making that sound, too. It is different from anything I have heard."

The donkey carried the cat on his back to a box near the stable door where the dog always slept. He wasn't there.

"Now that's funny," said the cat. "He was there when I went out to hunt for rats. He even barked as I passed."

"Yes," replied the donkey. "Something very important must be going on to take the dog away from his watching place. Let us go and see if the cow knows anything about this."

They found the cow awake and trembling.

"What is happening?" the cow asked as the donkey with the cat on his back approached.

"That is what we came to ask you," replied the donkey.

"Something very important must be happening because the dog is not in his box," said the cat.

"My, my," said the cow, shaking her head, "that is very strange."

Just then the ox who lived in the next stall put his head around the side and said, "I have lived in this stable longer than any of you and this sound is different from any I have ever heard. I am going to find out what it is and not stand here talking about it all night."

"It seems to be coming from the far corner," said the cat, pointing his paw in that direction. "There is a dim light there, too."

The animals all looked where the cat pointed.

"Sure enough," said the donkey. "Let's all go that way and find out what it is."

"Oh, yes," said the cow. "That's a good idea. "Wait for me."

And so the donkey with the cat on his back, the cow and the ox started in the direction of the low, sweet sound and the dim light. When they got to the sheepfold, they heard the mother sheep trying to quiet her lamb.

"Hush," she said. "Do not be afraid. Look, here come the other animals of the stable. They will tell us what is happening."

Turning to the approaching animals, the mother sheep said, "Excuse me, but my lamb is frightened by the new sound we hear. Can you tell us what it is?"

The ox, being the oldest, answered. "We don't know ourselves, but we are going to find out. I'm sure it can do us no harm so do not be afraid. Why don't you and your lamb come with us?"

"Thank you, that would be nice," said the mother sheep. "Come, my lamb, we shall go and see for ourselves what is making this new sound."

And so the donkey with the cat on his back, the cow, the ox, and the mother sheep with her lamb at her side, slowly, quietly moved toward the faint glow of light and the low, sweet sound.

In the stall next to the sheep lived a family of pigs. They were awake and excited. When the animals came by their stall, the father pig grunted, "What's going on here? Where are you going?"

"We are going to find out what the new sound is," said the ox. "As I get closer it sounds to me like singing."

"Singing, you say! Humph!" grunted the father pig.

"I want to see what is making the singing," said one of the little pigs.

"Me too," said another.

So the father pig, mother pig and the five little pigs followed the ox, the cow, and the donkey with the cat on his back, the mother sheep with her lamb at her side, toward the low sweet sound, and the soft, dim light.

As they drew closer, they saw that the light was coming from a shaded lantern hanging on the side of a stall. Resting against a bale of hay in front of the manger sat a lady. She was holding a tiny baby in her arms. A man stood nearby her and at her other side sat the dog.

Hearing the approach of the animals, the dog turned and wagged his tail. "Come, my friends, and see the newborn Baby. His name is Jesus."

A new feeling of love and peace filled the animals as they drew closer to look at the Mother and her sleeping Baby.

The grey and white doves flew from the rafters and sat on the edge of the manger.

"Look, Mary," said the man to the Gentle Lady, "the animals of the stable are the first to come and worship the Baby King."

Mary smiled. "Yes," she said. "The animals are the first, but someday people everywhere will love and worship Him."

And snuggling the Baby closer, Mary began to sing another soft lullaby.

WICKED JOHN AND THE DEVIL

Richard Chase

One time there was an old blacksmith that folks called Wicked John. They say he was right mean: never would join the church, never did go to meetin', always laughed about folks gettin' saved and bein' baptized and sech. One thing about him, though, mean as he was, he always did treat a stranger right. And one mornin' a old beggar came along: crippled up, walkin' on two sticks, all bent over with rheumatism, looked right tired and hungry-like. Stood there in the door, and Wicked John fin'lly hollered at him, says, "Come on in! Whyn't ye come on in and sit down?" So the old beggar he heaved over the doorsill, sat down on it, and they talked a while. Wicked John he kept right on workin', talkin' big, and directly he throwed his hammer down and went to the house. Come back with a big plate of vittles: boiled sweet potato, big chunk of ham-meat, greens, beans, big slice of cake, and a glass of sweet milk. Says, "Here, old man! You might make out with these rations —if there's anything here you can eat."

The old beggar thanked him and started in eatin', and old John he went on with his work. Well, he was a-hammerin' around over there, sort of watchin' the beggar man, and pretty soon he saw him lay that plate and the glass to one side and start to get up. He let them two sticks fall to the ground and commenced straightenin' up, straightenin' up, and all the kinks come out of him, till the next thing Wicked John knowed, a big stout-lookin' man was r'ared up there in the door: had a long white beard and white hair, white robe right down to his feet, and a big key in his hand. Old John had done dropped his hammer and was a-standin' there with his mouth hangin' open and his eyes popped out. So the old man says to him, says, "Well, John, I'm Saint Peter. Yes, that's who I am, and once every year I walk the earth to see can I find any decent folks left down here, and the first man treats me right I always give him three wishes. Anything you've a mind to, you can just wish for it and hit'll be that-a-way."

Wicked John looked over there at Saint Peter sort of grinnin' like he didn't think it was really so, says, "Well, Peter, you better let me study on it a minute. Three wishes. Aaa Lord!"

Looked around, started wishin' on the first thing popped into his head. He didn't care!

"Well now, I've got a fine old high-back rockin' chair there by the door, and when I get my work done up I like to sit in my rocker; but, don't you know, every day nearly, blame if there ain't somebody done gone and got there ahead of me—one of these loafers hangs around in here of a evenin'. Makes me mad! And I just wish: —that anybody sits in my old rocker would have to stay there and rock right on till I let 'em get up.

"Aaa Lord!—Lemme see now.—Well, there's my old sledge hammer. It's these blame boys come in here and get to messin' with it, take it out there across the road, see how big a rock they can bust; and—con-found!—if I don't have to go out there ever' time I need it and hunt for it where them feisty boys have done gone and dropped it down in the grass somewhere. And I jest wish:—that anybody teches my sledge hammer would have to pound with it, and keep right on a-poundin' till I let 'em stop."

Well, Saint Peter he looked kind of sorry like he thought old John was a-wastin' his wishes pretty bad, but that old blacksmith he was mean, like I said, just didn't care about nothin' or nobody. Looked around at Saint Peter right mischievous-like, grinned sort of devilish, says, "One more wish, huh? Well, all right. Now:—I got a fine thorn-bush jest outside the door there, fire bush, gets full of red blooms real early in the spring of the year; and I like my old fire thorn, but—con-found!—ever'body comes here to get their horses shoed, blame if they don't tromple all over that bush, back their wagons into it, break it down; and—Aaa Lord!—these high-falutin' folks comes over the mountain a-fox-huntin'—Humph! fox-huntin' in red coats!—looks like they jest got to have ridin' switches off my bush, break off ridin' switches ever' time they pass. And I jest wish:— anybody teches my fire thorn, it 'uld catch'em and hold 'em right down in the middle of all them stickers till I let 'em out."

Well, Saint Peter he stepped over the doorsill and he was gone from there and Wicked John couldn't tell which-a-way he went nor nothin'.

So that old blacksmith he kept on blacksmithin' in his blacksmith shop, and it wasn't long till John and his old woman they got to fussin'. Well, she was jawin' at him and jawin' at him, and he jawed right back at her, till fin'lly she told him, says, "The Devil take ye anyhow, old man! I jest wish he would!"

So that day the old man was a-workin' in his shop, looked up and there was a little devil a-standin' in the door, says, "Daddy said he'd take ye now. Said for me to bring ye right on back."

"All right, son. I'll be ready to go with ye in jest a few more licks. Reckon you can let me finish this horseshoe. Come on in. I'll not be but a minute or two."

Well, the little devil he stepped over in the shop, hung around awhile, and then he went straight and sat down in that old high-back rockin' chair, commenced rockin'. Wicked John he finished the horseshoe, soused it in the coolin' tub, throwed it on the ground and picked him up another'n.

"Hey, old man! You said jest finish that one!" And he tried to get out of that rocker, but the more he tried to get up the worse that old chair rocked him, till that little devil's head was just a-goin' whammity-bang! against the chairback. And fin'lly he got to beggin' and hollerin' for Wicked John to let him go.

"All right. I'll let ye go if you get on out of here and not bother me no more."

So the little devil said yes, he'd go, and when the chair quit rockin', he jumped out of it and—a-whippity-cut! out the door he flew.

Well, not long after that the old woman she lit into the old man again about somethin' or other; and they was a-havin' it! She was just a-fussin', and he was just a-laughin' at her, till fin'lly she stomped around, says "I'll jest tell ye, old man! The Devil can have ye right now for all I care! He shore can! He can send for ye and take ye off from here, and the sooner the better. That's all there are to it now!" Stomped on out to the kitchen, slammed the door.

So that day another little devil come to the door of the shop, little bigger'n the first 'un, says, "Come on, old man. Daddy sent me for ye. Said for me not to wait for nothin', bring ye right on back. So come on now, and we'll go."

"All right, son. Yes, in-deed. I'm jest about ready. Come in, and I know you'll let me hit a few more licks on this wagon-tire. I'm bound to finish hit 'fore we start."

Well, that little devil he come on inside the shop, got to hangin' around lookin' at what old John was doin', seen he was havin' it kind of awkard the way he had to hold on to that wagon tire and beat it with one hand, says, "Here, old man, you hold it and let me beat it. We got to hurry or Daddy'll get after me for stayin' so long." Picked up that old sledge hammer layin' there on the ground, started in poundin'.

So Wicked John he held the wagon tire up and turned it where he wanted it fixed, and when it was done he pulled it out from under the hammer between licks, set it up against the wall. And when the little devil tried to let go the hammer handle, he just stuck to it and hit a-poundin' right on. Well, the way the old sledge swung that little devil around in there, a-jerkin' him up and down with his legs a-flyin' ever' which-a-way—hit was a sight in this world! So he got to beggin', "Please let me go! Please, sir! Make this thing turn loose of me!"

"All right. I'll let ye go if you get on out of here and don't never come back. Ye hear?"

The little devil said yes, he heard and no, he'd not be back never no more; and then he fell off the hammer-handle and out the door he streaked.

Well, a few days after that the old woman she started raisin' another racket. They hadn't spoke many words 'fore she r'ared back and stuck her hands on her hips, hollered at him, says, "Old man! I jest wish—the puore-old-Devil himself would come on and git ye! I shore do! Now you get on out of here 'fore I knock ye in the head with this stick of firewood!"

So old John he dodged the stick of wood and laughed at the old lady, and went on out to his shop, and—sure enough—he hadn't any more'n got started workin' fore he looked up and there standin' in the door was the Old Boy himself, with his horns and his tail and that old cow's foot of his'n propped up on the sill, says, "COME ON NOW, OLD MAN! AND I AIN'T A-GOIN' TO TAKE NO FOOLISHNESS OFF YE NEITHER!"

"Yes, sir! No, sir! I'm ready to go, mister, right now. I jest got to finish sharpenin' this mattick. Promised a man I'd get it done first thing this mornin'. Come on in and sit down."

"NO! I'LL NOT SIT IN NO CHAIR OF YOUR'N!"

"All right, sir. All right. We'll be ready to go quicker'n you can turn around if you'd jest give this mattick blade a lick or two while I hold it here. There's the sledge hammer leanin' there on the door-sill."

"NO! I AIN'T GOIN' TO TECH NO SLEDGE HAMMER!" says the old Devil. Says, "YOU DONE MADE ME MAD ENOUGH ALREADY, OLD MAN! I DIDN'T LIKE A BIT THE WAY YOU DONE MY BOYS, AND I'M A-TAKIN' YOU OFF FROM HERE RIGHT NOW. YOU HEARD ME!"

And the old Devil reached in and grabbed Wicked John by the back of his collar, started draggin' him out. So old John he started in fightin'; punchin', knockin', beatin', poundin', scratchin', kickin', bitin'. They had several rounds there just outside the door, made the old Devil awful mad, says, "CONFOUND YE, OLD MAN! I'M GOIN TO LICK THE HIDE OFF YOU RIGHT NOW. JEST SEE IF I DON'T—WHERE'LL I GET ME A SWITCH?"

The old Devil looked around and reached for that bush, and time he touched it, hit grabbed him and wropped around him, jerked him headforemost right down in the middle of that bush where them thorns was the thickest. The old Devil he tried to get loose but the more he thrashed around in there, the worse he got scratched up till fin'lly he just stayed right still, with his legs a-stickin' out the top of the bush.

"Mister?"

"What ye want?"

"Please, sir, let me out of here."

"All right. I'll let ye go on one condition:—you, and none of your boys, don't none of ye never come up here a-botherin' me no more. Ye hear? You promise me that and I might let ye go."

"Heck yes, I'll promise," says the old Devil. "I'll not come, and I'll not send nobody neither—not never no more."

So the bush turned him loose, and sech a kickin' up dust you never did see. The Old Boy left there and he wasn't moseyin' neither.

Well, Wicked John he kept on blacksmithin' and he wasn't bothered by no more devils. And after a long time he died and went on up to the pearly gates. When he got there he knocked, and Saint Peter opened up a little crack, looked out, says, "Oh, it's you, is it? What ye want?"

"Well," old John told him, "I thought I might stand some little show of gettin' in up here."

"You? Why, old man, don't you know we got your record in yonder? I'll tell ye right now: I was lookin' at your accounts just the other day; and on the credit side—yes—you have a few entries 'way up at the top of the page; but over on the other side—why, man! hit's filled up right down to the bottom line. There hain't a chance in the world of your gettin' in this place." And Saint Peter started shuttin' the gates to.

So old John turned around and down the stairsteps he went. Got down there on the road to hell, a-staggerin' along with his hands in his pockets a-whistlin'. And when he come in sight of the gates of hell, one of them little devils happened to peek out.

"Daddy! O Daddy! Look a-yonder!"

The old Devil come runnin' and when he saw who it was a-comin', he hollered out, says, "Bar the door, boys! Bar the door!"

Them little devils grabbed the big gates and slammed 'em to quick, turned the key in the lock. So when Wicked John come on up and looked through the bars there stood the old Devil with his young 'uns crowdin' around behind him just a-tremblin'.

"Un-unh!" the old Devil says. "Get on away from here now! No, indeed, you ain't comin' in! I'll not have ye! Don't ye come no closer! You just turn around right there now, and put off from here."

Wicked John studied a minute, says, "Well, con-found! I don't know what'n the nation to do now. Saint Peter wouldn't let me in up yonder, and here you've done locked me out. Why, I don't know where to go to!"

So the Devil he looked around, grabbed him up a set of tongs, reached in the furnace, and got holt on a hot coal. Handed it out the bars, says, "Here, old man, you jest take this chunk of fire, and go on off somewhere else, and start you a hell of your own."

Old John he took it; and they tell me that if you go down in the Great Dismal Swamps, you can look out of a night and see a little bob of a light a-movin' along out there. And some folks call it the Jacky-my-lantern, and some call it the will-o'-the-whisp—but I reckon you know now who it is.

HOW PECOS BILL BEGAN

Leigh Peck

Everywhere and at all times men have worked hard and tried to do their best, but sometimes have failed. Then they have comforted themselves for their failures by making up stories of a hero, a man like themselves, but able to do all the things they wanted to do and could not. The Greeks, long ago, told stories of Odysseus and of Prometheus. The Saxons called their hero Beowulf.

The men that work in the North Woods of our country call him Paul Bunyan. Their hero is a giant whose voice roars like the thunder and whose step shakes the ground like an earthquake.

The ranch men of the Southwest call him Pecos Bill. He is no giant like Paul Bunyan, but he is as strong and brave as any hero that men have ever dreamed of anywhere. Of all the heroes, he is the gayest. He tosses a jest no less lightly than he tosses his lariat, and he laughs in the face of death itself.

When cowboys sit by their campfires at night, they like to tell each other stories about Pecos Bill. They say that he has done all the things that they would like to do. He is what all the real cowboys would like to be. No matter how tired and worried they are, they feel better after they have told each other the brave deeds of Pecos Bill.

There is a reason why they call their hero "Pecos" Bill. To call him "Pecos" Bill is to say that he is "plenty good" and "plenty tough," because the land along the Pecos River is a very rough ranching country, and many cattle thieves and warlike Indians used to live there. A cowboy had to be "plenty good" and "plenty tough" to run cattle along the Pecos River. Pecos Bill was so good that he could ride the lightning, and so tough that the cyclones learned to keep out of his way.

Here are some of the stories that the cowboys tell each other about their hero, Pecos Bill.

Pecos Bill's Youth

No wonder Pecos Bill was so brave. His mother was a very brave woman. One morning before breakfast she swept forty-five Indian chiefs out of her yard with her broom.

When Davy Crockett heard how brave she was, he sent her a Bowie knife as a present. All her eighteen children cut their teeth on that Bowie knife.

Her nearest neighbor lived one hundred miles away. When one day she heard that a new neighbor had moved in only fifty miles away, she decided, "This part of Texas is getting too crowded. We must move out where we will have more room."

So Pecos Bill's father hitched the old spotted cow and the old red mule to the old covered wagon. The father and mother put their eighteen children into the wagon, and they started out over the prairie. Their son Bill was four years old then. He sat in the very end of the wagon, with his feet hanging out.

When they were driving through the low waters of the Pecos River, one wheel of the wagon hit a rock, and the jolt threw Bill right out of the wagon and into the sand of the river. No one saw him fall or heard him call, "Wait for me!"

After Bill saw that the wagon was going on without him, he got up and ran after it. But his short little legs could not go so fast as the wagon. Soon it was gone, and Bill was left all alone.

There were still seventeen children in the wagon, and no one noticed that little Bill was gone, until his mother counted the children at dinner time.

"Where is Bill?" she asked.

No one had seen him since they crossed the river. So the family hurried back to the river and hunted for little Bill. They looked and looked, but could not find him. Because they had lost him at the Pecos River, they always spoke of him after that as their little lost Pecos Bill.

Little Pecos Bill was not lost long. His father and mother never did find him, but he was found by an old grandfather Coyote, named Grampy.

Grampy showed little Pecos Bill berries to eat, dug up roots for him, and found mesquite beans for him, too. At night Grampy led Pecos Bill to his cave in the mountain where he could sleep safe and warm.

Grampy showed his man-child to each of the other hunting animals, and asked them not to hurt little Pecos Bill. The Bear grunted, "W-f-f-f! I will not hurt your man-child. I will show him where to find wild honey in the bee trees."

The Wolf yelped, "I will not hurt your man-child. Let him come play with my cubs."

The Polecat purred, "I will not hurt your man-child if he will promise not to pull my lovely long tail. I will not put any of my perfume on him."

But the Rattlesnake shook his rattles, "Th-r-r-r!" and hissed, "SS-s-s-s! Keep him out of my way! I bite anybody that crosses my path, but I give fair warning first. Th-r-r-r! S-s-s-s!"

The Mountain Lion yowled, "Get your child out of my way before I eat him up! A nice fat man-child is what I like to eat best of all!"

So all the hunting animals except the Rattlesnake and the Mountain Lion promised to be good to little Pecos Bill. He learned to talk to all the animals and birds in their own languages.

But the Coyotes liked Pecos Bill best of all. They taught him how to hunt. When he grew older, he was able to run so fast that he could catch the long-eared Jack Rabbit and the long-tailed Road-Runner. Finally he grew big enough to catch the Deer, and even the Antelope, which runs fastest of any animal. He grew strong enough to pull down a Buffalo for his brother Coyotes.

The Coyotes were all very proud of their brother and very fond of him. At night he went out on the prairie with the Coyotes and howled at the moon. He thought he was a Coyote.

Pecos Bill Becomes a Cowboy

In all the years while Pecos Bill was living with the Coyotes, he had never seen a human being. Then one day, Bill's brother Chuck came riding along on his cowpony and found Bill. Bill was a tall young man now, his skin was a dark brown color, and his black hair hung long and tangled. But Chuck knew him at once, and cried, "Why, you are my long-lost brother, Pecos Bill!"

Even though Pecos Bill had learned all the animal and bird languages, he could still talk to people, too. He said, "I'm not your brother! I am the brother of the Coyotes.

"If you were a Coyote, you would have a tail. Look in the spring with me here, and see yourself and me in the water. See, you have no tail! You are no brother of the Coyotes—you are my brother, for you look like me."

Bill looked at himself and Chuck in the water, and agreed, "We do look alike, and it is true that I have no tail. Perhaps I am your brother!"

Chuck said: "Brother, you must put on some clothes and come with me to the ranch where I work and be a cowboy too. But I don't have any extra clothes with me. I don't know what we can do!"

Pecos Bill laughed. "If anything has to be done, I can do it! Just wait a minute, and I'll have some clothes!"

He looked around until he found a big old steer with horns measuring six feet from tip to tip. He grabbed it by the tail, yelled loudly, and scared it so badly that it jumped clear out of its skin! From the hide Pecos Bill made himself a leather jacket, using a yucca thorn for a needle. He made some boots, too. Then he made himself a pair of leather pants, the kind that are now called chaps. Other cowboys wear them now, to keep from getting scratched when riding through thorny bushes. They learned that from Pecos Bill.

When Bill had put on his clothes, Chuck told him, "Get up behind me on my cowpony, and he will carry both of us to the ranch."

But Pecos Bill laughed. "Ride your pony, and I'll go afoot, and I'll beat you to the ranch."

Sure enough, Bill galloped along easily, faster than Chuck's cowpony could run.

Chuck argued, though: "You really must not go up to the ranch on foot. Nobody walks in the ranch country. We must find you some old pony to ride and a quirt to whip him along with."

Just then Pecos Bill nearly stepped on the Rattlesnake that lay in the trail. It was fifteen feet long, and had thirty rattles on the end of its tail.

"Get out of my way," hissed Pecos Bill in snake language.

"I won't," the Snake hissed back. "I told Grampy long ago to teach you to stay out of my way."

The Snake spit poison at Pecos Bill, hitting him right between the eyes. Bill said, "I'll give you three chances at me, before I even begin to fight."

The three shots of poison didn't even blister Pecos Bill's skin.

Next, Bill spit back at the Snake, right on top of the Snake's head, and the Snake fell over, unable to move for a moment.

Bill jumped on the Snake and stamped it before it had time to bite him. He caught the Snake up by the throat and asked, "Had enough yet?"

The Snake cried "I give up!" Pecos Bill wrapped it around his arm and galloped on ahead of Chuck's pony.

Soon they met the Mountain Lion. He was the largest Mountain Lion in all the world, twice as large as Chuck's cowpony. The Mountain Lion growled, "I said I would eat you up if ever you got in my way, and now I will!"

He jumped at Pecos Bill, but Bill dodged and pulled out a hand-ful of the Mountain Lion's fur as he went by. The fight lasted for two hours. Every time the Mountain Lion tried to jump on Pecos Bill, Bill pulled out some more of his hair. The sky was so full of the Mountain Lion's hair that it was almost as dark as night. Finally the Lion lost all of his hair except just a little on the tips of his ears and under his chin. Then he begged, "Please, Pecos Bill, will you not hurt me any more?"

"Very well," agreed Pecos Bill, "but you must let me ride you for a cowpony."

So Pecos Bill jumped on the Mountain Lion's back, and using the Rattlesnake for a quirt to whip him along with, rode on to the ranch with Chuck.

Just at sundown, Pecos Bill rode up to the cowboys' camp on the Mountain Lion, twice as big as a cowpony, and he was still using the Rattlesnake fifteen feet long for a quirt. The cowboys around the campfire were too surprised to say a word. Chuck an-nounced proudly, "Boys, this is my brother, Pecos Bill."

Bill shouted, "Who is the boss around here?"

A big man seven feet tall and wearing three guns stepped forward. "I was," he said, "but you are now, Pecos Bill. Anybody that can ride a Mountain Lion and use a Rattlesnake for a quirt is boss here as long as he wants to be."

Bill became the greatest cowboy that ever was. And everything a cowboy does, he does, because of Pecos Bill.

—from *Pecos Bill and Lightning*

HOW OLD STORMALONG CAPTURED THE MOCHA DICK
Irwin Shapiro

Way back in the days of clipper ships there was always someone who knew someone, who knew someone, who knew someone who

had seen a white whale. Now because they only saw this whale
on the trip to Mocha, where they went after coffee, they got to calling the whale the Mocha Dick (or Moby Dick as he was sometimes
called).

In those days they burned whale oil in lamps (it was before the
days of electricity, you know). Whaling ships sailed all over the
high seas in search of whales. Every sailor wanted to get a berth on
a whaling ship because the profits from the sale of the oil were
divided among the crew. So the bigger the whale, the more oil and
the bigger the profit of which you got your share.

These whaling ships used as their home port the island of Nantucket, off the coast of Massachusetts. One of the ships which used
Nantucket as a home port was the good ship Dolphin. One member
of its crew was a famous sailor known as Old Stormalong. He stood
four fathoms tall in his stocking feet. His eyes were as blue as the
calm sea, his hair as black as a storm cloud. He could whistle shrill
like the wind in the rigging; he could hoot like a fog horn; and he
could talk ordinary, just like anyone else.

One windy night he and some members of the crew and Captain
Skinner of the good ship Dolphin were sitting in the Sailors' Snug
Haven, the inn that served the best shark soup in the town of Nantucket. They were all boasting and bragging of all the things they
could do—or thought they could do.

"This trip I'm going to capture Mocha Dick," boasted Stormalong.

"Hm, you've said that five times," said Captain Skinner.

"Aye, 'tis easy to capture the white whale with words," jeered a
little sailor with red whiskers.

"If you are so sure of yourself, you'd better write it down. Then
you'll have to do it," said the innkeeper.

He handed Old Stormalong a slate and Stormalong wrote "This
trip I will capture Mocha Dick" and signed his full name, Alfred
Bulldozer Stormalong. They put it up on the wall over the fireplace
for everyone to see.

Next morning the ship set sail. A cheer went up as the Dolphin
caught the wind in her sails and went out to the open sea. She sailed
clear across the Atlantic, down around the Cape of Good Hope, and
into those cold waters that come up from the south Arctic just before you get to the Indian Ocean. These are good whaling waters.
The captain put an extra lookout in the crow's nest high on the mast,
his only responsibility being to keep on the lookout for the spout of
a whale, always hoping for a big one.

One day out—no whales!

Two days out—no whales!

Three days—and just after sunrise the lookout called, "Thar she blows! Whale off the port side. Thar she blows and breathes!"

They looked and it was a huge spout and there was the white whale in the blue waters.

"The Mocha Dick! The Mocha Dick!" The cry rang out all over the ship. The men grabbed their harpoons, went aft on the ship, lowered the boats to the waters and hurried after the great white whale.

"After him, me hearties!" shouted Stormalong.

"Faster, lads, faster. There he is." But it was just as if the whale had heard Old Stormalong's boast, for he lashed his tail this way and lashed his tail that way, until the waters were so churned up the men had never a chance to get near him. They had to save their boats, some of them swim for their lives to get back to the good ship Dolphin again.

Old Stormalong was the last to give up. The Mocha Dick pushed his way close to Stormalong and opened his mouth in a big grin. His body shook as though he were laughing. Then he spouted a stream of water right into Stormalong's face, grinned again and swam away.

The red-whiskered sailor was standing at the top of the ship's ladder as Old Stormalong came along side.

"Ha! Ha!" he laughed. "Mocha Dick laughed at Old Stormalong and spit in his eye."

All the sailors laughed until their sides ached and then they laughed some more. Old Stormalong did not like to come up on deck the rest of that trip. When they got back to port he did not want to go near the Snug Haven Inn, but it was the only place to eat and he got so hungry that he just had to. Sure enough, underneath his proud boast they had written, "But the Great Whale just laughed at him and spit in his eye."

"Always thought I was the world's best whaler. Do you suppose I'm not?"

"Always knew I was the world's best sailor. Do you suppose I'm not? It's a big world. There must be a lot of things to do. There must be something else I could do. Why don't I find out?"

So he started walking across the states and across the states to the great Mississippi River. He stepped across into the state of Missouri where he saw farmers clearing the land.

"Are you farmers, mateys? I aim to be a farmer and I'd thank you for telling me what to do," shouted Stormalong.

"Where did you come from?"

"How tall did you say? Four fathoms! Hm! Well, you'd better get an axe and clear the land the way we're doing."

Old Stormalong borrowed the biggest axe they had and before nightfall he had cleared enough land for a hundred farms.

"Now what do you do?"

"Plow your land."

By nightfall he had the hundred farms all plowed.

"Now what do you do?"

"Plant the seed; corn, wheat, oats, rye."

By nightfall he had the hundred farms all planted.

"Now what?"

"Well, now you have to wait for the sun and the wind and the rain to help things grow."

Old Stormalong settled down to wait. He got restless.

"I don't like waiting and waiting!"

Just then a black storm came up. The winds grew stronger and stronger, the clouds grew darker and darker. Suddenly the rains broke and Old Stormalong shouted, "Avast! Avast there mateys! Storm ahead! What do you do on a farm in a storm?"

"Wait until it's over," the farmers answered.

"Too much waiting," grumbled Stormalong. "I guess I just wasn't cut out to be a farmer. It's a big world. There must be other things I could do. Why don't I find out?"

So he started walking, southwest this time—across the states and across the states until he came to Texas. Ah, there he saw what he wanted, cowboys.

"Are you cowboys, mateys? I aim to be a cowboy and I'd thank you for telling me what to do," he shouted.

"Who are you?" asked one as they crowded around and looked up at him. "How tall did you say?"

"Four fathoms? Well you're plenty big! Better get you an outfit first."

Old Stormalong went to town and asked for an outfit.

The storekeeper looked him over and said, "I can give you a ten-gallon hat right now but the rest I'll have to have made special."

Old Stormalong liked his ten gallon hat and swaggered around town in it until his outfit came. Then he got dressed up, went back to the range and got himself a job on the Triple Star ranch as a cowboy.

He asked the cowboys, "Now mateys, what does a cowboy do?"

"Work!" they replied.

"What can I do?"

"Get a horse and round up cattle."

Old Stormalong found a horse and came in next morning with a thousand head of cattle.

"You're good!"

"I know it! Now what do I do?"

"Brand your horses. Build corrals if you don't want them all going back on the range."

Old Stormalong set to work. He didn't mind this kind of work. He liked it. It was fun.

He hadn't been working many days when another storm blew up. A huge black cloud filled the sky, and the rain poured down. Lightning flashed and the thunder raced across the plain like wild horses.

"Avast! Avast there! What do you do on the range in a storm? On a ship you have to furl sail—and fast!"

"Take it easy, mate. You're not on a ship. Just wait until the storm is over."

"But I don't like waiting—all this waiting," grumbled Stormalong as he sat and pondered.

"My first love was the sea. Maybe I'd better go back. There's always something to do on a ship."

So he started walking back East—across the states and across the states and across the states until he came to Boston. One step over and he was in Nantucket.

There was his old ship the Dolphin in port and his old captain, Captain Skinner.

"Captain! Captain! May I sign on for the next trip?"

"Oh, you again," said the captain looking up at Stormalong. "Certainly not with that ten-gallon hat."

"Aw, Captain . . . say, Captain, could I make a bargain with you? If I capture the Mocha Dick this trip, may I keep this ten gallon hat?"

"What a bargain! Ho!"

Stormalong began to hop up and down so that the Dolphin rocked in the water.

"Belay there, Stormalong," shouted the sailors.

"Stop Stormalong! You'll sink the ship," cried the captain.

Stormalong kept hopping up and down.

"I won't stop until you say it's all right for me to wear my ten gallon hat," he said, "and you can lay to that!"

"All right," said the captain. "Wear what you like, you stubborn walrus! I can use you, so come sign the crew papers."

Stormalong signed the crew papers. The captain signed Stormalong's papers, the two men shook hands on the bargain and Stormalong was again a member of the crew of the good ship Dolphin.

Next morning they set sail on the same trip to Mocha, clear across the Atlantic ocean, down around the Cape of Good Hope, and into those cold waters that come up from the south Arctic, just before you get to the Indian Ocean. Those are good whaling waters, you remember, and again the captain put that extra lookout in the crow's nest, high in the mast, his only responsibility to be on the lookout for the spout of a whale, always hoping for a big one.

Day after day of sailing. No whales. Five days gone. Almost sundown.

"Thar she blows! Thar she blows and breathes!" called the lookout. The sailors looked. A huge spout! The white one again.

"The Mocha Dick! The Mocha Dick!" they shouted.

This time as agreed they let Old Stormalong go alone.

He grabbed his harpoon, went aft on the ship and they lowered his boat to the water.

Easily, easily through the waters, scarcely a ripple.

Quietly, quietly through the water, scarcely a sound, until he got right alongside the Mocha Dick.

He leaped on the back of the whale.

The whale dove to the bottom of the ocean. Up he came. He dove to the bottom of the ocean. Up he came. Three days and three nights Old Stormalong rode that whale before he could jab his harpoon in its back.

Plenty of whale oil they took home from that trip—plenty.

The captain was glad, the crew was glad, all the crowd at the dock in Nantucket were glad when they heard how Old Stormalong captured the Mocha Dick.

They say around Nantucket Island, you can still see an old sailor walking and he walks with a rolling gait from having walked the decks of a ship that sailed the rolling seas. But—you can never be quite sure he's a sailor, because always he wears—

A ten gallon hat!

—Adapted

Ballads and Story Poems

BARBARA ALLEN'S CRUELTY

In Scarlet town, where I was born,
    There was a fair maid dwellin'
Made every youth cry Well-a-way!
    Her name was Barbara Allen.

All in the merry month of May,
    When green buds they were swellin',
Young Jemmy Grove on his death-bed lay,
    For love of Barbara Allen.

He sent his man in to her then,
    To the town where she was dwellin';
"O haste and come to my master dear,
    If your name be Barbara Allen."

151

So slowly, slowly rase she up,
    And slowly she came nigh him,
And when she drew the curtain by—
    "Young man, I think you're dyin',"

"O it's I am sick and very very sick,
    And it's all for Barbara Allen."—
"O the better for me ye'se never be,
    Tho' your heart's blood were a-spillin'!

"O dinna ye mind, young man," says she,
    "When the red wine ye were fillin',
That ye made the healths go round and round,
    And slighted Barbara Allen?"

He turn'd his face unto the wall,
    And death was with him dealin':
"Adieu, adieu, my dear friends all,
    And be kind to Barbara Allen!"

As she was walking o'er the fields,
    She heard the dead-bell knellin';
And every jow the dead-bell gave
    Cried "Woe to Barbara Allen."

"O mother, mother, make my bed,
    O make it saft and narrow:
My love has died for me today,
    I'll die for him tomorrow.

"Farewell," she said, "ye virgins all,
    And shun the fault I fell in:
Henceforth take warning by the fall
    Of cruel Barbara Allen."

                            —Traditional: English

ROBIN HOOD AND ALAN A DALE

Come listen to me, you gallants so free,
    All you that love mirth for to hear,
And I will you tell of a bold outlaw,
    That lived in Nottinghamshire.

As Robin Hood in the forest stood,
    All under the green-wood tree,
There was he ware of a brave young man,
    As fine as fine might be.

The youngster was clothed in scarlet red,
    In scarlet fine and gay,
And he did frisk it over the plain,
    And chanted a roundelay.

As Robin Hood next morning stood,
    Amongst the leaves so gay,
There did he espy the same young man
    Come drooping along the way.

The scarlet he wore the day before,
    It was clean cast away;
And every step he fetcht a sigh,
    "Alack and a well a day!"

Then stepped forth brave Little John,
    And Much, the miller's son,
Which made the young man bend his bow,
    When as he saw them come.

"Stand off, stand off!" the young man said,
    "What is your will with me?"—
"You must come before our master straight,
    Under yon green-wood tree."

And when he came bold Robin before,
    Robin askt him courteously,
"O hast thou any money to spare,
    For my merry men and me?"

"I have no money," the young man said,
    "But five shillings and a ring;
And that I have kept this seven long years,
    To have it at my wedding.

"Yesterday I should have married a maid,
    But she is now from me tane,
And chosen to be an old knight's delight,
    Whereby my poor heart is slain."

"What is thy name?" then said Robin Hood,
    "Come tell me, without any fail."—
"By the faith of my body," then said the young man,
    "My name it is Alan a Dale."

"What wilt thou give me," said Robin Hood,
    "In ready gold or fee,
To help thee to thy true-love again,
    And deliver her unto thee?"

"I have no money," then quoth the young man,
    "No ready gold nor fee,
But I will swear upon a book
    Thy true servant for to be."—

"But how many miles to thy true-love?
   Come tell me without any guile."—
"By the faith of my body," then said the young man,
   "It is but five little mile."

Then Robin he hasted over the plain,
   He did neither stint nor lin,
Until he came unto the church
   Where Alan should keep his wedding.

"What dost thou do here?" the Bishop he said,
   "I prithee now tell to me:"
"I am a bold harper," quoth Robin Hood,
   "And the best in the north countrey."

"O welcome, O welcome!" the Bishop he said,
   "That musick best pleaseth me."—
"You shall have no musick," quoth Robin Hood,
   "Till the bride and the bridegroom I see."

With that came in a wealthy knight,
   Which was both grave and old,
And after him a finikin lass,
   Did shine like glistering gold.

"This is no fit match," quoth bold Robin Hood,
   "That you do seem to make here;
For since we are come unto the church,
   The bride she shall chuse her own dear."

Then Robin Hood put his horn to his mouth,
   And blew blasts two or three;
When four and twenty bowmen bold
   Come leaping over the lee.

And when they came into the churchyard,
   Marching all on a row,
The first man was Alan a Dale,
   To give bold Robin his bow.

"This is thy true-love," Robin he said,
   "Young Alan, as I hear say;
And you shall be married at this same time,
   Before we depart away."

"That shall not be!" the Bishop he said,
   "For thy word it shall not stand;
They shall be three times askt in the church,
   As the law is of our land."

Robin Hood pull'd off the Bishop's coat,
   And put it upon Little John;
"By the faith of my body," then Robin said,
   "This cloath doth make thee a man."

When Little John went into the quire,
    The people began for to laugh;
He askt them seven times in the church,
    Least three should not be enough.

"Who gives me this maid?" then said Little John;
    Quoth Robin, "That do I!
And he that doth take her from Alan a Dale
    Full dearly he shall her buy."

And thus having ended this merry wedding,
    The bride lookt as fresh as a queen,
And so they return'd to the merry green-wood,
    Amongst the leaves so green.

                       —Traditional: English

MOY CASTLE

There are seven men in Moy Castle
    And merry men this night;
There are seven men in Moy Castle
    Whose hearts are gay and light.

Prince Charlie came to Moy Castle
    And asked for shelter there,
And down came Lady M'Intosh,
    As proud as she was fair.

"I'm a hunted man, Lady M'Intosh—
    A price is on my head!
If Lord Loudon knew thou'dst sheltered me,
    Both thou and I were sped."

"Come in! come in, my prince!" said she,
    And opened wide the gate;
"To die with Prince Charlie Stuart,
    I ask no better fate."

She's called her seven trusty men,
    The blacksmith at their head:
"Ye shall keep watch in the castle wood,
    To save our prince from dread."

The lady has led the prince away,
    To make him royal cheer;
The seven men of M'Intosh
    Have sought the forest drear.

And there they looked and listened,
    Listened and looked amain;
And they heard the sound of the falling leaves,
    And the soft sound of the rain.

The blacksmith knelt beside an oak,
    And laid his ear to the ground,
And under the noises of the wood
    He heard a distant sound.

He heard the sound of many feet,
    Warily treading the heather—
He heard the sound of many men
    Marching softly together.

"There's no time now to warn the prince,
    The castle guards are few;
'Tis wit will win the play tonight,
    And what we here can do."

He's gi'en the word to his six brethren,
    And through the wood they're gone;
The seven men of M'Intosh
    Each stood by himself alone.

"And he who has the pipes at his back,
    His best now let him play;
And he who has no pipes at his back,
    His best word let him say."

It was five hundred Englishmen
    Were treading the purple heather,
Five hundred of Lord Loudon's men
    Marching softly together.

"There's none tonight in Moy Castle
    But servants poor and old;
If we bring the prince to Loudon's lord,
    He'll fill our hands with gold."

They came lightly on their way,
    Had never a thought of ill,
When suddenly from the darksome wood
    Broke out a whistle shrill.

And straight the wood was filled with cries,
    With shouts of angry men,
And the angry skirl of the bagpipes
    Came answering the shouts again.

The Englishmen looked and listened,
    Listened and looked amain,
And nought could they see through the murk night,
    But the pipes shrieked out again.

"Hark to the slogan of Lochiel,
    To Keppoch's gathering cry!
Hark to the rising swell that tells
    Clanranald's men are nigh!

"Now woe to the men that told us
    Lochiel was far away!
The whole of the Highland army
    Is waiting to bar our way.

"It's little we'll see of Charlie Stuart
    And little of Loudon's gold,
And but we're away from this armed wood,
    Our lives have but little hold."

It was five hundred Englishmen,
    They turned their faces and ran,
And well for him with the swiftest foot,
    For he was the lucky man.

And woe to him that was lame or slow,
    For they trampled him on the heather!
And back to the place from whence they came
    They're hirpling all together.

Lord Loudon's men, they are gone full far,
    Over the brow of the hill;
The seven men of M'Intosh,
    Their pipes are crying still.

They leaned them to a tree and laughed,
    'Twould do you good to hear,
And they are away to Moy Castle
    To tell their lady dear.

And who but Lady M'Intosh
    Would praise her men so bold?
And who but Prince Charlie Stuart
    Would count the good French gold?

There are seven men in Moy Castle
    Are joyful men this night;
There are seven men in Moy Castle
    Whose hearts will aye be light.

                          —Traditional: Scots

DUNKIRK

Will came back from school that day,
And he had little to say.
But he stood a long time looking down
To where the gray-green Channel water
Slapped at the foot of the little town,
And to where his boat, the Sarah P.,
Bobbed at the tide on an even keel,
With her one old sail, patched at the leech,
Furled like a slattern down at heel.

He stood for a while above the beach,
He saw how the wind and current caught her;
He looked a long time out to sea.
There was steady wind, and the sky was pale,
And a haze in the east that looked like smoke.

Will went back to the house to dress.
He was halfway through, when his sister Bess
Who was near fourteen, and younger than he
By just two years, came home from play.
She asked him, "Where are you going, Will?"
He said, "For a good long sail."
"Can I come along?"
                                    "No, Bess," he spoke.
"I may be gone for a night and a day."
Bess looked at him. She kept very still.
She had heard the news of the Flanders rout,
How the English were trapped above Dunkirk,
And the fleet had gone to get them out—
But everyone thought it wouldn't work.
There was too much fear, there was too much doubt.

She looked at him, and he looked at her.
They were English children, born and bred.
He frowned her down, but she wouldn't stir.
She shook her proud young head.
"You'll need a crew," she said.

They raised the sail on the Sarah P.,
Like a pennoncel on a young knight's lance,
And headed the Sarah out to sea,
To bring their soldiers home from France.

There was no command, there was no set plan,
But six hundred boats went out with them
On the gray-green waters, sailing fast,
River excursion and fisherman,
Tug and schooner and racing M,
And the little boats came following last.

From every harbor and town they went
Who had sailed their craft in the sun and rain,
From the South Downs, from the cliffs of Kent,
From the village street, from the country lane.
There are twenty miles of rolling sea

From coast to coast, by the seagull's flight,
But the tides were fair and the wind was free,
And they raised Dunkirk by the fall of night.

They raised Dunkirk with its harbor torn
By the blasted stern and the sunken prow;
They had raced for fun on an English tide,
They were English children bred and born,
And whether they lived, or whether they died,
They raced for England now.

Bess was as white as the Sarah's sail,
She set her teeth and smiled at Will.
He held his course for the smoky veil
Where the harbor narrowed thin and long.
The British ships were firing strong.

He took the Sarah into his hands,
He drove her in through fire and death
To the wet men waiting on the sands.
He got his load and he got his breath,
And she came about, and the wind fought her.

He shut his eyes and he tried to pray.
He saw his England where she lay,
The wind's green home, the sea's proud daughter,
Still in the moonlight, dreaming deep,
The English cliffs and the English loam—
He had fourteen men to get away,
And the moon was clear, and the night like day
For planes to see where the white sails creep
Over the black water.

He closed his eyes and he prayed for her,
For England's hope and for England's fate;
He prayed to the men who had made her great,
Who had built her land of forest and park,
Who had made the seas an English lake;
He prayed for a fog to bring the dark;
He prayed to get home for England's sake.
And the fog came down on the rolling sea,
And covered the ships with English mist.
And diving planes were baffled and blind.

For Nelson was there in the Victory,
With his one good eye, and his sullen twist,
And guns were out on The Golden Hind,
Their shot flashed over the Sarah P.
He could hear them cheer as he came about.

By burning wharves, by battered slips,
Galleon, frigate, and brigantine,
The old dead Captains fought their ships.
And the great dead Admirals led the line.
It was England's night, it was England's sea.
The fog rolled over the harbor key.
Bess held to the stays, and conned him out.

And through the dark, while the Sarah's wake
Hissed behind him, and vanished in foam,
There at his side sat Francis Drake,
And held him true, and steered him home.

—Robert Nathan

Bibliography

Bibliography

Just as the stories told by anyone must be his own, the stories and books discussed in this book are those with which I have lived and do live. All the adult books mentioned have been building stones in my house of life. The children's stories are those I love to tell. There is some folk material and there are some anthologies I know better through other people whose experience I treasure. In the field of language, this is a good list for any lay person. The children's literature list contains many of the best books available today.

The books of poetry and of ballads, many of which tell a

story, are invaluable to know and good to live with through the years. Because music is so closely akin to storytelling, especially folk music and folklore, many books of and about music as well as song collections are given. The folklore list is a full one—not a folklorist's research one, but a fine list of folklore from all over the world, real treasure for a storyteller. The children's stories by modern authors have been found good to tell by many storytellers today.

This is not a definitive bibliography of books in any area, but a list of many books that are rich resource for a creative storyteller.

CREATIVE LIVING

Brown, Rollo Walter	*The Creative Spirit: An Inquiry into American Life*	Harper
Bryson, Lyman	*The Next America*	Harper
Cole, Natalie R.	*Arts in the Classroom*	Day
Dewey, John	*Art as Experience*	Minton Balch
Eichenberg, Fritz	*Art and Faith*	Pendle Hill
Ellis, Havelock	*The Dance of Life*	Houghton
Fry, Roger	*Transformations*	Anchor
Gasset, Ortega y	*Dehumanization of Art and Other Writings on Art and Culture*	Anchor
Ghiselin, Brewster	*The Creative Process*	Mentor
Krutch, Joseph Wood	*Experience and Art*	Houghton
Lowenfeld, Viktor	*Creative and Mental Growth*	Macmillan
Maurois, Andre	*The Art of Living*	Harper
Mearnes, Hughes	*The Creative Adult*	Doubleday
	Creative Power	Doubleday
	Creative Youth	Doubleday
Santayana, George	*The Sense of Beauty: The Outline of Aesthetic Theory*—Good general background in aesthetics	Scribner
Whitehead, Alfred North	*Adventure of Ideas*	Macmillan

LANGUAGE

Bodiner, F.	*The Loom of Language*	Norton
Gray, Louis H.	*Foundations of Language*	Macmillan
Hayakawa, S. I.	*Language in Action*	Harcourt
Jesperson, Otto	*Language: Its Nature, Development and Origin*	Holt
Laird, Charlton	*The Miracle of Language*	World
Mencken, H. L.	*The American Language*	Knopf
Pei, Mario	*The Story of Language*	Lippincott
Piaget, Jean	*Language and Thought of the Child* (especially pp. 140-148 in Meridian edition)	Harcourt Meridian
Pyles, Thomas	*Words and Ways of American English*	Random
Walpole, H. R.	*Semantics: The Nature of Words and Their Meanings*	Norton

LANGUAGE BOOKS FOR YOUNG PEOPLE

Laird, Charlton and Helene	*The Tree of Language*	World
Lambert, Eloise	*All About Language*	Lippincott
Pei, Mario	*About Language*	Lothrop

LANGUAGE ARTS

Dawson, Mildred	*Teaching Language in the Grades*	World
Hatchett, Ethel L., and Donald H. Hughes	*Teaching Language in the Elementary School*	Ronald
Herrick, Virgil, Leland Jacobs, and others	*Children and the Language Arts*	Prentice-Hall
National Council of Teachers of English	*Language Arts for Today's Children*	Appleton
Strickland, Ruth G.	*Language Arts in the Elementary School*	Heath

LITERATURE

Auslander, Joseph, and Frank E. Hill	*The Winged Horse*	Doubleday
Chute, Marchette	*Ben Jonson of Westminster*	Dutton
	Geoffrey Chaucer of England	Dutton
	Shakespeare of London	Dutton
	Introducing Shakespeare	Dutton
Coffin, Robert P. Tristram	*On the Green Carpet*	Bobbs
Drew, Elizabeth	*The Enjoyment of Literature*	Norton
	Discovering Poetry	Norton
Drinkwater, John	*The Outline of Literature*	Putnam
Eastman, Max	*The Enjoyment of Poetry*	Scribner
	The Sense of Humor	Scribner
Gordon, Caroline	*How to Read a Novel*	Viking
Guerard, A. L.	*Preface to World Literature*	Holt
Hart, J. D.	*Oxford Companion to American Literature*	Oxford U.P.
Harvey, P.	*Oxford Companion to English Literature*	Oxford U.P.
Housman, A. E.	*The Name and Nature of Poetry*	Cambridge U.P.
Lewis, B. Roland	*Creative Poetry*	Stanford U.P.
Powys, John Cowper	*The Enjoyment of Literature*	S. and S.
Quiller-Couch, Sir Arthur	*On the Art of Reading*	Putnam
West, Rebecca	*The Strange Necessity Essays on Literary Interests*	Doubleday
Wilson, Edmund	*A Literary Chronicle*	Anchor
Woolf, Virginia	*The Common Reader*	Harcourt
	The Second Common Reader (especially the chapter "How Should One Read a Book")	Harcourt
	A Room of One's Own	Harcourt

CHILDREN'S LITERATURE

Adams, Bess Porter	*About Books and Children*	Holt
Arbuthnot, May Hill	*Children and Books* (rev. 1957)	Scott Foresman
Darton, F. J. H.	*Children's Books in England* *Five Centuries of Social Life*	Macmillan
Duff, Annis	*Bequest of Wings: A Family's Pleasure With Books*	Viking
	Longer Flight	Viking
Eaton, Anne Thaxter	*Reading With Children*	Viking
	Treasure for the Taking (1957 Edition)	Viking
Hazard, Paul	*Books, Children and Men*	Horn Book
Hewins, Caroline M.	*The Mid-century Child and Her Books*	Macmillan
Hollowell, Lillian	*A Book of Children's Literature*	Houghton
Huber, Miriam B.	*Story and Verse for Children* (rev. 1956)	Macmillan
Johnson, Edna, E. Sickels Sayers, and Francis Clark	*Anthology of Children's Literature*	Houghton
Jordan, Alice M.	*From Rollo to Tom Sawyer*	Horn Book
Mahoney, Bertha, and	*Realms of Gold*	Doubleday
Elinor Whitney	*Five Years of Children's Books*	Doubleday
	Horn Book Papers, Vol. II	Caldecott Medal Books
Meigs, C., A. T. Eaton, and Ruth Viguers	*Critical History of Children's Literature*	Macmillan
Miller, Bertha Mahoney, and Elinor Whitney	*Newbery Medal Books,* *Horn Book Papers,* Vol. I	Horn Book
Moore, Annie Carroll	*My Roads to Childhood*	Doubleday
	Three Viols Notebook, 1st. 2nd, and 3rd books	Coward

Smith, Lillian	*The Unreluctant Years*	American Library Assn.
White, Dorothy Neal	*About Books for Children*	Oxford U.P. (from New Zealand Council for Education Research and New Zealand Library Association)

MAGAZINES

(Concerned with children's books)

The Horn Book	A bi-monthly magazine devoted to children's books	Horn Book
Elementary English and *Childhood Education*	These two magazines have excellent book reviews and articles on children's books and authors	National Council of Teachers of English, Association on Childhood Education

CHILD GROWTH AND DEVELOPMENT

d'Evelyn, Katherine	*Meeting Children's Emotional Needs*	Prentice-Hall
Gesell, Arnold, and Frances Ilg	*Infant Child in Culture of Today*	Harper
	The Child from Two to Six	Harper
	The Child from Five to Ten	Harper
	Youth, the Years from Ten to Sixteen	Harper
Hopkins, L. Thomas	*The Emerging Self*	Harper
Mitchell, Lucy Sprague	*Here and Now Story Book* (Introduction)	Dutton
Rugg, Harold	*Culture and Education in America*	Harcourt

Warner, Ruby	*The Child and the Elementary School World*	Prentice-Hall
Wickes, Frances G.	*The Inner World of Childhood, A Study in Analytical Psychology*	Appleton
	White House Conference Report 1956	Appleton

STORYTELLING

Bryant, Sara Cone	*How to Tell Stories to Children*	Houghton
Mitchell, Lucy Sprague	*Here and Now Story Book*	Dutton
Sawyer, Ruth	*The Way of a Story-Teller*	Viking
Shedlock, Marie	*The Art of Story-Telling*	Appleton

RELATED ARTS

GENERAL

Mumford, Lewis	*The Arts in Revival*	U. of Pa.
Tooze, Ruth, and Beatrice Krone	*Literature and Music as Resources for Social Studies*	Prentice-Hall
Van Loon, Hendrik Willem	*The Arts*	S. and S.

ART

| Bergson, Henri | *Laughter: An Essay on the Meaning of the Comic* — Wonderful analysis of humor and the comic element in art | Macmillan |
| Gardner, Helen | *Art Through the Ages*— Each cultural era considered in terms of its art | Harcourt |

Kainz, Luise C., and Olive K. Riley	*Exploring Art*	Harcourt
Maritain, Jacques	*Creative Intuition in Art and Poetry*	Meridian
Parkhurst, Helen H.	*Beauty: An Interpretation of Art and Imaginative Life*	Harcourt
Read, Herbert	*Education Through Art*	Pantheon
	Art and Society	Macmillan
Riley, Olive L.	*Your Art Heritage*	Harper

ARCHITECTURE

Hudnut, Joseph	*Architecture and the Spirit of Man*	Harvard U.P.
Neutra, Richard	*Survival Through Design*	Oxford U.P.
Wright, Frank Lloyd	*An American Architecture*	Seven Arts Society

DRAMA, SPEECH, AND DANCE

Barber, Sara M.	*Speech Education*	Little
Boleslavsky, Richard	*Acting: The First Six Lessons* (Training the body like tuning an instrument)	Theatre Arts, Inc.
H'Doubler, Margaret N.	*The Dance, A Creative Art Experience*	F. S. Crofts

CHILDREN'S THEATRE

Lease, Ruth G, and Geraldine Siks	*Creative Dramatics*	Harper
Robertson, Hazel	*Children's Theatre*	Stanford U.P.
Ward, Winifred	*Playmaking with Children*	Appleton

MUSIC

Andrews, Gladys	*Creative Rhythmic Movement for Children*	Prentice-Hall
Bauer, Marion, and Ethel Payon	*How Music Grew*	Putnam
Bekker, Paul	*The Story of Music*	Norton
Biancolli, L., and R. Bagar	*Victor Book of Operas*	S. and S.

Coleman, Satis	*Creative Music for Children*	Day
Cross, Milton	*Complete Stories of the Great Operas*	Doubleday
Cross, Milton, and David Ewen	*Encyclopedia of Great Composers and Their Music*	Doubleday
Copland, Aaron	*What to Listen for in Music* (Especially discussion of rhythm)	McGraw
Dike, Helen	*Stories from the Great Metropolitan Operas*	Random
Downes, Olin	*Olin Downes on Music*	S. and S.
Fox, Lillian, and L. Thomas Hopkins	*Creative School Music*	S. and S.
Hindemith, Paul	*A Composer's World*	Harvard U.P.
Howard, John Tasker	*Our American Music: Three Hundred Years of It*	Crowell
Kinscella, Hazel G.	*Music Appreciation Readers, I-VI*	University Publ. Co.
Luther, Frank	*Americans and Their Songs*	Harper
McKinney, Howard D.	*Music and Man*	Am. Book Co.
Mursell, James L.	*Education for Musical Growth*	Ginn
	Music and the Class Room Teacher	Silver Burdett
	Practices and Principles in Music Education	Prentice-Hall
Ritchie, Jean	*Singing Family of the Cumberlands* (for folk background)	Oxford U.P.
Rolland, Romain	*Essays in Music*	Allen, Towne & Heath
Sachs, Curt	*Our Musical Heritage*	Prentice-Hall
Spaeth, Sigmund	*Read 'Em and Weep*	Arco
Surette, Thomas Whitney, and D. G. Mason	*The Appreciation of Music*	H. W. Gray
Taylor, Deems	*Of Men and Music*	S. and S.
	The Well-Tempered Listener	S. and S.
Trapp, M.	*Around the Year with the Trapp Family*	Pantheon

SONG COLLECTIONS

Boni, M. B., and N. Lloyd	*Fireside Book of Folk Songs*	S. and S.
	Fireside Book of Favorite American Songs	S. and S.
	Fireside Book of Christmas Carols	S. and S.
Botsford, Frances	*Collection of Songs*, Vols. I and II	G. Schirmer
Brand, Oscar	*The Singing Holidays—* The calendar in folk song	Knopf
Colcord, Joanna	*Songs of American Sailormen*	Norton
Ewen, David	*Songs of America*	Ziff-Davis
Felton, Harold	*Cowboy Jamboree*	Knopf
Ives, Burl	*Burl Ives Song Book*	Ballantine
Kapp, Paul	*A Cat Came Fiddling*	Harcourt
(Krone, Max, and Beatrice P.)	*Songs to Sing with Descants*	Neil Kjos
	Descants and Easy Basses	Neil Kjos
	Inter Americana	Neil Kjos
	Folksongs of Brazil	Neil Kjos
	Mexican Folksongs	Neil Kjos
	Spanish and Latin American Songs	Neil Kjos
	Songs from Many Lands	Neil Kjos
Landeck, Beatrice	*Songs to Grow on: Collection of American Folk Songs for Children*	Sloane
	More Songs to Grow On	Sloane
Lomax, John and Alan	*Best Loved American Songs*	Grosset
	Folk Song, U. S. A.	Duell, Sloane, Pierce
Ritchie, Jean	*Swapping Song Book*	Oxford U.P.
Sandburg, Carl	*The American Songbag*	Harcourt
Seeger, Ruth C.	*American Folk Songs for Children*	Doubleday
	Animal Folk Songs for Children	Doubleday
Siegmeister, Elie	*Treasury of American Song*	Knopf

Wheeler, Opal	*Sing for America; Sing in Praise; Sing for Christmas*—Interesting backgrounds for all the songs are given in all three books	Dutton

The Recreation Services of Delaware, Ohio, publish a series of small paper-bound collections of the best folk songs, hymns, and songs: *Songs of Many Nations, Songs for the Open Road, Lift Every Voice, Let Us be Joyful,* and so on. These offer, in inexpensive form, one of the richest resources of folk songs, ballads, and songs from all over the world.

All the basic music series commonly used in schools today have an excellent selection of folk music and the world's great music. Frequently background is given.

	American Singer Series (8 Vols.), especially *Together We Sing*	Am. Bk. Co.
	A Singing School (10 Vols.), especially *Sing Out!*	Birchard-Summy
Fullerton, Wolfe, Krone (eds.)	*Together We Sing* (3 Vols.), especially the enlarged edition	Follett
Fullerton, Wolfe (ed.)	*New Series* (6 Vols.), especially *Voices of America* and *Voices of the World*	Follett
	Our Singing World (8 Vols.), especially *Singing Together*	Ginn
	Music for Living (6 Vols.)	Silver Burdett
	New Music Horizons (8 Vols.)	Silver Burdett

POETRY FOR CHILDREN AND YOUNG PEOPLE

(Verse by individual poets)

Becker, John	*New Feathers for the Old Goose*	Pantheon

Behn, Harry	*The Little Hill*	Harcourt
	Windy Morning	Harcourt
Benet, Rosemary, and Stephen	*A Book of Americans*	Farrar & Straus
Blake, William	*Songs of Innocence*	Holt
Coatsworth, Elizabeth	*Poems*	Macmillan
	Hide and Seek	Pantheon
	Mouse Chorus	Pantheon
Daugherty, James	*West of Boston*	Viking
De La Mare, Walter	*A Child's Day*	Holt
	Bells of Grass	Holt
	Peacock Pie	Holt
Dickinson, Emily	*Poems for Youth*	Little
Farjeon, Eleanor	*Eleanor Farjeon's Poems for Children*	Lippincott
Field, Rachel	*Poems*	Macmillan
	Taxis and Toadstools	Doubleday
Fyleman, Rose	*Fairies and Chimneys*	Doubleday
Lear, Edward	*Edward Lear's Nonsense Book*	Garden City
	Complete Nonsense Book	Dodd
Lindsay, Vachel	*Johnny Appleseed and Other Poems*	Macmillan
Millay, Edna St. Vincent	*Poems for Young People*	Harper
Miller, Mary Brittain	*Give a Guess*	Pantheon
	All Aboard	Pantheon
Milne, A. A.	*When We Were Very Young*	Dutton
	Now We Are Six	Dutton
Roberts, Elizabeth Maddox	*Under the Tree*	Viking
Rossetti, Christina	*Sing Song*	Macmillan
Stephens, James	*Collected Poems*	Macmillan
Teasdale, Sara	*Stars Tonight*	Macmillan
Whitman, Walt	*Leaves of Grass*	Modern Library

POETRY ANTHOLOGIES

Association for Childhood Education	*Sung Under the Silver Umbrella*	Macmillan

Adshead, Gladys, and Annis Duff	*Inheritance of Poetry*	Houghton
Anthony, Edward	*Oddity Land*	Doubleday
Arbuthnot, May Hill	*Time for Poetry*	Scott Foresman
Auslander, Joseph, and Frank E. Hill	*The Winged Horse Anthology*	Doubleday
Brewton, John and Sara	*Gaily We Parade*	Macmillan
	Sing a Song of Seasons	Macmillan
	Bridled with Rainbows	Macmillan
	Under the Tent of the Sky	Macmillan
Ferris, Helen	*Favorite Poems Old & New*	Doubleday
Friedman, Albert B.	*The Viking Book of Folk Ballads of the English Speaking World*	Viking
Geismer, Barbara, and Antoinette Suter	*Very Young Verses*	Houghton
Harrington, Mildred	*Ring Around*	Macmillan
Hazeltine, Alice, and Eloise E. Smith	*The Year Around: Poems for Children*	Abingdon
Huffard, G., and others	*My Poetry Book*	Winston
Love, Katherine	*A Little Laughter*	Crowell
	A Pocketful of Rhymes	Crowell
McEwen, Catherine S.	*Away We Go!*	Crowell
McFarland, Wilma	*For a Child*	Westminster
Parker, Elinor	*100 Story Poems*	Crowell
	100 Poems about People	Crowell
Peterson, Isobel	*First Book of Poetry*	Watts
Plotz, Helen	*Imagination's Other Place —Poems of Science and Mathematics*	Crowell
	Untune the Sky—Poems of Music and the Dance	Crowell
Read, Herbert	*This Way Delight*	Pantheon
Sechrist, Elizabeth	*One Thousand Poems for Children*	Macrae Smith
Sharp, Cecil	*Old English Ballads in the Southern Appalachians*	H. W. Gray
Suter, Antoinette, and Barbara Geismer	*Very Young Verses*	Houghton

Taylor, Margaret	*Did You Feed My Cow? Rhymes From City Streets and Country Lanes*	Crowell
Thompson, Blanche	*Silver Pennies*	Macmillan
	More Silver Pennies	Macmillan
Tobitt, Janet, and Alice White	*Dramatized Ballads*	Dutton
	The Saucy Sailor and Other Dramatized Ballads	Dutton
Untermeyer, Louis	*Rainbow in the Sky*	Harcourt
	Stars to Steer by	Harcourt
	This Singing World	Harcourt
	The Magic Circle	Harcourt
Withers, Carl, and Alta Jablow	*Rainbow in the Morning* (Folk Rhymes)	Abelard Schuman

RELIGION

The Bible		
Bro, Margueritte H.	*Every Day a Prayer*	Harper
Jones, Jessie Orton, and Elizabeth Orton Jones	*Small Rain*	Viking
	This is the Way	Viking
Smith, Ruth	*The Tree of Life*	Viking

ANTHOLOGIES OF STORIES NEW AND OLD

(The following symbols, preceding the titles, indicate the age level for which the books are appropriate: *y,* for children under 8; *m,* for children 8 to 11; *o,* for children 12 or over. The letter *h* indicates that the book has humorous appeal.)

Association for Childhood Education, International	(*m*) *Told Under the Green Umbrella* — Traditional Tales	Macmillan
	(*m*) *Told Under the Blue Umbrella* — Realistic Stories	Macmillan
	(*m*) *Told Under the Magic Umbrella*—Tales of Imagination	Macmillan

	Told Under Spacious Skies—Stories of the United States	Macmillan
Bacmeister, Rhoda	(y) *Stories to Begin On*	Dutton
Bailey, Caroline Sherwin	(m) *Tell Me a Birthday Story*—Stories for birthdays of famous people	Lippincott
Baker, Augusta (ed.)	*The Talking Tree and Other Stories*—Fairy Tales from the Islands	Lippincott
Baker, Margaret and Mary	*Tell Them Again Tales*	Dodd
	Fifteen Tales for Lively Children	Dodd
Baldwin, James	*Favorite Tales of Long Ago*	Dutton
Barksdale, Lena	*The Treasure Bag: Stories and Poems*	Knopf
Beston, Henry	*Henry Beston's Fairy Tales*	Dutton
	Firelight Fairy Book	Little
Bleecker, Mary Noel	*Big Music: Twenty Merry Tales to Tell*	Viking
Brock, Emma C., and others	(m) *Spooks and Spirits and Shadowy Shapes*	Dutton
Brown, Frances	(m) *Granny's Wonderful Chair*	Macmillan
Bryant, Sara Cone	(m) *Stories to Tell Children*	Houghton
	(y) *Stories to Tell Littlest Ones*	Houghton
Buck, Pearl	(y) *Stories for Little Children*	Day
Cavanah, Frances, and Ruth C. Weir	*Twenty-four Horses; A Treasury of Stories*	Rand McNally
Carpenter, Frances	*Wonder Tales of Cats and Dogs*	Doubleday
	Wonder Tales of Horses and Heroes	Doubleday
Child Study Association	(y) *Read-to-me-Story Book*	Crowell
	(y) *Read Me More Stories*	Crowell
	(y) *Read Me Another Story*	Crowell
Clark, Barrett and M. Jagendorf	*A World of Stories for Children*	Bobbs

Cothren, Jean	(m) *Magic Bells*	Dutton
Courlander, Harold (ed. for U.N. Women's Guild)	*Ride With the Sun*—Folk Tales and Stories from the United Nations	Whittlesey
Dalgliesh, Alice	*The Enchanted Book*	Scribner
De La Mare, Walter	*Told Again*	Knopf
	Animal Stories	Scribner
Dobbs, Rose	*Once Upon a Time: Twenty Cheerful Tales*	Random
Du Laney, Peggy	*The Golden Grab Bag*	S. and S.
Emrich, M. W., and G. Korson	*Child's Book of Folklore*	Dial
Emerson, Caroline D.	*Merry Go Round of Modern Tales*	Dutton
Evans, Pauline	*The Family Treasury of Children's Stories*, Vols. I, II, III	Doubleday
Fenner, Phyllis	(o) *Adventure Rare and Magical*	Knopf
	Circus Parade: Stories of the Big Top	Knopf
	Fools and Funny Fellows	Knopf
	Crack of the Bat: Stories of Baseball	Knopf
	Giants and Witches and a Dragon or Two	Knopf
	Magic Hoop: Horse Stories from Many Lands	Knopf
	Princesses and Peasant Boys: Tales of Enchantment	Knopf
	Stories of the Sea	Knopf
	Ghosts, Ghosts, Ghosts	Watts
	Time to Laugh: Funny Tales from Here and There	Watts
	Fun, Fun, Fun	Watts
	Yankee Doodle: Stories of the Brave and the Free	Watts
Frost, Frances	(o) *Legends of the United Nations*	Whittlesey
Fyleman, Rose	*Tea Time Tales*	Doubleday
Green, Roger	*Modern Fairy Stories*	Dutton

Gruenberg, Sidonie M.	(*y, m*) *Favorite Stories Old and New*	Doubleday
	(*o*) *More Favorite Stories Old and New*	Doubleday
	Let's Read a Story	Garden City
Harper, Wilhelmina	*Easter Chimes*	Dutton
	The Harvest Feast	Dutton
	Ghosts and Goblins	Dutton
	Down in Dixie	Dutton
	The Gunniwolf and Other Merry Tales	McKay
Hazeltine, Alice I.	*Easter Book of Legends and Stories*	Lothrop
	(*o*) *Just for Fun*	Lothrop
Housman, Lawrence	*Moonshine and Clover*	Harcourt
Hutchinson, Veronica S.	*Candlelight Stories*	Putnam
	Fireside Stories	Putnam
Justus, May, and others	(*m*) *Big Meeting Day and Other Festival Tales*	Dutton
Kramer, Nora	(*y*) *Nora Kramer's Story Book for 3's and 4's*	Messner
	(*y*) *Nora Kramer's Story Book for 5's and 6's*	Messner
Lawson, Marie	(*o*) *Strange Sea Stories*	Viking
Leekley, Thomas B.	(*o*) *King Herla's Quest and Other Stories from Walter Map*	Vanguard
Martignoni, Margaret	*A Treasury of Children's Literature*	Grosset
Mitchell, Lucy Sprague	(*y*) *Here and Now Story Book*	Dutton
	(*y*) *Another Here and Now Story Book*	Dutton
Mitchell, Lucy Sprague, and others	(*y*) *Believe and Make Believe*	Dutton
O'Connor, Betty	(*y*) *Better Homes and Gardens Story Book*	Better Homes & Gardens
Olcott, Frances J.	*The Wonder Garden*	Houghton
	Good Stories for Great Anniversaries, Birthdays and Holidays	Houghton
Power, Effie	*Bag O' Tales*	Dutton

Pyle, Howard	*The Wonder Clock*	Harper
	Pepper and Salt	Harper
Rackham, Arthur	*The Arthur Rackham Fairy Book*	Lippincott
Ross, Eulalie Steinmetz	*The Buried Treasure and Other Picture Tales*	Lippincott
Scoggin, Margaret	(o) *Chucklebait*	Knopf
	More Chucklebait	Knopf
Sechrist, Elizabeth	(o) *Thirteen Ghostly Yarns*	Macrae Smith
Shannon, Terry, and Charles Payzant	*Today is Story Day*	Dutton
Smith, Elva	(o) *Adventure Calls*	Lothrop
Smith, Helen R.	*Laughing Matter*	Scribner
Stockton, Frank	*Ting-a-Ling Tales*	Scribner
Tenggren, Gustav	(y) *The Tenggren Tell-it-again Book*	Little
Tyler, Anna C.	*Twenty-four Unusual Stories*	Harcourt
Wiggin, Kate Douglas	*Tales of Laughter*	Doubleday
	The Fairy Ring	Doubleday
Young, Barbara	(m) *The Puppet Man and Other Stories*	Reynal

COLLECTIONS OF STORIES WRITTEN BY INDIVIDUAL AUTHORS

Bacon, Peggy	(y) *The Lion Hearted Kitten and Other Stories*	Macmillan
Dolbier, Maurice	*The Half Pint Jinni and Other Stories*	Random
Farjeon, Eleanor	*The Little Book Room*	Oxford U.P.
Irving, Washington	(o) *The Bold Dragoon and Other Ghostly Tales*	Knopf
Kipling, Rudyard	*Just So Stories*	Doubleday
	Jungle Books I and II	Doubleday
Potter, Miriam Clark	(y) *Mrs. Goose and Three Ducks*	Lippincott
	(y) *Mrs. Goose of Animal Town*	Lippincott
	(y) *Here Comes Mrs. Goose*	Lippincott

	(y) *Our Friend Mrs. Goose*	Lippincott
	(y) *Just Mrs. Goose*	Lippincott
Sandburg, Carl	*Rootabaga Stories*	Harcourt
Shakespeare, William		
Chute, Marchette	*Stories from Shakespeare*	World
Lamb, Charles and Mary	*Lamb's Tales from Shakespeare*	Dutton
Wilde, Oscar	*The Happy Prince and Other Fairy Tales*	Putnam
	The Happy Prince—All of Wilde's lovely fairy tales	Macmillan

MYTHS, LEGENDS, HERO STORIES, AND EPICS

Alexander, Beatrice	*Famous Myths of the Golden Age*	Random
Anderson, R. B.	*Norse Mythology*	Scott, Foresman
Baldwin, James	*Story of Roland*	Scribner
	Story of Siegfried	Scribner
Benson, Sally	*Stories of the Gods and Heroes*	Dial
Brown, Abbie Farwell	*In the Days of the Giants* (Norse)	Houghton
Buff, Mary and Conrad	*The Arrow and the Apple* (Story of William Tell)	Houghton
Bulfinch, Thomas	*Mythology*	Modern Library
Cervantes, Miguel de (retold by Eric Kastner)	*Don Quixote*	Macmillan
	Don Quixote (Harlequin book)	Messner
Chidsey, Alan Lake	*Rustam, Lion of Persia*	Putnam
Church, Alfred	*Iliad of Homer*	Macmillan
	Odyssey of Homer	Macmillan
Colum, Padraic	*Children of Odin*	Macmillan
	Children's Homer: The Adventures of Odysseus and the Tale of Troy	Macmillan
	Golden Fleece and the Heroes before Achilles	Macmillan
Cooke, Donald	*Silver Horn of Robin Hood*	Winston
	The Firebird	Winston

Coolidge, Olivia	*Greek Myths*	Houghton
	Legends of the North	Houghton
	Trojan Horse	Houghton
Dasent, G. W.	*Popular Tales from the North*	Blackie, London
Dawson, Warren R.	*The Bridle of Pegasus; Studies in Magic, Mythology and Folklore*	Methuen
de Selincourt, Aubrey	*Odysseus, the Wanderer*	Criterion
Deutsch, Babette	*Heroes of the Kalevala (Finland)*	Messner
Echols, Ula W.	*Knights of Charlemagne*	Longmans
Elgin, Kathleen	*First Book of Myths*	Watts
	First Book of Norse Legends	Watts
Fiske, John	*Myths and Myth Makers*	Houghton
Frazer, J. G.	*The Golden Bough*	Macmillan
French, Allen	*Story of Grettir the Strong*	Dutton
Funk and Wagnalls (Marie Leach, ed.)	*Funk & Wagnall's Standard Dictionary of Folklore, Mythology, and Legends*	Funk
Gaer, Joseph	*The Adventures of Rama (India)*	Little
Gaster, Theodore H.	*The Oldest Stories in the World*	Viking
Gayley, C. N.	*Classic Myths in English Literature and Art*	Ginn
Gilbert, H.	*Robin Hood*	Lippincott
Gorska, Halina, and Irena Lorentowicz	*Prince Godfrey: the Knight of the Star of the Nativity*	Roy
Graves, Robert	*The Greek Myths,* Vols. I and II	Penguin Books
Guerber, H. A.	*Book of the Epic*	Lippincott
	Legends of the Middle Ages	Am. Bk. Co.
Hadfield, A. M.	*King Arthur and the Round Table*	Dutton
Hamilton, Edith	*The Greek Way*	Norton
	Mythology	Norton
Hawthorne, Nathaniel	*Tanglewood Tales*	Dutton
	The Wonder Book	Dutton
	The Wonder Book	Houghton

Hosford, Dorothy	*Thunder of the Gods* (Norse)	Holt
	Songs of the Volsungs (Norse)	Holt
	By His Own Might (Beowulf)	Holt
Hutchinson, W. M. L.	*The Golden Porch*	Longmans
	Orpheus with His Lute	Longmans
Kingsley, Charles	*The Heroes*	Macmillan
Koht, Halodan	*The Old Norse Sagas*	American Scandinavian Foundation
Lang, Andrew	*Custom and Myth*	Longmans, London
Lanier, Sidney	*King Arthur and His Knights of the Round Table*	Grosset
Lowry, Janette	*In the Morning of the World—Some of the Greek Myths Retold*	Harper
Lum, Peter	*The Stars in Our Heavens —Myths and Fables*	Pantheon
Mabie, Hamilton W.	*Myths Every Child Should Know*	Garden City
MacLeod, Mary	*The Book of King Arthur and His Noble Knights*	World
Malcolmson, Anne (ill. Virginia Lee Burton)	*The Song of Robin Hood*	Houghton
Malory, Sir Thomas	*Morte d'Arthur*	Dutton
McSpadden, J. Walker	*Robin Hood*	World
Mukerji, Dhan Gopal	*Rama, the Hero of India*	Dutton
Norton, André	*Huon of the Horn* (part of Charlemagne Saga)	Harcourt
Oman, Carola	*Robin Hood*	Dutton
Pyle, Howard	*Merry Adventures of Robin Hood*	Scribner
	Merry Adventures of Robin Hood	Grosset
	Story of King Arthur and His Knights	Scribner
	Story of the Champions of the Round Table	Scribner

	Story of Sir Launcelot	Scribner
	Story of the Grail and the Passing of Arthur	Scribner
Schwab, Gustav	*Gods and Heroes*	Pantheon
Seeger, Elizabeth	*Five Brothers: The Story of the Mahabharata* (India)	Day
Sellew, Catherine F.	*Adventures with the Gods* (Greek)	Little
	Adventures with the Heroes (Norse)	Little
	Adventures with the Giants (Norse)	Little
Seredy, Kate	*The White Stag* (Hungary)	Viking
Sewell, Helen	*Book of Myths*	Macmillan
Sherwood, Merriam (tr.)	*El Cid Campeador, The Tale of The Warrior Lord; El Cantor del mio Cid*	Longmans
Stone, Eugenia	*Page Boy for King Arthur*	Follett
	Squire for King Arthur	Follett
	Robin Hood's Arrow	Follett
Watson, J. W. (ill., The Provensens)	*The Iliad and the Odyssey*	S. and S.

FABLES

Aesop	*Twelve Fables of Aesop*	Museum of Modern Art
	Aesop for Children	Rand McNally
Aesop—Artzybasheff (ill.)	*Aesop's Fables*	Viking
—Jacobs, Joseph	*The Fables of Aesop*	Macmillan
—Kredel, Fritz (ill.)	*Aesop's Fables*	Grosset
—Rackham, Arthur (ill.)	*Aesop's Fables*	Heritage Press
—Stone, Elizabeth	*Aesop's Fables*	Garden City
—Townsend, G. T., and Thomas James (tr.)	*Aesop's Fables*	Lippincott

Bulfinch, Thomas	*The Age of Fable*	Dutton
La Fontaine (Margaret Wise Brown, tr.)	*Fables of La Fontaine*	Harper
Norton, Andre	*Rogue Reynard*	Houghton
Ruskin, John	*King of the Golden River*	Macmillan
Scudder, Horace	*Book of Fables and Folk Stories*	Houghton

FOLK TALES AND FAIRY TALES

GENERAL COLLECTIONS

Abell, Elizabeth	*First Book of Fairy Tales*	Watts
Carey, M. C.	*Fairy Tales of Long Ago*	Dutton
Green, Roger L.	*Modern Fairy Tales*	Dutton
Mabie, Hamilton M.	*Folk Stories Every Child Should Know*	Houghton
Rhys, Ernest	*Fairy Gold*	Dutton
Scudder, Horace	*Book of Fables and Folk Stories*	Houghton
Sumner, William Graham	*Importance of Usages, Manners, Customs, Mores and Morals*	Ginn

UNITED STATES OF AMERICA

Ball, Zachary	*Young Mike Fink*	Holiday
Blair, Walter C.	*Tall Tale America*	Coward
	Davy Crockett: Frontier Hero	Coward
Bloch, Marie H.	*Big Steve: The Double Quick Tunnelman*	Coward
Bontemps, Arno, and Jack Conroy	*Sam Patch, the High, Wide and Handsome Jumper*	Houghton
	Slappy Hooper, the Wonderful Sign Painter	Houghton
Botkin, Benjamin Albert	*Treasury of American Folklore*	Crown
	New York City Folklore	Random
	Folk-Say, A Regional Miscellany	U. of Okla.

	Sidewalks of America—Folklore, legends, sagas, traditions, customs, songs, stories, and sayings of city folk	Bobbs
	A Treasury of Mississippi River Folk Lore—stories, ballads, traditions of Yankee people	Crown
	A Treasury of Railroad Folklore	Crown
	A Treasury of Southern Folklore—stories, ballads, traditions	Crown
Bowman, James C.	*Pecos Bill*	Albert Whitman
	Mike Fink	Little Brown
	John Henry, the Rambling Black Ulysses	Albert Whitman
Carmer, Carl	*America Sings*	Knopf
Chase, Richard	*Grandfather Tales*	Houghton
	Jack Tales	Houghton
	Jack and Three Sillies	Houghton
	Wicked John and the Devil	Houghton
Cober, Mary E.	*The Remarkable History of Tony Beaver*	McKay
Cothran, Jean	*With a Wig and a Wag*	McKay
Credle, Ellis	*Tall Tales from the High Hills*	Nelson
Davidson, L. J., and Blake,	*Rocky Mountain Tales*	U. of Okla.
Davis, A. K. (ed.)	*Traditional Ballads of Virginia*	Harvard U.P.
Dobie, J. F.	*Coronado's Children: Tales of Lost Mines and Buried Treasure of the Southwest*	Grosset
Dorson, R. M.	*Jonathan Draws the Long Bow: New England Popular Tales and Legends*	Harvard U.P.
Felton, Harold	*Legends of Paul Bunyan*	Knopf
	Pecos Bill: Texas Cowpuncher	Knopf

	John Henry and His Hammer	Knopf
	Bowleg Bill, Seagoing Cowpuncher	Prentice-Hall
Field, Rachel	*American Folk and Fairy Tales*	Scribner
Gorham, Michael	*The Real Book of Tall Tales*	Garden City
Harris, Joel Chandler	*Complete Tales of Uncle Remus*	Houghton
	Uncle Remus, His Songs and His Sayings	Appleton
Irving, Washington	*The Bold Dragoon and Other Ghostly Yarns*	Knopf
	Rip Van Winkle and the Legend of Sleepy Hollow	Macmillan
Jagendorf, M.	*American Folk Stories to Read and Tell*	Vanguard
	Marvelous Adventures of Johnny Darling	Vanguard
	New England Bean Pot	Vanguard
	Sand in the Bag, Folk Stories of Ohio, Indiana and Illinois	Vanguard
	Upstate, Downstate, Folk Stories of the Middle Atlantic States	Vanguard
	The Merry Men of Gotham, New York	Vanguard
Jones, Louis C.	*Spooks of the Valley,* Stories of Hudson River Valley	Houghton
Justus, May	*Peddler's Pack,* Stories of southern mountains	Holt
Leach, Maria	*Rainbow Book of American Folk Tales and Legends*	World
Le Sueur, Meridel	*Little Brother of the Wilderness* (Johnny Appleseed)	Knopf
	Chanticleer of Wilderness Road (Davy Crockett)	Knopf

Lomax, John A.	*Adventures of a Ballad Hunter*	Macmillan
McCormick, Dell	*Paul Bunyan Swings His Axe*	Caxton
	Tall Timber Tales	Caxton
Malcolmson, Anne, and Dell McCormick	*Yankee Doodle's Cousins*	Houghton
	Mr. Stormalong	Houghton
Meine, F. G. (ed.)	*Tall Tales of the Southwest: An Anthology of Southern and Southwestern humor*	Knopf
Miller, Olive B.	*Heroes, Outlaws and Funny Fellows*	Doubleday
Peck, Leigh	*Don Coyote*	Houghton
	Pecos Bill and Lightning	Houghton
Petersham, Maud and Miska	*The Rooster Crows: American Rhymes and Jingles*	Macmillan
Rounds, Glen	*Ol' Paul the Mighty Logger*	Holiday
Shapiro, Irwin	*Casey Jones and Locomotive No. 638*	Messner
	How Old Stormalong Captured the Mocha Dick	Messner
	Joe Magerac and His Citizenship Papers	Messner
	Steamboat Bill and the Captain's Top Hat	Messner
	Yankee Thunder: Legendary Life of Davy Crockett	Messner
Shephard, Esther (ill., Rockwell Kent)	*Paul Bunyan*	Harcourt
Shippen, Katherine	*Big Mose*	Harper
Skinner, C. M.	*Myths and Legends of Our Own Country*	Lippincott
Steele, William O.	*Daniel Boone's Echo*	Harcourt
	Davy Crockett's Earthquake	Harcourt
Suddeth, R. E., and C. G. Moremus	*Tales of the Western World*	Steck

Swayne, Sam and Zoa	*Great Grandfather in the Honey Tree*	Viking
Turney, Ida V.	*Paul Bunyan the Work Giant*	Binford & Morse
Wadsworth, Wallace	*Paul Bunyan and His Great Blue Ox*	Doubleday
White, E. B. and K. S. A.	*Subtreasury of American Humor*	Modern Library
Withers, Carl	*Rocket in My Pocket: Rhymes and Chants of Young Americans*	Holt

NORTH AMERICAN INDIAN

Beck, Ethel F.	*Lummi Indian How Stories*	Caxton
Bowman, James C.	*Winabojo*	Albert Whitman
Buckley, Elsie F.	*Children of the Dawn*	Stokes
Cushing, Frank	*Zuni Folk Tales*	Knopf
de Angelo, James	*Indian Tales*	A. A. Wyn
De Huff, Elizabeth Wills	*Tay Tay's Tales*	Harcourt
Fisher, Anne B.	*Stories California Indians Told*	Parnassus
Gale, Albert	*Songs and Stories of the American Indians*	Neil Kjos
Grinnell, G. B.	*Blackfoot Lodge Tales*	Scribner
	Pawnee Hero Tales	Scribner
Hazeltine, Alice I.	*Red Man, White Man*	Lothrop
Hogner, Dorothy C.	*Navajo Winter Nights*	Nelson
Linderman, Frank B.	*Indian Why Stories*	Cadmus
Lyback, J. R. M.	*Indian Legends*	Lyons
Martin, Fran	*Nine Tales of Coyote*	Harper
	Nine Tales of Raven	Harper
Marriott, Alice	*Winter Telling Tales*	Crowell
Mason, Bernard	*Dances and Stories of the American Indian*	A. S. Barnes
Palmer, William R.	*Why the North Star Stands Still and Other Indian Legends*	Prentice-Hall
Penny, Grace J.	*Tales of the Cheyennes*	Houghton
Running, Corinne	*When Coyote Walked the Earth*	Holt

Wilson, Gilbert L.	*Myths of the Red Children*	Ginn

CANADA

Carlson, Natalie Savage	*The Talking Cat and Other Stories of French Canada*	Harper
	Sashes Red and Blue, 9 New French Canadian Tales	Harper
Gilham, Charles E.	*Beyond the Clapping Mountains* (Indian Tales)	Macmillan
Hooke, Hilda Mary	*Thunder in the Mountains* (Indian Tales)	Macmillan
Macmillan, Cyrus	*Glooskapo's Country* (Indian Tales)	Oxford U.P.

EUROPE

Albania

Wheeler, Post	*Albanian Wonder Tales*	Doubleday

Czechoslovakia

Fillmore, Parker	*Czechoslovak Fairy Tales*	Harcourt

Finland

Bowman, James C.	*Tales from a Finnish Tupa*	Albert Whitman
Deutsch, Babette	*Heroes of the Kalevala*	Messner
Fillmore, Parker	*Mighty Mikko*	Harcourt

France

Baldwin, James	*Song of Roland*	Scribner
Brown, Marcia, (ill.)	*Puss in Boots*	Scribner
Kastimer, Erich (tr. Winston)	*Puss in Boots*	Messner
Norton, Andre	*Rogue Reynard*	Houghton
Perrault, Charles	*All the French Fairy Tales Retold by Louis Untermeyer*	Didier
Perrault, Charles, and Countess D'Aulnoy	*Fairy Tales*	Dutton

Picard, Barbara L.	*French Legends, Tales and Fairy Stories*	Oxford U.P.
Pourat, A.	*A Treasury of French Tales*	Houghton
Todd, Mary Fidelis	*The Juggler of Notre Dame*	Whittlesey

Germany

Benary-Isbert, Margo	*The Wicked Enchantment*	Harcourt
Chapin, Anna Alice	*Story of the Rhinegold*	Lippincott
Cooke, David	*Nutcracker of Nuremberg*	Winston
Grimm, Brothers	*Household Tales*	Macmillan
	Grimm's Fairy Tales (ill., Jean O'Neill)	World
	Grimm's Fairy Tales (ill., Fritz Kredel)	Grosset
	Tales from Grimm (ill., Wanda Gag)	Coward
	More Tales from Grimm (ill., Wanda Gág)	Coward
	Grimm's Fairy Tales (ill., Charles Folkard)	Dutton
Henderson, Gertrude	*Ring of the Nibelung*	Knopf
Jagendorf, M.	*Tyll Eulenspiegel's Merry Pranks*	Vanguard
Kastner, Erich (tr. Winston)	*Baron Münchausen*	Messner
	Till Eulenspiegel, the Clown	Messner

Great Britain

England

Baring-Gould, S.	*Old English Fairy Tales*	A. L. Burt
Brooke, Leslie	*Golden Goose Book*, Vols. I, II, III, IV	Warne
Farjeon, Eleanor	*Tales of Chaucer—* the Canterbury Tales done in prose	Branford, London
Lang, Andrew	*Fairy Tale Books* (Blue, Green, Red, etc.)	Longmans
Jacobs, Joseph	*English Fairy Tales*	Putnam
	More English Fairy Tales	Putnam
Reeves, James	*English Fables and Fairy Stories*	Oxford U.P.

| Steele, Flora A. | *English Fairy Tales Retold* | Macmillan |
| Tregarthen, Enys | *Piskey Folk, A Book of Cornish Legends* | Day |

Channel Islands

| Campbell, Alfred S. | *The Wizard and His Magic Powder* | Knopf |

Ireland

Bennett, Richard	*Little Dermot and the Thirsty Stones and Other Irish Folk Tales*	Coward
Buck, Alan	*The Harper's Daughter*	Oxford U.P.
Campbell, Alice	*Tales My Father Told*	Whittlesey
Colum, Padraic	*The Big Tree of Bunlahy*	Macmillan
	The Boy Who Knew What the Birds Said	Macmillan
	The Girl Who Sat by the Ashes (another Cinderella)	Macmillan
Cormack, M. Grant	*Animal Tales from Ireland*	Day
Curtin, Jeremiah	*Myths and Folklore of Ireland*	Little
Dunbar, Aldis	*The Sons O' Cormac an' Tales of Other Men's Sons*	Dutton
Jacobs, Joseph	*Celtic Fairy Tales*	Putnam
	More Celtic Fairy Tales	Putnam
MacMahon, Bryan	*Jack O'Moora and the King of Ireland's Son*	Dutton
Mac Manus, Seumas	*The Bold Heroes of Hungry Hill* (12 Irish folk and fairy tales)	Farrar & Straus
	Donegal Fairy Stories	Doubleday
	Donegal Wonder Book	Lippincott
	In Chimney Corners	Doubleday
	Heavy Hangs the Golden Grain	Macmillan
Mason, Arthur	*Wee Men of Bally Wooden*	Viking
O'Faolain, Eileen	*Irish Sagas and Folk Tales*	Oxford U.P.
Stephens, James	*Irish Fairy Tales*	Modern Library

Yeats,
   William Butler
	*Irish Fairy and Folk
	   Tales*
		Modern Library

Young, Ella	*Wonder Smith and His Son*	Longmans
	The Tanglecoated Horse	Longmans
	The Unicorn and the Sil- ver Shoes	Longmans

Scotland

Grierson,
   Elizabeth W.
	*Tales of Scottish Keeps
	   and Castles*
		Macmillan

Wilkerson, Barbara	*Scottish Folk Tales and Legends*	Oxford U.P.
Jones, Gwyn	*Welsh Legends and Folk Tales*	Oxford U.P.

Greece

(see Myths and Epics)

Italy

Botsford,
   Florence N.
	*Picture Tales from the
	   Italian*
		Lippincott

Jagendorf, M.	*The Priceless Cat and
	   Other Italian Folk
	   Stories*
		Vanguard

Mincieli,
   Rose Laura
	Tales Merry and Wise
	   (from Adriatic coast of
	   Italy)
		Holt

Toor, Frances	*The Golden Carnation and Other Stories*	Lothrop

Netherlands

Hart, John	*Picture Tales from Holland*	Lippincott

Poland

Bernhard, J. B.	*9 Cry Baby Dolls*	Roy
Borski, L. M.	*Polish Folk Tales*	Sheed & Ward
	The Jolly Tailor	Longmans
	Gipsy and the Bear	Longmans

Roumania

Jagendorf, M.	*The Gypsies' Fiddle and Other Gypsy Tales*	Vanguard

Nandris, Mabel	*Folk Tales from Roumania*	Roy

Russia

Carpenter, Frances	*Tales of a Russian Grand-mother*	Doubleday
Carrick, Valery	*Picture Tales from the Russian*	Lippincott
	More Picture Tales from the Russian	Lippincott
Deutsch, Babette	*Tales of Faraway Folk*	Harper
	The Steel Flea	Harper
Downing, Charles	*Russian Tales and Legends*	Oxford U.P.
Gottschalk, Fruma	*The Runaway Soldier and Other Tales of Old Russia*	Knopf
Grishina, N.	*Peter Pea*	Lippincott
Houghton, L. S.	*The Russian Grand-mother's Wonder Tales*	Scribner
Papashvily, George and Helen	*Yes and No Stories*	Harper
Ransome, Arthur	*Old Peter's Russian Tales*	Nelson
Tolstoi, A-N.	*Russian Tales for Children*	Dutton
Wheeler, Post	*Russian Wonder Tales*	Appleton
Zeitlin, Ida	*Skaski, Tales and Legends of Old Russia*	Farrar & Rhinehart

Scandinavia; Norway, Sweden, Denmark

Asbjornsen, Peter C.	*Fairy Tales from the North*	A. L. Burt
Asbjornsen, Peter C., and Jorgen E. Moe	*East of the Sun and West of the Moon*	Macmillan
Dasent, George M. (tr.)	*East of the Sun and West of the Moon*	Macmillan
d'Aulaire, Edgar and Ingri (ed. and ill.)	*East of the Sun and West of the Moon*	Viking
Thorne-Thomsen, Gudrun (ed.)	*East of the Sun and West of the Moon*	Row

Andersen, Hans Christian

Virginia Lee Burton (ill.)	*The Emperor's New Clothes*	Houghton
G. D. Hauman (ill.)	*Fairy Tales and Stories* (Children's Classics)	Macmillan
Keigwin (tr.)	*The Ugly Duckling*	Macmillan
Paul Leyssac (tr.)	*It's Perfectly True*	Harcourt
E. Lucas (tr.)	*Andersen's Fairy Tales* (Children's Illustrated Classics)	Dutton
Jean O'Neill (ill.)	*Andersen's Fairy Tales* (Rainbow Classics)	World
Arthur Szyk (ill.)	*Andersen's Fairy Tales* (Illustrated Junior Library)	Grosset
Bay, J. Christian	*Danish Fairy and Folk Tales*	Harper
Braekstad, Hans L.	*Fairy Tales from the Swedish*	Lippincott
Hatch, Mary C.	*13 Danish Tales*	Harcourt
	More Danish Tales	Harcourt
Jones, Gwyn	*Scandinavian Legends and Folk Tales*	Oxford U.P.
Norman, Einar	*Fairy Tales from the North*	Knopf
Owen, Ruth Bryan	*Picture Tales from Scandinavia*	Lippincott
	Castles in the Silver Wood and Other Scandinavian Fairy Tales	Dodd
Sandys, E. V.	*Peer Gynt*	Crowell
Sperry, Margaret	*The Hen That Saved the World and Other Norwegian Folk Tales*	Day
Thorpe, Benjamin, and Thomas Keightley	*Tales on the North Wind* (Norse Collection)	Roy
Topelius	*Canute Whistlewinks*	Dutton
Undset, Sigrid	*True and Untrue and Other Norse Tales*	Knopf

Spain

Boggs, Ralph T.	*Three Golden Oranges*	Longmans
Davis, Robert	*Padre Porko*	Holiday
Eells, Elsie S.	*Tales of Enchantment from Spain*	Lippincott

Gunterman, Bertha	*Castles in Spain*	Longmans
Irving, Washington	*The Alhambra*	Macmillan
Kastner, Erik	*Don Quixote* (A Harle-quin Book)	Messner
Marks, John	*Spanish Fairy Tales*	Knopf
Sawyer, Ruth	*Picture Tales from Spain*	Lippincott

Switzerland

| Carpenter, Frances | *Tales of a Swiss Grand-mother* | Doubleday |
| Duvoisin, Roger A. | *Three Sneezes and Other Swiss Tales* | Knopf |

Yugoslavia

| Curcija-Prodanovic, Nada (compiler) | *Yugoslav Folk-Tales* | Oxford U.P. |

THE NEAR EAST

Arabia

Arabian Nights

Burton, Sir Richard	*Tales from the Arabian Nights*	Lothrop
Colum, Padraic (ill. Lynd Ward)	*The Arabian Nights*	Macmillan
Dixon, E.	*Fairy Tales from Arabian Nights*	Dutton
Goodenow, Earl (ill.)	*Arabian Nights*	Grosset
Houseman, Lawrence	*Stories from the Arabian Nights*	Doubleday
Lang, Andrew	*Arabian Nights' Enter-tainment*	Longmans
Soifer, Margaret, and Irwin Shapiro	*Tenggren's Golden Tales from the Arabian Nights*	S. and S.
Tietgen, Eunice	*The Romance of Antar*	Coward
Wiggin, Kate Douglas	*Arabian Nights: Their Best Known Tales*	Scribner

Persia

| Gibson, Katherine | *The Golden Bird and Other Stories* | Macmillan |
| Kelsey, Alice Geer | *Once the Mullah* | Longmans |

Turkey

Kelsey, Alice Geer	*Once the Hodja*	Longmans

THE FAR EAST

Australia

Ewers, John	*Written in Sand*	Dutton

Burma

Russell, Maurice	*Told to Burmese Children*	Roy

China

Carpenter, Frances	*Tales of a Chinese Grand-mother*	Doubleday
Chrisman, Arthur B.	*Shen of the Sea*	Dutton
	Treasures Long Hidden	Dutton
Lim, Sian-Tek	*Folk Tales from China*	Day
	More Folk Tales from China	Day
Metzger, Berta	*Picture Tales from the Chinese*	Lippincott
Ritchie, Alice	*The Treasure of Li Po*	Harcourt

India

Aspinwall, F.	*Jataka Tales out of Old India*	Putnam
Babbitt, Ellen C.	*Jataka Tales*	Appleton
	More Jataka Tales	Appleton
Gaer, Joseph	*The Fables of India*	Little
Inayat, Noir	*Twenty Jataka Tales*	McKay
Metzger, Berta	*Picture Tales from India*	Lippincott
Mukerji, Dhan Gopal-	*Hindu Fables for Little Children*	Dutton
Pyle, Katherine	*Fairy Tales from India*	Lippincott
Rouse, W. H. D.	*The Talking Thrush: Stories of Birds and Beasts Retold*	Dutton
Steel, Flora A.	*Tales of the Punjab*	Macmillan

Indonesia

Courlander, Harold, and Richard Kane	*Kantchil's Lime Pit*	Harcourt

Japan

Coatsworth, Elizabeth	*The Cat Who Went to Heaven*	Macmillan
Hearn, Lafcadio	*Japanese Fairy Tales*	Liveright
Kiyooka, Chiyone	*Picture Tales from the Japanese*	Lippincott
Uchida, Yoshiko	*The Dancing Kettle and Other Japanese Folk Tales*	Harcourt
	The Magic Listening Cap —More Folk Tales from Japan	Harcourt

Korea

Carpenter, Frances	*Tales of a Korean Grandmother*	Doubleday
Jewett, Eleanore M.	*Which was Witch?—Tales of ghosts and magic from Korea*	Viking

Philippines

Sechrist, Elizabeth	*Once in the First Time*	Macrae Smith

WEST INDIES

Haiti

Courlander, Harold	*Uncle Bongni of Haiti*	Morrow

Jamaica

Sherlock, Philip N.	*Anansi the Spider Man*	Crowell

AFRICA

Courlander, Harold	*Terrapin's Pot of Sense*	Holt
Courlander, Harold, and George Herzog	*The Cowtail Switch and Other West African Stories*	Holt
Courlander, Harold, and A. K. Prempeh	*The Hat-Shaking Dance and Other Tales from the Gold Coast*	Harcourt
Graham, Lorenz	*Tales of Momolu*	McKay
Jewett, Eleanore M.	*Egyptian Tales of Magic*	Little
Kalibala, E. B., and Mary Gould Davis	*Waikaima and the Clay Man*	Longmans

| Marais, Josef | *Koos the Hottentot* | Knopf |
| Smedley, Constance | *Tales from Timbuktu* | Harcourt |

MEXICO

Brewer, Anita	*The Boy Who Could Do Anything*—Mexican folk tales	Scott
Campbell, Camilla	*Star Mountain and Other Legends of Mexico*	McGraw
Martinez del Rio, Amelia	*The Sun, The Moon and a Rabbit*—Mexican Indian Tales	Sheed and Ward
Ross, Patricia F.	*In Mexico They Say*	Knopf
Storm, Dan	*Picture Tales from Mexico*	Lippincott
Toor, Frances	*A Treasury of Mexican Folkways*	Crown

SOUTH AMERICA

Eells, Elsie Spicer	*Fairy Tales from Brazil*	Dodd
Finger, Charles	*Tales from Silver Lands*	Doubleday
Henius, Frank	*Stories from the Americas*	Scribner
Hudson, W. H.	*Tales of the Gauchos*	Knopf
	Tales of the Pampas	Knopf
Levy, Harry	*The Bombero, Tales from Latin America*	Knopf
Lovelace, Delio	*The Golden Wedge, South American Indian Tales*	Crowell
Rhoads, Dorothy	*Bright Feather and Other Mayan Tales*	Doubleday

STORIES TO TELL YOUNG CHILDREN
(*Selected from modern writers*)

Adshead, Gladys	*Brownies—Hush!* — The brownies come to the shoemaker's help	Oxford U.P.
Bannerman, Helen	*Little Black Sambo*—Fantastic adventure of a boy and tiger!	Lippincott
Beatty, Hester	*The Little Wild Horse*— Peter tames a wild horse on a western ranch	Houghton

Bemelmans, Ludwig	*Hansi*—A small boy's adventures in the Austrian Tyrol	Viking
	(h) *Madeline*—Madeline has appendicitis, so in this school in Paris every girl wants it	S. and S.
Beskow, Elsa	*Pelle's New Suit* (from the Swedish)—The story of a suit from sheep's back to boy's back	Harper
Bill, Helen	*The Shoes Fit for a King*—A pair of hand-made shoes in a cobbler's shop decide that only the King is worthy of them and hurry off to the palace to see about it	Watts
Bishop, Claire Huchet	(h) *The Man Who Lost His Head*—He really did! But woke up	Viking
Bright, Robert	(h) *Georgie*—A friendly little ghost loses his home	Doubleday
	Georgie to the Rescue—Georgie's visit to the city	Doubleday
Brown, Margaret	*The Noisy Book*	Harper
	The Country Noisy Book	Harper
	The Indoor Noisy Book	Harper
	The Summer Noisy Book	Harper
	The Winter Noisy Book—Adventures of little dog Muffin and the sounds he hears	Harper
	The Noon Balloon—A balloon sailing over the countryside can tell from the sounds what goes on below	Harper
	The Little Brass Band—They came over the hill and made music	Harper

	Sneakers—Seven tales of a cat	Scott
	Willie's Adventures— Three funny stories of a small boy. Willie's walk to Grandmama is especially good for telling	Scott
	Two Little Trains—Two little trains go west	Scott
Brown, Palmer	*Cheerful*—A city church mouse sets forth to find the beautiful country for which his mother longs and finds at last he can be what his name is—Cheerful	Harper
Bryant, Sara Cone	(*h*) *Epanminondas and His Auntie*—Hilarious tale of a small boy who always did the wrong thing	Houghton
Burton, Virginia Lee	*Choo Choo* — Rollicking adventures of a locomotive	Houghton
	Mike Mulligan and His Steam Shovel — Mary Anne, the steam shovel, builds many things	Houghton
	The Little House—A big city grows up about the little house which is at last moved out to the country again	Houghton
Chalmers, Audrey	(*h*) *Hundreds and Hundreds of Pancakes*—Mrs. Fizzlewit feeds the zoo —a wonderful nonsense story	Viking
Cook, Bernadine	(*h*) *The Little Fish that Got Away*—The usual fish story in reverse, great fun, delightful repetition	Scott

	The Curious Little Kitten—The kitten sees a turtle for the first time. More delightful repetition	Scott
Credle, Ellis	*Down, Down the Mountain*—Hetty and Hank in their log cabin in the Blue Ridge mountains	Nelson
d'Aulaire, Edgar and Ingri	*Ola*—A small boy's adventures in Norway	Doubleday
	Leif the Lucky—Thrilling story of the Viking who first discovered America	Doubleday
DuBois, William Pene	(h) *Three Policemen*—International complications in wonderful non-season	Viking
Duvoisin, Roger	*The House of Four Seasons*—Four members of the family each paint one side of the house a different color, but each is right for a different season.	Lothrop
	(h) *Petunia*	Knopf
	(h) *Petunia and the Song*	Knopf
	(h) *Petunia Takes a Trip*—Hilarious adventures of a wonderfully stupid duck	Knopf
Elkin, Benjamin	(h) *The Loudest Noise in the World*—Builds to an unexpected quiet surprise at the end	Viking
	(h) *Six Foolish Fishermen*—Six foolish brothers count to see that all are there and each counts the others and gets only 5! Great fun in this re-telling of old folk tale	Children's Press
Ets, Marie Hall	(h) *Mr. Penny*	Viking
	Mr. Penny's Race Horse—Hilarious adventures of Mr. Penny and his animals	Viking

Fischer, Hans	*The Good For Nothings*	Harcourt
	The Traveling Musicians —Delightful versions of these Grimm folk tales	Harcourt
Flack, Marjorie	*Ask Mr. Bear*—Danny finds a birthday present for his mother	Macmillan
	Angus and the Ducks— Angus, a scottie, explores the other side of the hedge	Doubleday
	Angus Lost and *Angus and the Cat* are other Angus stories	Doubleday
	The Story about Ping—A little duck's night of adventure on the Yangtze river	Viking
Flora, James	(h) *The Day the Cow Sneezed*—Hilarious tall tale of cumulative adventure, the sneeze involving a mouse, a cat, a goat, a pig, a mailman and dozens of other things	Harcourt
Gág, Wanda	*Millions of Cats*	Coward
	Gone is Gone	Coward
	The Funny Thing	Coward
	Nothing at All—Animal tales with true folk flavor, and the kind of repetition little children love	Coward
Garrett, Helen	(h) *Angelo the Naughty One*—Children find the mischievous adventures of this small Mexican boy irresistible	Viking
Gramatky, Hardie	(h) *Little Toot*—Adventures of a tugboat in New York Harbor	Putnam
Hader, Berta and Elmer	*The Big Snow*—The animals find food in a severe winter	Macmillan

	Home on the Range—A small boy's exciting summer on a ranch	Macmillan
	The Mighty Hunter—A little Indian boy goes hunting	Macmillan
	Pancho—A little Mexican boy captures a bull	Macmillan
Hall, Rosalys	(h) *The Tailor's Trick*—The tailor outwits his neighbors in this humorous tale with genuine folk flavor	Lippincott
Handforth, Thomas	*Mei Li*—A little Chinese girl runs away to see the New Year Fair	Doubleday
Heyward, Dubose	*The Country Bunny and the Little Gold Shoes*—Cottontail realizes her great ambition to be an Easter Bunny	Houghton
Ivens, Dorothy	*The Long Hike*—Charming episodic adventuring on their own of two children and how they eat up most of their picnic on the way	Viking
Jupo, Frank	(h) *Hinkldinkl*—Some wise men try to be fools. Has true folk quality	Macmillan
Kahl, Virginia	(h) *The Duchess Bakes a Cake*—Amusing tale of a cake that rises and rises with the Duchess on top	Scribner
	Maxie—A small dachshund achieves his ambition to be successful. See Miss Kahl's other wonderful humorous tales, *The Habits of Rabbits, Away Went Wolfgang*	Scribner
Kingman, Lee	*Peter's Long Walk*—A little boy goes in search	Doubleday

	of playmates. Charming episodic story for the very young	
Koch, Dorothy	*Gone is My Goose*—A little girl's adventures in the barnyard, hunting for her goose. Delightful for the very young	Holiday
Krasilovsky, Phyllis	(h) *The Cow Who Fell in the Canal*—Hilarious adventures of the cow who saw the city, the cheese market and captured her own hat told with gay folk-tale quality	Doubleday
	The Man Who Didn't Wash His Dishes—A comic tale of a lazy man who solves his problem in a delightful way	Doubleday
Krum, Charlotte	*The Four Riders*—Charming repetitive story with folk quality of how all four animals finally ride on the old horse's back	Follett
Lathrop, Dorothy	*Who Goes There?*—A picnic for the little animals of the wood	Macmillan
Leaf, Munro, and Robert Lawson	(h) *The Cock and the Mouse and the Little Red Hen*—A cumulative tale with folk quality, a great favorite	Macrae Smith
LeWitt, Jan	(h) *The Vegetabull*—Wonderful nonsense tale	Harcourt
MacDonald	*Whistle for the Train*—The little train whistles everything from children to a bumblebee out of its way	Doubleday

Mammen, Edward S.	(h) *The Buttons Go Walking*—Lively story of a family who have fun together	Harper
Marino, Dorothy	*Song of the Pine Tree Forest*—Three children living beside a mountain hear a lovely tune coming from the forest	Lippincott
Martin, Dahris	*Little Lamb*—A little lamb finds out where his new coat is coming from	Harper
McCloskey, Robert	*Make Way for Ducklings*—A Boston policeman near the Commons stops all traffic while a mother duck gets her family across the street	Viking
	Blueberries for Sal—Sal and her mother go blueberrying and meet a mother bear and her cub who are also blueberrying	Viking
	One Morning in Maine—Family adventures on the morning Sal loses her first tooth	Viking
McGinley, Phyllis	(h) *The Horse Who Lived Upstairs*—Joey, a discontented city horse longs for the country	Lippincott
Norman, Charles	(h) *Mr. Upstairs, Mr. Downstairs*—Wonderful nonsense — fun with words	Harper
Parrish, Helen Rand	*At the Palace Gates*—A Peruvian Indian boy sets himself up as a bootblack in front of the President's palace in Lima	Viking
Paull, Grace	*Pancakes for Breakfast*—Gay story of children	Doubleday

	going to the country at sugaring-off time and making the maple syrup for their pancakes for breakfast	
Payne, Emmy	(h) *Katy No-Pocket*—A pocketless kangaroo, in search of a pocket for her son finds a shoe-maker's apron with a dozen pockets on it and out-pockets the other kangaroos	Houghton
Petersham, Maud and Miska	*Off to Bed*—Seven stories for little wide-awakers	Macmillan
Politi, Leo	*The Butterflies Come*— The Monarch butter-flies' annual migration to Monterey	Scribner
	Song of the Swallows— Juan rings the Mission bells to welcome the swallows back again to San Juan Capistrano	Scribner
Potter, Beatrix	*The Tale of Peter Rabbit* —This beloved tale of adventuresome Peter in Mr. McGregor's garden is a classic story of a small rabbit. So, too, are	Warne
	The Tale of Benjamin Bunny	Warne
	The Tale of Jemima Pud-dle Duck	Warne
	The Tale of Squirrel Nut-kin	Warne
	The Tale of Mrs. Tiggy-winkle	Warne
Prokofieff, Sergei	*Peter and the Wolf*— Charming retelling of the old folk tale with some of Prokofieff's mu-sic giving the theme which belongs to each character	Knopf

Rey, H. A.   *(h) Curious George*   Houghton
                      Curious George Gets a   Houghton
                          Medal—The adventures
                          of a small curious mon-
                          key delight all children

Sawyer, Ruth   *(h) Journey Cake, Ho!*—   Viking
                          Rollicking rhythmic ver-
                          sion of small Johnny
                          and his journey cake
                          which came to be
                          called Johnny cake

Schlein, Miriam   *Big Talk*—An understand-   Scott
                          ing mother kangaroo
                          believes in her boastful
                          baby and encourages
                          him to believe he can
                          do big things. Excellent
                          for children who like to
                          tell tall tales about
                          themselves

Seeger, Ruth   *Let's Build a Railroad*—   Dutton
                          Delightful use of music
                          and story

Seuss, Dr.   *(h) The 500 Hats of Bar-*   Vanguard
                          tholomew   Cubbins—
                          Every time Bartholo-
                          mew takes off his hat to
                          the King another is
                          there in its place

                      (h) And To Think that I   Random
                          Saw It on Mulberry
                          Street—A small boy
                          builds up a marvelous
                          tale of all that he saw
                          coming home from
                          school, only to have the
                          whole marvelous tale
                          collapse when he runs
                          up the steps to meet his
                          father

                      (h) Horton Hatches the   Random
                          Egg—An elephant sits
                          on an egg, willing to do
                          her best

	(These are only three of Dr. Seuss' 14 riotously funny stories)	
Skaar, Grace	*The Little Red House*—A reassuring family story for very young children in cumulative pattern	Scott
Stone, Amy	*P-Penny and His Little Red Cart*—Everyday adventure which little children love	Hale
Tresselt, Alvin S.	*Rain Drop Splash* — Charming simple story of water cycle, from rain to the sky and back again. Children love the rhythmic pattern and interesting use of words	Lothrop
Ward, Nanda	*High Flying Hat*—Whoever heard of a garden on a hat brim? Here it is with real adventures	Farrar, Straus
Watson, Nancy D.	*Annie's Spending Spree*—Annie spends a whole dollar in a country store on the day before her birthday party	Viking
Weil, Lisl	*Jacoble Tells the Truth*—A small boy with a large imagination learns to bring his exaggerated tale down to what he really saw	Houghton
Wiese, Kurt	*The Cunning Turtle*—How the turtle comes to have a cracked back	Viking
Will and Nicolas	*Finders Keepers*—Two dogs claim the same bone in this amusing tale	Harcourt
Worm, Piet	*Three Little Horses*—A delightful tale from Holland	Random

Yashima, Taro	*Crow Boy*—A shy little boy is finally encouraged by a new teacher in this sensitive Japanese school story. It will help many to understand that some slow learners are made not born	Viking
Young, Evelyn	*Wu and Lu and Li*—Grandmother comes to visit the family and gives each child a penny. They go to the village to spend it. The family happens to be Chinese, but they could be a family anywhere	Oxford U. P.
Zimnik, Reiner	*The Proud Circus Horse*—The proud beautiful horse wanders away from the circus to be free, but learns there is no such thing as a free life without work and without friends	Pantheon

STORIES TO TELL TO SLIGHTLY OLDER CHILDREN

(Selected from modern writers)

Atwater, Richard and Florence	*Mr. Popper's Penguins*—Amusing story of a family of penguins who came to live with a house painter's family	Little
Averill, Esther	*The Cat Club*—This is the first of a series of ten stories of the resourceful cat, Jenny Linsky and all her adventures fitting into this world	Harper

Barksdale, Lena	*The First Thanksgiving*— Grandmother tells the story of the first Thanksgiving as she remembers how the Indians came, to grandchildren returning to visit her	Knopf
Batchelor, Julie F.	*A Cap for Mul Chaud*— An East Indian boy's adventures in getting the red cap he so desires	Harcourt
	Tim and the Purple Whistle—Delightful story of young Tim who travels as a peddler assistant in Connecticut in 1790. His father gave him a purple whistle to help him to be brave, and the summer's adventures really tested him	Harcourt
Barrie, Sir James	*Peter Pan*—A beloved modern fairy tale in which Peter Pan takes three children to the Never Never Land	Scribner
Bianco, Margery	*The Velveteen Rabbit*— The wish of this stuffed rabbit to be real, comes true	Doubleday
Bigham, Madge A.	*Sonny Elephant*—A little boy of India and his pet, "the fattest baby elephant you ever saw"	Little
Bontemps, Arna	*The Fast Sooner Hound* —A long-legged, flopeared hound proves he would sooner run than eat when he outruns the Cannon Ball Express	Houghton
Brock, Emma C.	*Drusilla*—A corn husk doll travels West in a covered wagon	Macmillan

Bronson, Wilfrid	*Pinto's Journey*—A Pueblo Indian boy goes alone to the mountains to get turquoise for his grandfather in time of need	Messner
Brown, Marcia	*Cinderella*	Scribner
	Dick Whittington and His Cat	Scribner
	The Flying Carpet	Scribner
	Puss in Boots	Scribner
	The Steadfast Tin Soldier	Scribner
	Stone Soup — Marcia Brown, a distinguished artist illustrates and tells each of these traditional tales with characteristic flavor	Scribner
Bryan, C., and M. Madden	*Pito's House*—A delightful Mexican version of the old crowded house story	Macmillan
Buff, Mary and Conrad	*The Apple and the Arrow* —Story of William Tell	Houghton
	Kobi: A Boy of Switzerland—Everyday life in Swiss mountain country	Viking
	Peter Pinto—Peter's dream of owning a horse of his own comes true at his uncle's ranch in Utah	Viking
Bulla, Clyde	*Riding the Pony Express*	Crowell
	Squanto, Friend of the White Man	Crowell
	John Billington, Friend of the White Man	Crowell
	The Sword in the Tree (King Arthur's sword)	Crowell
	Eagle Feather (Modern Indian story)	Crowell
	A Ranch for Danny	Crowell
	The Secret Valley	Crowell
	Star of Wildhorse Canyon	Crowell
	Surprise for a Cowboy	Crowell

	Clyde Bulla is a born storyteller. Here are wonderful stories to tell, full of the action this age group so enjoys, whether the story comes out of history as do the first four above, or out of modern western ranch life as do the later ones	
	Vanilla Village — Little brother solves the mystery of who is stealing the vanilla beans in a Mexican village	Farrar & Straus
Clark, Ann Nolan	*In My Mother's House*— Memorize or read aloud this beautiful poetic story of how Tesuque Indians live	Viking
	Magic Money—A small Costa Rican boy finds a way to earn money to replace grandfather's cow	Viking
Clark, Margery	*The Poppy Seed Cakes*— Andrewshek's and Erminka's adventures	Doubleday
Coatsworth, Elizabeth	*Dancing Tom*—A pioneer family and their dancing pig	Macmillan
	First Adventure (1600-1680)—A little Pilgrim boy gets lost and is rescued by Indians	Macmillan
	The Wishing Pear (1650-1700)—Lydia Ten Eyck helps Peter Stuyvesant in New Amsterdam	Macmillan
	Boston Bells (1700-1750) —John Singleton Copley wins his right to be an artist	Macmillan

	Aunt Flora (1750-1800)— Nepsie has adventures with Flora MacDonald, her aunt from Scotland, friend of Bonnie Prince Charlie	Macmillan
	Old Whirlwind (1800-1850)—Davy Crockett's trip East as a young boy	Macmillan
	The Peddler's Cart— George and his father travel and trade on a summer's trip	Macmillan
	Away Goes Sally—Sally's family moves to Maine, house and all	Macmillan
Coblentz, Catherine C.	*Martin and Abraham Lincoln*—A little shoemaker's son takes a nail from Lincoln's shoe	Children's Press
Colum, Padraic	*The Boy Who Knew What the Birds Said*— Stories the birds told	Macmillan
	The Girl Who Sat by the Ashes—Another version of the Cinderella story beautifully told	Macmillan
Creekmore, Raymond	*Ali's Elephant*—A boy trains a baby elephant in India	Macmillan
	Fujio—A little Japanese boy fulfills his ambitions to climb the great Mount Fuji	Macmillan
	Little Fu—A Chinese boy has an exciting adventure on the river	Macmillan
	Lokoshi—An Eskimo boy goes on his first seal hunt	Macmillan
Dalgliesh, Alice	*The Columbus Story*— Columbus really comes alive	Scribner
	The Fourth of July Story	Scribner

	The Thanksgiving Story— Authentic stories of the origins of these holidays which will help children understand their significance	Scribner
	Ride on the Wind—Exciting story of Lindbergh's flight to Paris	Scribner
	The Courage of Sarah Noble—True story of an 8-year old girl in pioneer Connecticut	Scribner
Daugherty, James	*Andy and the Lion* —Based on the old fable of Androcles and the Lion. A modern boy meets a lion and then?!!	Viking
Davis, Norman	*Picken's Great Adventure* —Small boy's trip down the river in Gambia, the African jungle	Oxford U.P.
DeAngeli, Marguerite	*Bright April* — Brownie Scout adventure	Doubleday
	Thee Hannah—A spirited little Quaker girl has adventures in old Philadelphia	Doubleday
	Yonie Wondernose—Yonie takes care of the farm, even with a fire while his father is away	Doubleday
Dobbs, Rose	*The Discontented Village* —An old folk tale of how the village learns to overcome its troubles and be happy	Coward
	No Room—Another good version of the folk tale of the peasant's crowded room	Coward
Embry, Margaret	*The Blue Nosed Witch*— Delightful imaginative tale of a witch who joins a trick or treat ad-	Holiday

	venture on earth on Halloween	
Estes, Eleanor	*The Hundred Dresses*—Her class at school come to appreciate the poor little girl with the odd Polish name who really could draw	Harcourt
Gannett, Ruth Stiles	*My Father's Dragon*—Wonderful imaginative journey of a small boy	Random
Godden, Rumer	*Impunity Jane*—A four-inch doll in a boy's pocket, a very special story	Viking
	The Mouse Wife—Hauntingly beautiful story of a mouse's friendship with a caged dove	Viking
	Mouse House—A real mouse evicts toy mice from their tiny toy home and makes a house for herself. The sensitivity and perceptiveness of all Rumer Godden's writing gives every story a special quality for children of all ages	Viking
Hader, Berta and Elmer	*Little Appaloosa*—Lively tale of a Western ranch horse	Macmillan
	Spunky—The many adventures of a Shetland pony	Macmillan
Haywood, Caroline B.	*B is for Betsy*—The first of several books about life in school which delight children who like to hear about children like themselves	Harcourt
	Eddie—The first of a group of books about a	Morrow

	typical American small boy with curiosity and a desire for adventure All of them are hilariously funny whether Eddie is getting out the vote for his father or traveling to Texas with Gardenia, a goat	
Howard, Alice W.	*Sokar and the Crocodile* —a boy's adventure in ancient Egypt	Macmillan
Hunt, Mabel Leigh	*Benjie's Hat*—A little boy and his hand-me-down hat in a thrifty Quaker family	Lippincott
	Little Girl with Seven Names—A little Quaker girl with seven names gives two of them away	Lippincott
Jaeger, Karl	*The Bull that was Terrifico*—Hilarious tale of the role of a docile but ferocious bull in the destinies of certain persons in a little Spanish village	Day
Johnson, Elizabeth	*The Little Knight*—A modern fairy tale of a very up-to-date princess	Little
King, Robin	*Burrito*—Delightful story of a special little burro and his own Mexican family	Dutton
Kipling, Rudyard	*Just So Stories*—All of these are favorites. Because of Kipling's special use of words, some people do better to read these aloud. Special favorites are "How the Elephant got his Trunk, How the Camel got his Hump, How the	Doubleday

	Leopard got his Spots," "Sing-Song of Old Man Kangaroo"	
Lathrop, Dorothy	*The Colt from Moon Mountain*—A delightful story based on the legend of the unicorn	Macmillan
Lattimore, Eleanor F.	*Little Pear*—Adventures of a small boy in pre-war China told by one who grew up in China	Harcourt
	Little Pear and His Friends, Peach Blossom and others are further charming tales of the China that Miss Lattimore knows so well. Her more recent books are about American children as well as more Chinese children whose everyday adventures she makes interesting to all children in books such as *Davy of the Everglades, Jeremy's Isle, Deborah's White Winter*	Harcourt

Morrow |
Lawson, Robert	*Rabbit Hill*—Small creatures of the Connecticut countryside are all excited when they learn new folks are coming to the house so long empty	Viking
	Ben and Me—Perhaps no one knew Benjamin Franklin so well as the mouse who lived in his fur hat	Little
	I Discover Columbus—This parrot tells Columbus' story	Little
	Mr. Revere and I—Paul Revere's horse tells the	Little

	Revere story with a slightly different understanding	
LeGrand, H.	*Cap'n Dow and the Hole in the Doughnut*—An hilarious tale of why we have holes in doughnuts that comes down to us from Maine	Abingdon
	Cats for Kansas—How Trader Gabe Slade collected a crate of cats to take back to Kansas	Abingdon
	Tom Benn and Black Beard the Pirate — Amazing inside story of how Black Beard was captured	Abingdon
	When the Mississippi was Wild—How Mike Fink tied up the tail of Old Al, the alligator, so settlers could cross the river	Abingdon
	Why Cowboys Sing in Texas—How Slim Jim Bean, the most silent of all cowboys began to sing and so changed things for all Texas cowboys. All these LeGrand tall tales are wonderful to tell	Abingdon
Liu, Beatrice	*Little Wu and the Watermelons*—Story of how Little Wu earned money to buy earrings for his beautiful mother and also land for the family	Follett
Lofting, Hugh	*The Story of Dr. Dolittle* —The adventures of a doctor who loved animals more than people. There are eleven more	Lippincott

	books telling the adventures of the famous doctor and his animal friends. Some lend themselves to telling more than others; choose your favorites	
McGinley, Phyllis	*The Plain Princess*—A modern story of a little girl who discovered that beauty comes from within. It belongs in the tradition of good fairy tales	Lippincott
Mason, Miriam	*Susannah, the Pioneer Cow*—Susannah proves not only useful but heroic on the wagon trip west of a pioneer family	Macmillan
	Miss Posy Longlegs—Susannah's calf has unusual adventures because she loves to jump	Macmillan
	Caroline and Her Kettle Named Maude—Even Caroline was surprised to find her kettle a better weapon than a gun	Macmillan
	Hominy—A blunt nosed arrow proves useful to this small Indian boy	Macmillan
	Timothy Has Ideas—A vivacious cocker spaniel gets into mischief	Macmillan
	Hoppity—A goat who likes to taste things gets into mischief	Macmillan
	A Pony Called Lightning—A wild pony of the plains loved to race the wind	Macmillan
	Broomtail—A wild pony's exciting adventures on the western prairie	Macmillan

	The Sugarbush Family— A pioneer family has plenty of fun and excitement	Macmillan
Meigs, Elizabeth	A *Cheese for Lafayette*— All the people of Nantucket save milk to make a 500-pound cheese to send to Lafayette in gratitude for his help at a critical time. Wonderful bit of American history to tell	Putnam
Meigs, Cornelia	*The Wonderful Locomotive*—A little boy takes old No. 44 on her last run	Macmillan
Merrill, Jean	A *Song for Gar*—Absalom, who can't carry a tune properly, helps his brother Gar win the Song Swapping Contest at Amity Hill	Whittlesey
Milne, A. A.	*Winnie the Pooh*—Pooh is Christopher Robin's understanding bear. Other friends are Piglet and Eeyore. If you have the kind of imagination that enjoys these whimsical stories, you will tell them with joy—especially Eeyore's birthday—or perhaps read that aloud on birthdays	Dutton
	The House at Pooh Corner has more stories of Pooh's friends and Christopher	Dutton
O'Faolain, Eileen	*Miss Pennyfeather and the Pookah*—Delightful story of a pookah (fairy) horse, an Irish tale for those with imagination	Random

Orton, Helen Fuller   *Treasure in the Little Trunk*   Lippincott

Mystery of the Little Red School House—These are two mystery stories with just enough mystery in the plot to delight 3rd and 4th graders   Lippincott

Parrish, Ann   *Floating Island*—Adventures of a doll family shipwrecked on a tropical island   Harper

Stong, Phil   *Honk the Moose*—A moose wanders into the main street of a Minnesota town. Hilariously funny!   Dodd

Travers, Pamela   *Mary Poppins*—This amazing baby sitter can take off into space on a moment's notice with exciting adventures. Children enjoy these adventures with rare delight. She has more of them in *Mary Poppins Comes Back, Mary Poppins in the Park, Mary Poppins Opens the Door*   Harcourt

Trevino, Elizabeth B. de   *Carpet of Flowers* — The persistence of a small blind boy in bringing blue flowers for the eyes of the Virgin of Guadalupe's carpet brings about a miracle—beautifully told   Dutton

Unnerstad, Edith   *Little O*   Macmillan

The Saucepan Journey   Macmillan

Pysen—This Swedish family, the Larsons, have great fun. They are rather like our Ameri-   Macmillan

	can Moffat family with a little more hilarity and whimsy	
Walsh, Mary	*Molly the Rogue*—Irish farm tale with genuine folk flavor	Knopf
Ward, Lynd	*The Biggest Bear*—Johnny wanted a bear skin on his barn like that of all his neighbors, so he starts out to find a big bear. He comes home with a little live one that grows	Houghton
Weston, Christine	*Bhimsa, the Dancing Bear* —Lively adventures of a boy and a performing bear in India	Scribner

STORIES TO TELL OLDER CHILDREN

(Selected from modern writers)

Alessios, Alison B.	*The Singing Shoemaker*— Manios wanders the Greek countryside getting stories and songs as he gathers grapes—and makes shoes	Scribner
Atkins, Elizabeth H.	*Treasures of the Medranos*—Early California about 1820 and the exciting story of how the wealthy aristocratic Medranos save their silver treasure	Parnassus
Bailey, Carolyn Sherwin	*Miss Hickory*—Miss Hickory, a tiny country woman made of twigs and a hickory-nut head has adventures in her apple orchard	Viking

| Barnes, Nancy | *The Wonderful Year*— Two English boys and an American girl, Ellen, in pioneer Colorado | Messner |

| Barringer, D. Moran | *When the Waters Prevailed*—Powerful story of the time when the Atlantic Ocean broke through the Spain to Africa coast, to form the Mediterranean, leaving only Gibraltar standing as the waters swirled around and past it | Dutton |

| Bauman, Hans | *Son of Columbus*—Fourteen-year old German accompanies his father on his fourth voyage to the West Indies. A powerful dramatic story which throws light on the sort of person Columbus was | Oxford U.P. |

| | *Caves of the Great Hunters*—Four boys and their dog discover an ice age cave in Lesceaux, France. Adventure, art, history all rolled into one | Pantheon |

| Benary-Isbert, Margo | *Blue Mystery*—Annegret and her friends clear up the mystery of who stole the priceless blue gloxinia. Like all of Mrs. Benary-Isbert's stories, the *Ark* and *Castle on the Border*, this story shows poignant understanding of adolescents and their courage in facing the world as it is | Harcourt |

Bennett, John	*Master Skylark*—Charming story of a boy in Shakespeare's England. Good to develop interest in Shakespeare	Grossett
Brink, Carol Ryrie	*Caddie Woodlawn*—Story of a lively girl in pioneer Wisconsin days	Macmillan
Bro, Margueritte Harmon	*Sarah*—True to life story of a modern girl's finding herself and developing her special artistic gifts. Rich background of music	Doubleday
	Su Mei's Golden Year—A modern Chinese girl backs her father's ideas of growing wheat learned in agricultural college against the superstitions of older villagers. Excellent for family values, for conflict between old and new mores and knowledge as well as for authentic Chinese background	Doubleday
Brooks, Walter R.	*Freddy Goes to Florida*—Freddy is a clever detective, the pig of Farmer Bean's Farmyard. This is the first of 22 clever fantastic tales of Freddy and all the animals on the farm. His latest adventures take him into outer space with *Freddy and the Flying Saucer Plans*. American whimsy, humor at its best	Knopf
Caudill, Rebecca	*The Tree of Freedom*—The Venable family's	Viking

	trek from Caroliny over into Old Kaintuck following Daniel Boone	
Ceder, Georgiana	*Ethan the Shepherd Boy* —Ethan joins the other shepherds in bringing a gift to the baby Jesus on the night of the wonderful star	Abingdon
	Ann of Bethany—Ann befriends the holy family in their journey to Egypt	Abingdon
	Joel, the Potter's Son— Joel learns much of the political struggle of his people when Jesus was living	Abingdon
Chute, Marchette	*The Wonderful Year*— Tom runs away from the strict home life at his aunts', to be picked up near London by one of the actors of the Globe Theatre. He helps at the theatre, even gets bit parts and comes to know Shakespeare	Dutton
Cluff, Tom	*Minute Men of the Sea*— Probably the first battle of the American Revolution was not Bunker Hill but the exciting struggle by the brave Maine seamen off the coast of Machias to capture a British ship	Follett
Coblentz, Catherine Cate	*The Blue Cat*—Charming story of a blue cat of Castleton, Vermont, and her efforts to find a human being who could hear and remember the river's song, "Sing your own Song"	Longmans

Daringer, Helen F.	*Adopted Jane*	Harcourt
	Stepsister Sally—Modern family stories of the typical problems faced by an adopted child and by adolescent girls whose parents remarry	Harcourt
DeAngeli, Marguerite	*Copper-Toed Boots*—In pioneer days, a Michigan boy earns the first copper toes on his shoes, a sign he is really grown up	Doubleday
	The Door in the Wall—Robin, the crippled son of a great lord of medieval England, swims the moat, gets through the door in the wall, and so saves the castle, winning even the King's recognition	Doubleday
	Jared's Island—Jared hunts not only his brother but lost treasure on the half-wild Jersey coast of the 1760's	Doubleday
De Jong, Meindert	*Hurry Home Candy*	Harper
	Shadrach—Two moving dog stories	Harper
	The Wheel on the School—Six children begin to wonder why storks do not come to their town of Shora and things happen from the wondering. They discover storks want a wheel for a nest and finally get one put upon the school's chimney	Harper
Donovan, Herbert	*The Desert Stallion*—An Arabian boy tames a wild stallion on the desert	Knopf

Eager, Edward	*Half Magic*	Harcourt
	A Knight's Castle	Harcourt
	Magic by the Lake—In their first adventure with magic, Jane and Mark and Katherine and Martha could order it by the pound or day or by halves or by threes, but it took a whole vacation to tame a whole lake full of magic. Here is a very special kind of enchantment	Harcourt
Enright, Elizabeth	*Gone Away Lake*—Julian and Portia discover the secrets of an old lake from Minnehaha Augusta Cheever and her brother Pindar Peregrine Payton who have retired to the deserted houses where long ago they had spent childhood summers	Harcourt
	The Saturdays	Rinehart
	Thimble Summer—Happy everyday adventures of children on a Wisconsin farm. Elizabeth Enright has a special genius for making everyday living interesting for her characters and all who share their adventures	Rinehart
Estes, Eleanor	*The Moffats*	Harcourt
	The Middle Moffat	Harcourt
	Rufus M—A happy family has much fun together in a Connecticut town. The first chapter of *Rufus M.* telling how he got his library card	Harcourt

	is wonderful to tell as a story by itself.	
Farjeon, Eleanor	*The Glass Slipper*—A delightfully told story of Cinderella in which the characters truly come alive	Lippincott
	The Silver Curlew—Tom Tit-Tot in only such talk as Eleanor Farjeon commands. Here is old wine in new bottles to savor and share with others. They are perhaps better for reading aloud than for telling because the exact words mean so much	Lippincott
Fenton, Edward S.	*Us and the Duchess*—Joel Evans brings home the Duchess, a prize dog lost from her kennel. Her staying involves the whole family and also helps solve a mystery	Doubleday
	Aleko's Island—A modern Greek boy, his pet goat, and a cherished bronze figurine, all combine to make a lively story	Doubleday
Forbes, Esther	*Johnny Tremain*—A young silversmith's apprentice is burned and no longer can work in silver. But he plays an important part in The Boston Tea Party and early days of the Revolution	Houghton
Forbus, Ina B.	*The Magic Pin*—Neelie and the animals save the Simmons baby's life because Neelie can understand what the animals say when she	Viking

	wears grandmother's golden horseshoe pin	
	The Secret Circle—Neelie makes a just-right decision about spending the five dollar gold piece her great-aunt Amanda had given her. Of course, it concerns the animals, too. Mrs. Forbus creates a very special blend of fantasy and the reality of life on a North Carolina farm of pioneer days	Viking
Franklin, George Cory	*Tricky*—True-to-life story of a mischievous red fox	Houghton
	Tuffy—True-to-life story of a beaver during a terrible drought and after a disastrous flood	Houghton
	Monte—Harvey turns his pet bear Monte back to the freedom of the forest	Houghton
Frost, Frances	*Windy Foot at the County Fair*—The whole Clark family is concerned with Toby and his wonderful pony's entrance in the race at the county fair	Whittlesey
	Sleigh Bells for Windy Foot	Whittlesey
	Maple Sugar for Windy Foot	Whittlesey
	Fireworks for Windy Foot Further adventures of the Clarks and Toby's pony. All of these stories are perhaps more valuable as family sto-	Whittlesey

	ries than as horse stories —a good family to know	
Garthwaite, Marion	*Tomas and the Red-headed Angel*—An Indian boy was devoted to a willful Spanish girl who was no angel, on a rancho in the early days of the California missions	Messner
	Coarse Gold Gulch—Madie and Jonathan make an exciting journey from San Francisco across the gold fields in search of their father	Doubleday
Gates, Doris	*Blue Willow*—Janey Larkin has only a beautiful blue willow plate as a symbol of the earlier years of her life. But it helps her find a permanent home and job for her father so that he need no longer be a migrant worker. Sensitive portrayal of a girl and fine human relationships	Viking
Gibson, Katherine	*Cinders*—How often as we lay down a book we wonder what happened next! This is the story of what happened next to Cinderella's coachman	Longmans
Goudge, Elizabeth	*The Little White Horse*—An exciting mystery story of the western part of England about 100 years ago in which fantasy and reality meet in a charming way	Coward

Grahame, Kenneth *Wind in the Willows*— Scribner
       Rat and Mole search
       for lost little Portly,
       meeting the piper at
       the gates of dawn in
       their joyous adventures
       in the world of River
       Bank and Wild Wood

Gray, Elizabeth *Adam of the Road*—A Viking
 Janet   minstrel boy's adven-
       tures in 13th century
       England

Grey, Eve   *Elsa's Secret*—More than Doubleday
       anything in all the
       world Elsa wanted to
       be Snow White in the
       Christmas play. Losing
       her first tooth created a
       serious predicament

Hale, Lucretia P. *Peterkin Papers*—An old Houghton
       favorite of funny ad-
       ventures of a family.
       Individual episodes de-
       lightful to tell

Harte, Bret   *Best Stories*—Several of Modern Library
       these beloved western
       stories such as "The
       Jumping Frog of Cala-
       veras County" are won-
       derful to tell

Hatch, Richard *The Lobster Books*—*Curi-* Houghton
       ous Lobster and *Curi-*
       ous Lobster's Island—
       Fine, spontaneous tales
       full of delightfully ab-
       surd logic which is the
       charm of the fanciful
       animal story

Havighurst, Walter *Song of the Pines*—Au- Winston
 and Marion thentic moving story of
       Norwegian family lum-
       bering in Wisconsin a
       century ago

Henry, Marguerite *Misty of Chincoteague*— Rand McNally
       Thrilling story of the
       capture and training of

	a banker pony mare and her colt	
	King of the Wind—Authentic story of the Godolphin Arabian, a founder of the entire thoroughbred strain	Rand McNally
	Brighty of the Grand Canyon—True story of a little burro who blazed trails for men in the Grand Canyon	Rand McNally
Henry, O.	*Best Short Stories*—Fine collection of stories of one of America's greatest story-tellers. One may be yours to tell	Modern Library
Hoff, Carol	*Johnny Texas*—Johnny's family come to Texas from Germany to make a home in a free land	Follett
	Head to the West—After being almost lost at sea, the Von Dohns reach their cabin in Texas. But farming in wild rough country is not for them, so Father finds a way to move them to a city and still be valuable to the growing state	Follett
Hudson, W. H.	*A Little Boy Lost*—Sensitive, imaginative story of a boy's childhood on the South American plains	Knopf
Jewett, Eleanore	*Hidden Treasure of Glaston*—Crippled Hugh is left at Glastonbury Abbey in medieval England, but a miracle happens when he rescues Brother John from the great fire	Viking

Kelly, Eric P.	*Trumpeter of Krakow*— Thrilling story of 15th century Poland in which the trumpeter saves his city	Macmillan
Kent, Louise Andrews	*He Went with Marco Polo*—Sharing the adventures of the young gondolier of Venice who went with Marco Polo to the land of Kublai Khan makes you feel you were there. The same sense of firsthand experience rings true in *He Went with Christopher Columbus* and *He Went with Magellan*	Houghton
Kipling, Rudyard	*Just So Stories* *Jungle Books I and II* To be told, these beloved famous stories of India have to be almost memorized; otherwise, read them aloud	Doubleday
Kjelgaard, Jim	*Big Red*—A trapper's son and champion Irish setter grow up together in this classic dog story. This is one of Kjelgaard's many fine animal stories. *Haunted Fox, Irish Red, Lion Hound, A Nose for Trouble, Outlaw Red, Snow Dog* and others. Kjelgaard is an outstanding teller of animal adventures	Holiday
Knight, Eric	*Lassie Come Home*—Now a classic, this is a moving story of a collie's determined long trek	Winston

	back home from Scotland to England	
Krumgold, Joseph	*And Now Miguel*—Twelve-year old Miguel at last has his chance to go to the mountains to help with the sheep in this authentic story of the sheep raising Chavez family in New Mexico	Crowell
Latham, Jean Lee	*This Dear Bought Land*— Exciting story of Jamestown beginnings in which John Smith really comes alive	Crowell
Lawrence, Isabelle	*Niko, Sculptor's Apprentice*—Authentic warm story of Niko who becomes an apprentice to Phidias when he is working on the sculptures for the Parthenon	Viking
	A Spy in Williamsburg— Ben Budge, who works in his father's blacksmith shop, captures a British spy and helps Patrick Henry save the city from the Tories. Authentic and exciting	Rand McNally
Lindquist, Jennie	*Golden Name Day*—Nancy has many adventures with her Swedish American friends before she finds her very own name day. Another warm family story with fine human relations	Harper
Lobdell, Helen	*Golden Conquest*—Dramatic story of a Castilian boy in Cortez' army who becomes a friend of Montezuma's brother. Told so that	Houghton

one feels both the Spanish and Mexican sides of this exciting conquest

Lownsberry, Eloise — *Boy Knight of Rheims*— Houghton
Vivid story of an apprentice who worked on the great cathedral at Rheims

Macgregor, Ellen — *Miss Pickerell Goes to Mars*—Another flying Whittlesey
baby sitter who has unusual adventures involving much knowledge of science has rare charm for all who become her friends. She lives in three more exciting adventures in *Miss Pickerell and the Geiger Counter, Miss Pickerell Goes Undersea, Miss Pickerell Goes to the Arctic*

McCloskey, Robert — *Homer Price* — Hilarious Viking
adventures of a typical American boy

McGraw, Eloise — *Mara*—Exciting mystery Coward
of a slave girl and the ambitious half-brother of an Egyptian queen

Meadowcroft, Enid — *Ship Boy with Columbus* Crowell
—Live with a lad on Columbus' first voyage of discovery

Silver for General Washington — Valley Forge Crowell
takes on new meaning from this realistic story of the general and his men

By Wagon and Flatboat— Crowell
The adventures of those who opened up the

West by sailing down the Ohio River. American history becomes a real human struggle in all Mrs. Meadowcroft's stories of those who have built our country

Meigs, Elizabeth	*Candle in the Sun*—Moving story of Joan of Arc	Dutton
	The Crusade and the Cup —One of the choice King Arthur stories	Dutton
Meigs, Cornelia	*Fair Wind to Virginia*— Exciting adventure in colonial Williamsburg. One of the best stories to tell of Cornelia Meigs' many fine historical narratives	Macmillan
Merwin, Decie	*Mostly the Meldons*— Sally gains a new concept of her family after spending a weekend in the city	Lippincott
Morrison, Lucile	*The Lost Queen of Egypt* —Stirring account of the wife of Tutankamen	Dodd
Norton, Mary	*The Borrowers*—Delightful imaginative tale of the little people who live under the floors of our homes	Harcourt
Poe, Edgar Allan	*Best Tales*—Some few may feel equal to telling one of the stories of this master of mystery and imaginative tales	Modern Library
Power, Rhoda	*From the Fury of the Northmen* — Historic English stories offering fine background material for story-telling, told by BBC broadcaster for young people	Houghton

Ransome, Arthur   *Swallows and Amazons—*   Lippincott
The lively adventures
of English children in
boats on the lakes.
There are more books
of their adventures such
as *Picts and Martyrs,
Great Northern Winter
Holiday*

Robertson, Keith   *The Wreck of the Sagi-*   Viking
*naw—*Authentic   dra-
matic true story of the
brave attempt made by
five men to go from
their wreck on an island
in the North Pacific
thousands of miles to
Hawaii, on a raft which
they built. Only one
man made it

*The Pinto Deer—*Exciting   Viking
story of how John
Michelson, a young
forestry student, with
the help of some pic-
turesque characters in
those New Jersey moun-
tains, captured a beau-
tiful deer alive. Mr.
Robertson has several
exciting tales of the
Sourland Mountain part
of New Jersey, *Outlaws
of the Sourland, The
Mystery of Burnt Hill*
and others

Sauer, Julia L.   *Fog Magic—*Sensitive im-   Viking
aginative story of the
Nova Scotia coast, past
and present

The Light at Tern Rock—   Viking
Both the isolation of a
lighthouse   and   the
power and beauty of

	the sea are captured in this story of a boy and his aunt stranded on Tern Rock at Christmas	
Seredy, Kate	*The Good Master*—All the richness of life on a horse farm in the plains of Hungary—fun, excitement, adventure, mystery, beauty are to be found in this modern classic. Other stories such as *A Tree for Peter, The Singing Tree* and many more are good to tell and live with	Viking
Simon, Charlie May	*Robin on the Mountain*— Interesting living in the Ozarks	Dutton
	Popo's Miracle — Lively story of a small boy eager to be a good potter in Mexico	Dutton
Skidmore, Hubert	*Hill Doctor*—York Allen returns to serve his own people in the Blue Ridge mountains after studying medicine	Doubleday
Sorensen, Virginia	*Miracles on Maple Hill*— Marly's father, ill from long war imprisonment, finds health up on Maple Hill—only one of the several miracles that take place on this farm in New Hampshire	Harcourt
Sperry, Armstrong	*Call It Courage*—The son of a Polynesian chieftain proves to his father he can conquer his fear of the water	Macmillan

Sprague, Rosemary — *Heir of Kiloran*—Exciting, authentic story of the Renaissance, in which a young Scots nobleman meets and falls in love with Gioia Gonzaga, daughter of the Duke of Mantua, when he goes to Florence in search of the heir to his grandfather's estates in Scotland. Her two tales of Viking days are also thrilling, *Heroes of the White Shield* and *A Kingdom to Win* — Oxford U.P.

Steele, William O. — *Flaming Arrows*—Realistic story of Chad Rabun, the Logans and Chickamauga Indians in the Tennessee mountains. Mr. Steele really makes pioneer days come alive, but also his characters are real people who face real problems —some of them problems we face today as we did then—in his fine stories of the long hunters and pioneers: *The Lone Hunt, Winter Danger* and *Wilderness Journey* — Harcourt

Stevenson, Robert Louis — *Treasure Island*—Real buccaneers come alive in this classic adventure story — Scribner / Grosset / World

Stuart, Jesse — *A Penny's Worth of Character*—A mountain boy, Shan, returns ten bags to the country storekeeper for a penny each when only nine — Whittlesey

	are usable. He confesses to his grandmother and to the storekeeper as he realizes the real meaning of honesty	
Sutcliff, Rosemary	*The Eagle of the Ninth*—A young centurion, invalided out of service in Britain, ventures beyond the Roman Wall to recover the eagle standard of the lost Ninth Legion. Roman times come alive in this and her other fine stories: *Outcast* and *The Silver Branch*. Vikings are true to life in *Heroes of the White Shield, A Kingdom to Win*, and *The Shield Ring*. You live again in Elizabethan England in *Brother Dusty-Feet* and *The Queen Elizabeth Story*	Oxford U.P.
Tolkien, J. R. R.	*The Hobbit; or, There and Back Again*—Rare beauty and imagination characterize this story of dwarfs and dragons	Houghton
Ullman, James	*Banner in the Sky*—A Swiss boy is determined to climb the inaccessible Citadel. Here is mountain climbing so real, so thrilling that *your* thighs ache, too, and *your* determination becomes invincible also	Lippincott
White, E. B.	*Stuart Little*—To have the new baby brother, a mouse, creates many	Harper

unusual problems and situations

Charlotte's Web—Tender   Harper
story of a small girl who loves animals, a pig and a spider. Mr. White's special brand of imagination, humor and tenderness is unique and has great appeal for certain human beings. See that these certain special children (of all ages) have the opportunity to know him

Wickenden, Dan   *The Amazing Vacation*—   Harcourt
The children go through a window to unusual adventure—reminiscent of Alice in Wonderland and only for those with active imaginations

Wilder, Laura Ingalls   *Little House in the Big*   Harper
Woods—This is the first of eight stories of the Ingalls family in Wisconsin, Nebraska, the Dakotas, Minnesota about 100 years ago. It is a great saga of American midwestern pioneers

Wilson, Holly   *Snowbound in Hidden*   Messner
Valley—Jo Shannon and her Indian classmate Oneta live through the exciting tense days of Michigan's great blizzard

Wilson, Leon   (o) *This Boy Cody*—Lively   Watts
story of a house raising in the mountains on Cody's tenth birthday

Worth, Katherine	*The Middle Button*—Maggid McArn, a Scotch girl in North Carolina of the 1880's wants to study medicine more than anything else in the world and proves her ability by traveling first with a country doctor	Doubleday
Yates, Elizabeth	*Patterns on the Wall*— Lively story of a boy who travels with a painter in colonial days in New England	Dutton

BIOGRAPHIES

Life stories of interesting, or successful, or great people are often good stories to tell. They do not have a plot comparable to that of a story, but the working out of life's problems is often as exciting as solving the complications of a plot. Here are a few life stories in which the incidents are selected so skillfully, and the life story told so well, that they bear telling.

FOR YOUNG CHILDREN

Averill, Esther	*Daniel Boone*—Exciting brief portrait of the famous pioneer	Harper
d'Aulaire, Ingri and Edgar	*Abraham Lincoln*	Doubleday
	Leif the Lucky	Doubleday
	Benjamin Franklin	Doubleday
	Christopher Columbus Skillful, understanding selection of what will interest children make these life stories vital	Doubleday

FOR SLIGHTLY OLDER CHILDREN

Foster, Genevieve	*Abraham Lincoln*	Scribner
	Andrew Jackson	Scribner

	George Washington—Interesting lively accounts of these three presidents	Scribner
Peare, Catherine	*Rosa Bonheur*	Holt
	Jules Verne	Holt
	Mark Twain	Holt
	Louisa May Alcott	Holt
	Henry Wadsworth Longfellow	Holt
	John James Audubon	Holt
	Stephen Foster	Holt
	Washington Irving	Holt

No one interprets these authors, whose contribution to cultural growth is so significant, with such lively charm as Miss Peare.

Makers of America

A series of fifteen brief dramatic life stories of important figures in our country's history with more in preparation. Here are a few especially good ones for telling. All are worth knowing.

Graham, Alberta P.	*Clara Barton, Red Cross Pioneer*	Abingdon
	Lafayette, Friend of America	Abingdon
Haines, Madge, and Leslie Merrill	*The Wright Brothers, First to Fly*	Abingdon
	John Muir, Protector of the Wilds	Abingdon
Weir, Ruth C.	*Leif Ericson, Explorer*	Abingdon
	Thomas Alva Edison, Inventor	Abingdon
Wright, Frances E.	*Sam Houston, Fighter and Leader*	Abingdon

Lives to Remember

A new series of interesting, authentic lives of interesting people.

Luce, H. K.	*St. Paul*	Putnam
Moore, Patrick	*Isaac Newton*	Putnam
Noel-Baker, Francis	*Fridtjof Nansen*	Putnam
Pain, Nesta	*Louis Pasteur*	Putnam
Thomas, Henry	*George Washington Carver*	Putnam

	Thomas Alva Edison	Putnam
Tibble, J. W. and Anne	*Helen Keller*	Putnam

Signature Books

Another series of life stories of forty great people of history. Written by many good authors, they are all skillfully edited by Enid Meadowcroft, who also has written a few of them. Here are a few especially good for telling. All are worth knowing.

Collier, Edmund	*Kit Carson*	Grosset
de Leeuw, Adele	*Amelia Earhart*	Grosset
Graham, Shirley	*Pocahontas*	Grosset
Malkus, Alida S.	*Louis Pasteur*	Grosset
Meadowcroft,	*Crazy Horse*	Grosset
Enid L.	*Davy Crockett*	Grosset
Nolan, Jeanette	*Joan of Arc*	Grosset
Price, Olive	*Marco Polo*	Grosset
Steele, William O.	*Daniel Boone*	Grosset
Vinton, Iris	*Robert E. Lee*	Grosset

Judson Biographies

Judson, Clara Ingram	*Abraham Lincoln, Friend of the People*	Follett
	George Washington, Leader of the People	Follett
	Theodore Roosevelt, Fighting Patriot	Follett
	Thomas Jefferson, Champion of the People	Follett
	Benjamin Franklin	Follett

FOR OLDER CHILDREN

There are a number of outstanding biographies of musicians such as:

Ewen, David	*George Gershwin*	Holt
Goss, Madeleine	*Deep Flowing Brook* (Bach)	Holt
Purdy, Claire Lee	*My Brother Was Mozart*	Holt

Messner has a long biographical bookshelf. Many titles are outstanding. The biographies of sports heroes by Gene Schoor are unique. There are life stories of Casey Stengel, Christy Mathewson, Jack Dempsey, Jackie Robinson, Jim Thorpe, Joe Di Maggio, Red Grange, Stan Musial, Ty Cobb, and others. It is worth exploring among the others to discover those of special interest.

There are many other good biographies for older children, such as Lisitzky's *Thomas Jefferson*, Simon's *Albert Schweitzer*, Marguerite Vance's *Flight of the Wildling: Elizabeth of Austria*, most of which are perhaps better read than told. These are listed in many places and are easy to find on the biography shelf of any library or bookstore.

COLLECTIONS OF STORIES FOR HOLIDAYS

Child Study Association	*Holiday Story Book*	Crowell
Cavanah, Frances, and Lucile Pannell	*Holiday Round Up*	Macrae Smith
Gaer, Joseph	*Holidays Around the World*	Little
McSpadden, J. Walker	*The Book of Holidays*	Crowell
Purcell, John W.	*True Book of Holidays*	Children's Press
Sechrist, Elizabeth H.	*Red Letter Days*—See also *Poems for Red Letter Days*	Lothrop

EASTER

Harper, Wilhelmina	*Easter Chimes*	Dutton
Hazeltine, Alice I., and Pamela Bianco	*Easter Book of Legends and Stories*	Lothrop

HALLOWEEN

Brock, Emma, and others	*Spooks, Spirits and Shadowy Shapes*	Dutton
Fenner, Phyllis	*Ghosts, Ghosts, Ghosts*	Watts
Harper, Wilhelmina	*Ghosts and Goblins*	Dutton

Irving, Washington	*Bold Dragoon and other Ghostly Tales*	Knopf
Jewett, Eleanore	*Which is Witch? Korean Ghostly Tales*	Viking
Linton, Ralph	*Halloween*	Abelard
Sechrist, Elizabeth H.	*Heigh-ho for Halloween!* —Thirteen ghostly yarns	Macrae Smith

THANKSGIVING

Harper, Wilhelmina	*The Harvest Feast*	Dutton
Linton,	*We Gather Together*	Abelard
Sechrist, Elizabeth H., and Janette Woolsey	*It's Time for Thanksgiving*	Macrae Smith

CHRISTMAS

A. C. E.	*Told Under the Christmas Tree*	Macmillan
Dalgliesh, Alice	*Christmas*	Scribner
Dickinson, Asa Don	*Children's Book of Christmas Stories*	Doubleday
Harper, Wilhelmina	*Merry Christmas to You*	Dutton
Hazeltine, Alice, and Elva Smith	*Christmas Book of Legends and Stories*	Lothrop
Lillie, Amy Morris	*The Book of Three Festivals*—Christmas, Easter, Thanksgiving	Dutton
Linton, Ralph and Adelin	*4000 Years of Christmas*	Abelard
Retan, Walter	*Santa's Footprints and Other Christmas Stories*	Dutton
Sawyer, Ruth	*The Long Christmas*	Viking
	This Way to Christmas	Harper
Sechrist, Elizabeth	*Christmas Everywhere*	Macrae Smith
Smith, Dorothy	*The Tall Book of Christmas*	Harper
Smith, Irene	*The Santa Claus Book*	Watts
	Golden Christmas Book	S. and S.
	Golden Book of Christmas Tales	S. and S.

INDIVIDUAL STORIES FOR HOLIDAYS

NEW YEAR'S DAY

Milhous, Katherine	*Patrick and the Golden Slippers*—Annual Mummer's Parade in Philadelphia	Scribner
Stillman, Dorothea	*When the New Year Began in March*	Dutton

VALENTINE'S DAY

Bianco, Pamela	*The Valentine Party*	Lippincott
Hays, Wilma P.	*The Story of Valentine*	Coward
Milhous, Katherine	*Appolonia's Valentine*	Scribner

LINCOLN'S BIRTHDAY

Andrews, Mary	*The Perfect Tribute*	Scribner
Coblentz, Catherine	*Martin and Abraham Lincoln*—small boy and Lincoln	Children's Press
d'Aulaire, Edgar and Ingri	*Abraham Lincoln*	Doubleday
Foster, Genevieve	*A. L., Abraham Lincoln*	Scribner
Judson, Clara I.	*Abraham Lincoln, Friend of the People*	Follett
Neyhart, Louise	*Henry's Lincoln*—a boy hears the Lincoln-Douglas Debate	Holiday
Pauli, Herta	*Lincoln's Little Correspondent*—a little girl's letter to Lincoln about his beard	Doubleday
Sandburg, Carl	*Abe Lincoln Grows Up*	Harcourt

GEORGE WASHINGTON'S BIRTHDAY

Ball, Elsie	*George Washington, First President*	Abingdon
d'Aulaire, Edgar and Ingri	*George Washington*	Doubleday

| Foster, Genevieve | *George Washington* | Scribner |
| Judson, Clara I. | *George Washington, Leader of the People* | Follett |

EASTER

Bianco, Pamela	*The Look-Inside Easter Egg*	Oxford U.P.
Brown, Margaret Wise	*The Golden Egg Book*	S. and S.
Foster, Doris T.	*Tell Me Little Boy*	Lothrop
Friedrich, Priscilla and Otto	*The Easter Bunny That Overslept*	Lothrop
Milhous, Katherine	*The Egg Tree*	Scribner
Schlein, Miriam	*Little Rabbit, the High Jumper*	Scott
Tresselt, Alvin S.	*The Rabbit Story*	Lothrop
Tudor, Tasha	*A Tale for Easter*	Oxford U.P.

JULY FOURTH

| Dalgliesh, Alice | *The Fourth of July Story* | Scribner |
| Judson, Clara I. | *(o) Thomas Jefferson, Champion of the People* | Follett |

COLUMBUS DAY

Bauman, Hans	*(o) Son of Columbus*	Oxford U.P.
Dalgliesh, Alice	*The Columbus Story*	Scribner
d'Aulaire, Edgar and Ingri	*Christopher Columbus*	Doubleday
Graham, Alberta P.	*Christopher Columbus, Discoverer*	Abingdon
Hodges, C. Walter	*(o) Columbus Sails*	Coward
Kent, Louise A.	*(o) He Went with Christopher Columbus*	Houghton
Meadowcroft, Enid	*Ship Boy with Columbus*	Crowell

HALLOWEEN

| Bennett, Anna Elizabeth | *(m) Little Witch* | Lippincott |
| Embry, Margaret | *(m) The Blue Nosed Witch* | Holiday |

Foster, Doris V.	*Tell Me, Mr. Owl*	Lothrop
Jones, Louis	*(o) Spooks of the Valley*	Houghton
Tudor, Tasha	*Pumpkin Moonshine*	Oxford U.P.
Weales, Gerald	*Miss Grimsbee is a Witch*	Little

THANKSGIVING

Barksdale, Lena	*The First Thanksgiving*	Knopf
Dalgliesh, Alice	*The Thanksgiving Story*	Scribner
Hays, Wilma P.	*Pilgrim Thanksgiving*	Coward

CHRISTMAS

Alden, Raymond	*Why the Chimes Rang*	Appleton
Adshead, Gladys	*Brownies, It's Christmas*	Oxford U.P.
Bro, M. H.	*Three-and Domingo*	Doubleday
Brown, M. W.	*The Little Fir Tree*	Crowell
	Christmas in the Barn	Crowell
	The Pussycat's Christmas	Crowell
Buck, Pearl	*Christmas Miniature*	Day
Ceder, Georgiana	*Ethan, the Shepherd Boy*	Abingdon
Dolbier, Maurice	*Torten's Christmas*	Little
Dorian, Edith	*Ask Dr. Christmas*	Whittlesey
Duryea, Elizabeth	*The Long Christmas Eve*	Houghton
Evers, Alf	*The Three Kings of Saba*	Lippincott
Fatio, Louise	*The Christmas Forest*	Dutton
Field, Rachel	*All Through the Night*	Macmillan
Forbus, Ina B.	*The Secret Circle*	Viking
Glover, Florida R.	*The First Christmas*	Harper
Godden, Rumer	*The Fairy Doll*	Viking
Gordon, Patricia	*The Heir to Christmas*	Viking
Goudge, Elizabeth	*The Reward of Faith —Eight Christmas legends*	Coward
Hays, Wilma P.	*Christmas on the Mayflower*	Coward
Howard, Joan	*The Light in the Tower*	Lothrop
Hull, Helen S.	*The Gift, a Tale for Christmas*	Macmillan
Jones, Elizabeth Orton	*Big Susan*	Macmillan
Kelly, Eric P.	*In Clean Hay*	Macmillan
	The Christmas Nightingale	Macmillan

Kingman, Lee	*The Best Christmas*	Doubleday
	The Magic Christmas Tree	Farrar & Straus
Lathrop, Dorothy	*An Angel in the Woods*	Macmillan
Lines, Kathleen	*Once in Royal David's City*	Watts
Lorentowicz, Irene	*Lullaby*	Roy
Lloyd, Mary E.	*Jesus the Little New Baby*	Abingdon
Menotti, Gian-Carlo (adapted by Frances Frost)	*Amahl and the Night Visitors*	Whittlesey
Milhous, Katherine	*Snow over Bethlehem*	Scribner
	With Bells On	Scribner
Morgan, Carol M.	*Hunt for the Yule Log*	Abelard
Politi, Leo	*Pedro, the Angel of Olvera Street*	Scribner
Potter, Beatrix	*The Tailor of Gloucester*	Warne
Sauer, Julia	*The Light at Tern Rock*	Viking
Sawyer, Ruth	*The Christmas Anna Angel*	Viking
	Maggie Rose	Harper
Seuss, Dr.	*How the Grinch Stole Christmas*	Random
Seymour, Alta	*The Christmas Camera* (Sweden)	Follett
	The Christmas Stove (Switzerland)	Follett
	Arnie and the Christmas Star (Norway)	Follett
	The Christmas Donkey (France)	Follett
	Kaatje and the Christmas Compass (Holland)	Follett
	The Top O' Christmas Morning (Ireland)	Follett
Thomas, Joan Gale	*One Little Baby*	Lothrop
Trent, Robbie	*The First Christmas*	Harper
Tudor, Tasha	*The Doll's Christmas*	Oxford U.P.
	Snow Before Christmas	Oxford U.P.
Vance, Marguerite	*The Boy on the Road*	Dutton
	Star for Hansi	Dutton
	While Shepherds Watched	Dutton
Welch, Jean	*The Animals Came First*	Oxford U.P.
Yates, Elizabeth	*Once in the Year*	Coward

THE SEASONS

GENERAL

Brewton, Sara and John	*Sing a Song of Seasons*	Macmillan
Gottlieb, William	*The Four Seasons—A Golden Book*	S. and S.
MacDonald, Golden	*Little Island*	Doubleday
Webb, Addison	*The Book of Seasons*	Morrow

SPRING

Lenski, Lois	*(y) Spring Is Here*	Oxford U.P.
Schlein, Miriam	*(y) Little Red Nose*	Abelard
Tooze, Ruth	*(m) Wires Up!*	Messner
Tresselt, Alvin S.	*(y) Hi! Mr. Robin*	Lothrop

SUMMER

Lenski, Lois	*(y) On a Summer Day*	Oxford U.P.
Loken, Anna Belle and Hjalmar	*(o) When the Sun Danced —A Norwegian tale*	Lothrop
Marcher, Marion	*(m) Bob's Summer Sleigh Ride*	Dutton
Simont, Marc	*(y) Lovely Summer*	Harper

AUTUMN

Lenski, Lois	*(y) Now It's Fall*	Oxford U.P.
Tresselt, Alvin S.	*(y) Autumn Harvest*	Lothrop
	Johnny Mapleleaf	Lothrop

WINTER

Falk, Elsa	*(m) Winter Journey*	Follett
Hader, Berta & Elmer	*(y) The Big Snow*	Macmillan
Lathrop, Dorothy	*(y) Who Goes There?*	Macmillan
Lenski, Lois	*(y) I Like Winter*	Oxford U.P.
	(o) Prairie School	Lippincott
Milhous, Katherine	*(m) Snow Over Bethlehem*	Scribner
Paull, Grace	*(m) Pancakes for Breakfast*	Doubleday

Schlein, Miriam	*(y) Go with the Sun*	Scott
	(m) Deer in the Snow	Abelard
Tresselt, Alvin S.	*(y) White Snow, Bright Snow*	Lothrop
Wilson, Holly	*(o) Snowbound in Hidden Valley*	Messner

CHILDREN'S BIBLES AND RELIGIOUS BOOKS

BIBLES

Barnhart, Nancy	*The Lord is My Shepherd*	Scribner
Doane, Pelagie	*The Small Child's Bible*	Oxford U.P.
Goodspeed, Edgar J.	*The Junior Bible*	Macmillan
Hurlbut, Jesse Lyman	*Hurlbut's Story of the Bible*	Winston
Loveland, Seymour	*The Illustrated Bible Story Book*	Rand McNally
Meyer, Edith Patterson	*Bible Stories for Children*	Abingdon
Sherman, H. A., and C. F. Kent	*The Children's Bible*	Scribner
Sypherd, Wilbur Owen	*The Book of Books*	Knopf

BIBLE STORIES

Jones, Rufus	*The Boy Jesus and His Companions*	Macmillan
Kunhardt, Dorothy	*Once There Was a Little Boy*	Viking
Lau, Josephine S.	*Story of Joseph*	Abingdon
Petersham, Maud and Miska	*David*	Macmillan
	Joseph	Macmillan
	Jesus' Story	Macmillan
	The Story of Jesus (for Catholic children)	Macmillan
Smither, Ethel L.	*Early Old Testament Stories*	Abingdon
	Later Old Testament Stories	Abingdon
	Stories of Jesus	Abingdon
	First to be Called Christians	Abingdon

Tippett, James   *Jesus Lights the Sabbath*   Abingdon
  Sterling   *Lamp*

STORIES WITH BIBLICAL BACKGROUND

Ceder, Georgiana D.	*Ann of Bethany*	Abingdon
	Ethan, the Shepherd Boy	Abingdon
	Joel, the Potter's Son	Abingdon
Lau, Josephine S.	*Beggar Boy of Galilee*	Abingdon
	Slave Boy in Judea	Abingdon
Lillie, Amy Morris	*Judith, Daughter of Jericho*	Dutton
	Nathan, Boy of Capernaum	Dutton
	Stephen, Boy of the Mountain	Dutton

STORIES OF SAINTS AND RELIGIOUS HEROES

Beebe, Catherine	*St. John Bosco and the Children's Saint*	Farrar Straus
	St. Dominic and the Rosary	Farrar Straus
Bishop, Claire Huchet	*Bernard and His Dogs*	Houghton
	Christopher the Giant	Houghton
	Martin de Porres, Hero	Houghton
Bulla, Clyde	*Song of St. Francis*	Crowell
Derleth, August	*St. Ignatius and the Company of Jesus*	Farrar Straus
De Wohl, Louis	*St. Joan, the Girl Soldier*	Farrar Straus
Farjeon, Eleanor	*Ten Saints*	Oxford U.P.
Gaer, Joseph	*Young Heroes of the Living Religions*	Little
Homan, Helen Walker	*Francis and Clare, Saints of Assisi*	Farrar Straus
	St. Anthony of Padua	Farrar Straus
Jewett, Sophie	*God's Troubadour* (St. Francis)	Crowell
Larnen, Brendan and Milton Lomask	*St. Thomas Aquinas and the Preaching Beggars*	Farrar Straus
Nevins, Albert J.	*St. Francis of the Seven Seas*	Farrar Straus
Pauli, Herta	*Bernadette and the Lady*	Farrar Straus
	Christmas and the Saints	Farrar Straus

OUTSTANDING SERIES OF CHILDREN'S CLASSICS
(*in print*)

CHILDREN'S CLASSICS (*published by Dutton*)

Alice's Adventures in Wonderland and Through the Looking Glass
Black Beauty
The Book of Nonsense
The Brownies and Other Stories
Children of the New Forest
The Coral Island
The Cuckoo Clock
Don Quixote
Fairy Tales of Long Ago
Fairy Tales from the Arabian Nights
Good Wives
Grimms' Fairy Tales
Gulliver's Travels
Hans Andersen's Fairy Tales
Hans Brinker, or the Silver Skates
Heidi
Huckleberry Finn

King Arthur and the Round Table
Little Women
Lorna Doone
Modern Fairy Tales
Pilgrim's Progress
Pinocchio: The Story of a Puppet
The Princess and Curdie
The Princess and the Goblin
Robin Hood
Robinson Crusoe
Tanglewood Tales
Tom Brown's School Days
Tom Sawyer
Treasure Island
A Wonder Book
At the Back of the North Wind
The Water Babies
Little Men

JUNIOR ILLUSTRATED CLASSICS (*published by Grosset and Dunlap*)

Adventures of Huckleberry Finn, The
Adventures of Pinocchio, The
Adventures of Tom Sawyer, The
Aesop's Fables
Alice in Wonderland and Through the Looking Glass
Andersen's Fairy Tales
Arabian Nights
Black Beauty
Five Little Peppers and How They Grew
Grimms' Fairy Tales
Gulliver's Travels

Hans Brinker
Heidi
Jo's Boys
Jungle Book, The
Kidnapped
King Arthur and His Knights of the Round Table
Little Lame Prince, The, and Adventures of Brownie, The
Little Men
Little Women
Merry Adventures of Robin Hood, The
Robinson Crusoe

Swiss Family Robinson, The
Tale of Two Cities, A
Three Musketeers, The

Treasure Island
Wizard of Oz, The

CHILDREN'S CLASSICS (published by Lippincott)

Aesop's Fables
Black Beauty
Hans Brinker, or The Silver
   Skates
Heidi

King Arthur
Pinocchio
Robin Hood
Robinson Crusoe
Treasure Island

CHILDREN'S CLASSICS (published by Macmillan)

Adventures of Pinocchio
The Alhambra
Alice's Adventures in Wonderland and Through the Looking Glass
The Arabian Nights
At the Back of the North Wind
A Christmas Carol
East of the Sun and West of the Moon
The Fables of Aesop
Fairy Tales and Stories

The Gold Bug and Other Tales and Poems
The Heroes
Household Stories
The Iliad of Homer
The Little Duke
The Odyssey of Homer
The Princess and the Goblin
The Princess and Curdie
Rip Van Winkle and the Legend of Sleepy Hollow
Tales from Shakespeare
Treasure Island

ILLUSTRATED CHILDREN'S CLASSICS (published by Scribner)

Arabian Nights
The Story of Roland
The Story of Siegfried
Drums
A Little Princess
The Deerslayer
The Last of the Mohicans
Robinson Crusoe
The Children of Dickens
Hans Brinker
Poems of Childhood
The Little Shepherd of Kingdom Come

Grimms' Fairy Tales
Lone Cowboy
Smoky
Westward Ho!
The Boy's King Arthur
The Scottish Chiefs
The Yearling
Quentin Durward
The Children's Bible
A Child's Garden of Verses
The Black Arrow
Treasure Island
Kidnapped

David Balfour
The Mysterious Island

Twenty Thousand Leagues Under the Sea

RAINBOW-CLASSICS *(published by World Publishing Co.)*

Adventures of Huckleberry Finn, The
Adventures of Tom Sawyer, The
Alice's Adventures in Wonderland and Through the Looking Glass
Andersen's Fairy Tales
Black Beauty
Book of Bible Stories, The
Book of Sherlock Holmes, The
Child's Garden of Verses
Christmas Stories
Eight Cousins
Five Little Peppers
Grimms' Fairy Tales
Gulliver's Travels
Hans Brinker or The Silver Skates
Heidi
Jack and Jill
Jane Eyre
Jo's Boys
Kidnapped

King Arthur and His Knights
King of the Golden River, The
Last of the Mohicans, The
Little Lame Prince, The
Little Men
Little Women
Mysterious Island, The
Old-Fashioned Girl, An
Pinocchio
Pride and Prejudice
Prince and the Pauper, The
Rainbow Mother Goose, The
Robin Hood
Robinson Crusoe
Swiss Family Robinson, The
Three Musketeers, The
Toby Tyler
Treasure Island
Twenty Thousand Leagues Under the Sea
Two Years Before the Mast
Wuthering Heights

Index